Straight Talk

"Rebecca Powell has written a powerful book that transforms the way we think about teaching and learning. *Straight Talk* speaks with incredible honesty and agency; it's a book about hope, about the potential for transformation, and about what can happen when we work together for change. *Straight Talk* is an eloquent, intimate conversation about teaching and learning and the critical roles our notions about class, race, and gender play in the school achievement of students of color. Powell's honesty about what it means to be an Anglo educator engaged in the struggle to make schooling the best part of each child's day is a living testimony that we need not be forever crippled by the insidious destructiveness of racism, classism, homophobia, and gender bias. Rather, Powell critically examines these tough issues as they operate in language, curricula, and social institutions, and thus strips them of their power to distort our vision and to confound our educational and social best intentions. *Straight Talk* offers pragmatic help to classroom practitioners and university faculty. *Straight Talk* is a timely text; it will serve us well in the struggle to walk our talk as we work to transform society into a fit place for human beings to teach, to learn, and to thrive."

Linda Spears-Bunton, Florida International University

"In an honest and clear, but firm and informed voice, Rebecca Powell addresses issues of teaching multiculturally. Many authors try to soft peddle the concept of multicultural education in an effort to win over select groups. Powell, however, refreshingly confronts issues that surround the teaching of cultural difference in teacher education in a no nonsense manner. She challenges readers to embrace the philosophy of multicultural education and to put its tenets into action. Her discussion of seminal studies as well as cutting edge research is a real plus for the reader."

Arlette Ingram Willis, University of Illinois

STRAIGHT TALK

Studies in the
Postmodern Theory of Education

Joe L. Kincheloe and Shirley R. Steinberg
General Editors

Vol. 149

PETER LANG
New York • Washington, D.C./Baltimore • Bern
Frankfurt am Main • Berlin • Brussels • Vienna • Oxford

Rebecca Powell

STRAIGHT TALK

Growing as
Multicultural Educators

PETER LANG
New York • Washington, D.C./Baltimore • Bern
Frankfurt am Main • Berlin • Brussels • Vienna • Oxford

Library of Congress Cataloging-in-Publication Data

Powell, Rebecca.
Straight talk: growing as multicultural educators / Rebecca Powell.
p. cm. — (Counterpoints; vol. 149)
Includes bibliographical references and index.
1. Multicultural education—United States. 2. Teachers—United States—
Attitudes. I. Title. II. Counterpoints (New York, N.Y.); vol. 149.
LC1099.3 .P69   370.117'0973—dc21   00-020155
ISBN 0-8204-4988-1
ISSN 1058-1634

Die Deutsche Bibliothek-CIP-Einheitsaufnahme

Powell, Rebecca:
Straight talk: growing as multicultural educators / Rebecca Powell.
–New York; Washington, D.C./Baltimore; Bern;
Frankfurt am Main; Berlin; Brussels; Vienna; Oxford: Lang.
(Counterpoints; Vol. 149)
ISBN 0-8204-4988-1

Cover design by Lisa Dillon

The paper in this book meets the guidelines for permanence and durability
of the Committee on Production Guidelines for Book Longevity
of the Council of Library Resources.

∞

© 2001 Peter Lang Publishing, Inc., New York

Printed in the United States of America

To my parents
who taught me the meaning of love

Table of Contents

Part Four: Straight Talk
about Equitable Schools and Classrooms

Acknowledgments

I wish to express my sincere gratitude to Linda Spears-Bunton and Arlette Ingram Willis, who kindly agreed to review this book. Their affirmation of my ideas and their insightful suggestions for revision are deeply appreciated. I also wish to thank Karen Simms, Maynard Thomas, Aukram Burton, and Ben Oldham, who read and responded to various portions of the manuscript. Their thoughtful comments helped me to see my words more objectively, which greatly enhanced the text.

I wish to thank D. Moritz, Kati Haycock, and Ray Melecio for allowing me to include information and stories that they shared in presentations that I have attended over the past couple of years. I am especially appreciative of the vital work that they do on behalf of our children. I am also grateful to the Kentucky Educational Television for permitting me to include material from one of their broadcasts. A special thanks goes to Sandra Adams, Barbara Greenlief, and their former students, who graciously allowed me to interview them on their experiences with the "Saving Black Mountain" project and to include what I learned in this and other publications. The insights I gained from researching this project have been invaluable.

Finally, I am indebted to Joe Kincheloe and Shirley Steinberg for their continuing encouragement of my work, and to Carl Henlein, whose gift to Georgetown College provided financial support for completing this book. I am also indebted all those individuals who have taught me over the years, whose wisdom is interwoven into the pages of this volume. Last but certainly not least, I am extremely grateful to my family and friends for their enduring love, patience, and encouragement.

Part One

Straight Talk about
Multicultural Education

Introductory Letter

Dear Readers,

Don't you just love getting mail? I often read my e-mail while I eat lunch so that I have time to savor the notes from friends and colleagues. In fact, the letter is one of my favorite written genres; for me, it even surpasses the novel! Through letters, we can get to know one another on a more informal basis. Over the years, I've formed many friendships through letter writing.

The letters that you will read from me through this book are all about human difference. I chose to write to you through letters, because I wanted the book to be less formal than the typical textbook. I wanted to establish a closer relationship with you, my readers, and to share some of my own experiences as an Anglo working in the area of multicultural education. We will be exploring some tough issues together—racism, classism, sexism, homophobia, and the nature and causes of educational failure. Talking about such potentially volatile issues requires a relationship of trust. We must be willing to listen to one another, to be challenged by the research, and to explore our own cultural assumptions, acknowledging that we are individuals who arrive on the educational stage with varying human experiences. That is, we must be willing to be open-minded so that we might learn from the experiences of others, and to be vulnerable enough to grow from those experiences.

To begin our communication, I felt that it was important that you get to know me a little. Therefore, I decided to begin my letters to you by telling you about some of my own experiences and by sharing the ways that I have changed through those experiences. (By the way, letters are meant to be a process of dialogue and not monologue; therefore, I would welcome getting a letter from you!) I grew up in an affluent suburb of Cleveland, Ohio, where my only experience with persons who were different from me was having a couple of Japanese American and Chinese American friends. Like my own parents, their families had undoubtedly moved to the suburbs to escape the city and to seek a better life, and had essentially assimilated into the dominant White, middle-class society. I do not recall ever talking about *their* culture; in fact, it seemed quite insignificant at the time, since they appeared to be like me in every way except for their distinctive facial features.

As a community, we were quite insulated from the impoverished areas of the inner city, although as a teen I spent two summers working with young children at an all-Black church there. The preschoolers I taught were delightful, yet it was evident that their lives had already been significantly affected by poverty and racism. I particularly remember a small boy who was severely withdrawn; we learned later from his mother that his father had been so overwhelmed by the harsh realities of the family's life that he had recently committed suicide by jumping off a pier into Lake Erie.

During one of these summers in the late 1960s, Cleveland was plagued with what were popularly referred to as "race riots," and the National Guard was called in to restore order. Many of the children fled with their families to safer locations, and every morning we would encounter more homes that had been burned and looted the night before. The children who remained expressed their fear through their paintings, which generally depicted bright reds, oranges, and yellows—the colors of burning buildings that they saw around them.

During these same years, I also had the opportunity to spend the night in an apartment building in this same neighborhood, as part of a youth exchange program arranged through my church. I will never forget this overnight experience, as it was so foreign to anything I had encountered during my sheltered life. The streets seemed to "come alive" after midnight, and there was the nearly constant sound of police sirens. About this same time, an African American couple purchased a house in my suburban neighborhood, undoubtedly in an effort to secure for themselves and their children the opportunities that we already enjoyed but took for granted. Yet before they moved in, the house was burned to the ground—a concrete expression of the racism that was pervasive in my community, but which we could choose to ignore. (After all, as Whites, such racism didn't impact us directly.)

It was through these early experiences that I came to realize that life in our society is far from equal, that my life was one of privilege, and that I was blessed by both my class position and my racial constitution. Nevertheless, my knowledge of race and class privilege was still quite limited, for my aim was not to change persons of my own race and class so that they might be more accepting of human difference; rather, my aspiration was to "uplift the downtrodden" so that they might become more like *us*. I joined "liberal" youth mission groups, cleaned up neighborhoods, attended Black churches, and mentored young people living in the projects. And while my heart was perhaps "in the right place"—to use a familiar phrase—in retrospect I realize that my motives were not entirely honorable. A benevolent spirit led me to "help" those who were impoverished, yet in my naiveté I generally failed to acknowledge the need to confront the social norms and political decisions that reinforced a system of White privilege—a system that allows me to continue to benefit from my race and class status. (Years later, I was to encounter the various stages of White racial identity development, and learned that I was in what Janet Helms calls the "pseudo-independent" stage during this time period. In this stage, White standards are used to define acceptability, and one's attention is devoted to persuading Blacks to adapt to White standards, versus educating Whites to recognize the many ways in which they are consciously or unconsciously racist.[1] I'll talk more about these stages in a future letter to you.)

Please don't misunderstand me; I believe those of us who have been richly blessed in this world are obliged to give assistance to those who require it. Indeed, this should be a responsibility of living in the human community. At the same time, however, I believe that we are also obliged to work toward the elimination of the social, economic, and psychological barriers in society that create the conditions that lead to human poverty. (I will be discussing many of these barriers throughout this book.) Teachers are in one of the best positions to do this, since they have the potential to socialize students to respect human differences and to become advocates for equity and justice.

In my early teaching career, I continued with this same paternalistic, "pseudo-independent" ideology. My first teaching job was in a small, working-class community, and my elementary children sponsored food drives for the hungry and collected gloves during the cold Ohio winters for children who could not afford them. Yet, I never considered teaching my students about the inequities in our society that necessitated such benevolence, nor did I ever digress from the standard curriculum in order to include the perspectives and experiences of Native Americans, African Americans, or even those from different religions or from lower socioeconomic classes. My next teaching job was providing what was referred to as "remedial reading" to elementary students in an urban neighborhood in the South. Once again, the idea was to "help" those who needed it—most of them African American males—to adapt to the school's (Anglo, middle-class) expectations of success through "compensating" for their weaknesses. And once again, it never occurred to me that my young students would have benefited from reading stories that related to their own lives, or from writing about their own experiences. I lived in a state of what James Banks has referred to as "cultural encapsulation"—existing in my own white, middle-class cocoon.[2]

Breaking out of that cocoon has not been easy. My two marriages to men who have had very different cultural experiences from my own have helped me to be aware of the many ways in which I have been (and we all are) culturally determined. I have learned firsthand about the Appalachian culture and have gained a respect for the creativity and tenacity of those who reside in the Appalachian region. My work with teachers from eastern Kentucky and my study of the professional literature have given me insights into how the process of schooling works both to promote and to hinder positive social transformation.[3] Finally, I am indebted to a number of African American friends who have supported my growth as an Anglo multicultural educator and who have significantly enriched my understanding of cultural diversity. Through a process of reeducation and much introspection, I have come to a place in my own life's journey where I have a desire and a commitment to effect change.

Becoming a multicultural educator is a process of continuous transformation, and I am still on that journey. I have found that many teachers and future educators embrace the "idea" of multicultural education, yet they are all at different stages of the journey. Some, like me, are farther along in the process, while others are just beginning to think about what multicultural education is all about. Where are you in this process? What experiences have you had in your own life that have affected your perceptions of human diversity? I would encourage you to take a moment to reflect on your own life and your experiences with persons who are different from you in terms of race, ethnicity, socioeconomic class, language, gender, age, religion, and sexual orientation. Do you feel uncomfortable talking about any of these human differences? If you do, be assured that you are not alone.

In my own experience, I have found that the true multicultural educator sees society differently. It is as if we are given new eyes and ears with which to perceive the world: television shows, movies, advertisements, newspaper articles, conversations with others, comments of friends or colleagues—all are read or heard with enhanced sensitivity to our diverse human experiences. I am reminded of a former student who entered my office one day exclaiming, "Dr. Powell, I'm really angry at you. Through your class, I now find so many things to be offensive that I never found offensive before; I know that I'll never be complacent again—and complacency is so *comfortable*! I *liked* being complacent!"

An education that is multicultural is not just a way of teaching; it is also a way of believing and of seeing the world. In these letters to you, I explore the *ideology* of multicultural education, and not just the "idea" of multiculturalism. I hope to challenge you to go outside of your own "comfort zone" and to think about what you really believe about human differences. For to become a true advocate of multicultural education, it is necessary to develop an understanding of what this means for you personally, and to adopt its ideology—one that embraces the democratic goals of equity, justice, and fairness, and that believes teachers can make a difference. I invite you, dear readers, to join me on this journey.

Until next time,
Becky

Notes

1. Janet E. Helms, ed., *Black and White Racial Identity: Theory, Research, and Practice* (Westport, CT: Praeger, 1993).

2. James A. Banks, *An Introduction to Multicultural Education* (Boston: Allyn and Bacon, 1994).

3. Rebecca G. Eller, "Teacher Resistance and Educational Change: Toward a Critical Theory of Literacy in Appalachia," unpublished doctoral dissertation, University of Kentucky, 1989.

Letter Two

Thinking about Multicultural Education

Dear Readers,

It seems that an appropriate way to begin our journey together is to talk about what we mean when we say "multicultural education." When you hear this term, what comes to mind? What do you think a multicultural classroom looks like?

In my multicultural education course, each of my students is assigned to a particular classroom for observations. One of the assignments that I give them is to look at the ways in which the school and the classroom reflect a multicultural identity. Often, they end up looking for the obvious things: pictures on the walls that represent human diversity, multicultural/ multieth- nic literature, and so forth. While all of this is an important part of an education that is multicultural, there is more to multicultural education than using particular materials.

Before you continue with this letter, I encourage you to stop for a moment and jot down your ideas about multicultural education. Your ideas may be a bit sketchy at this point, but you undoubtedly have some concep- tion of what an education that is multicultural is all about. I invite you to take a minute to reflect; in a later letter, I'll ask you to come back to these ideas and see if they have changed.

Throughout my letters to you, I think you'll find that I have some very definite ideas about multicultural education. You may not agree with me. More than likely, however, you may find that you agree on some points, and not others. What I ask you to do is to keep an open mind. It seems that sometimes when we read and come across an idea that elicits in us a strong negative reaction, this reaction tends to affect the rest of what we read. That is, it causes us to read from one perspective rather than to try to see all sides of an issue. Has that ever happened to you?

Talking about issues relating to human diversity is not easy; it can produce controversy because we are forced to deal with our differences. On the other hand, unless we talk about those differences, we can never reach common ground. I also believe that we can never truly understand our similarities until we are able to get past the things that tend to divide us. In talking about our differences, we have to be willing to listen to the ideas of those with whom we might differ. So, I have just given you a clue about one characteristic of an education that is multicultural: it involves talk— dialogue—about our similarities and differences as human beings and the social (and political and economic) issues that evolve from those differences.

At this point, you are probably expecting me to give you a definition or two. I'm not going to do that, for a couple of reasons. First, an education that is multicultural has so many dimensions that I think to define it in a brief statement would be an exercise in futility. For instance, multicultural scholars have emphasized various facets of multicultural education, viewing it as a social movement,[1] as a means for fighting racism,[2] and as curriculum transformation.[3] I agree with all of these ideas, and I'll be talking about them in my letters to you. (Besides, if I were to suggest a definition, I can just imagine some well-meaning teacher asking you to memorize it for a quiz!)

But in all seriousness, I think it's important that you come to your own definition as you read these letters and reflect on the ideas presented. In fact, you would be doing that anyway—I could never *make* you accept my definition! Further, in giving you a definition, I would be sending a subtle message that I expect you to make your ideas conform to mine. Herein lies another characteristic of an education that is multicultural: it welcomes diverse perspectives and shared inquiry, and resists the imposition of ideas.

It's often interesting to talk with others about how we conceptualize multicultural education, though, because doing so can open our minds to the many ways in which it can be viewed. I am an active member of a group of higher educators in Kentucky called the Alliance for Multicultural Education, and one of our first discussions was on the topic, "What is Multicultural Education?" Some members of the group (myself included) see it as a means for fighting oppression. A colleague from the Middle East responded with the query, "What oppression? Do we really have oppression here in the

United States?" Of course, it depends upon your point of view. One of the reasons I chose letter writing as the genre for this book is that I wanted to encourage you to read actively—that is, to think critically as you read—and to come up with your own viewpoints.

I think you will find that my own ideas come through in these letters, and I am very passionate about them. As you shall see, I have strong beliefs about multicultural education. At the same time, I don't have the right to impose my beliefs on you. What I do have the right to do, however (and indeed, I feel that this is my *obligation* as an educator), is to get you to think critically about the issues associated with human difference and about your role as a teacher in a diverse nation and world.

At the outset, I think it's important to point out that we are all biased. Actually, I prefer to say that we all have "cultural assumptions" that have been formed through our own unique experiences. As I mentioned in my introductory letter, James Banks calls this "cultural encapsulation"; it is as if we grow up in a capsule of sorts, and we must break out of it in order to become truly educated. Perhaps it is trite to say that we are all "products" of our experiences, but to a large extent it is true. A primary argument for a multicultural education is that it takes students beyond their limited experiences and expands their thinking. Ideally, this process involves direct encounters with persons who differ from ourselves, but sometimes our experiences can also be vicarious, as in learning about the lives of others through literature or the media.

Often at the beginning of my course in multicultural education, many of my White students are silent. When I encourage them to share their thoughts, they typically state that they feel that their ideas will be seen as less valuable because they simply haven't experienced as much as others in the class. What they mean by this is that they haven't had many encounters with persons from different cultural backgrounds. Yet I think it is important to acknowledge that our experiences are just that—*our experiences*. Talking about those experiences can help us to understand why we feel the way we do, and can lead to a greater awareness and understanding of our own cultural assumptions. To state it another way, an important part of multicultural education is to understand who we are, and how our identities as men, women, Whites, African Americans, Asian Americans, members of the middle or working class, and so on shape the way that we see the world. We must validate our experiences and "own" them so that we can become aware of our own cultural assumptions. (If all of these ideas are a bit elusive to you at this point, don't worry. I'll come back to them in future letters!)

Take a minute at this point to think about who you are as a person. Let's begin with your gender. A popular topic throughout the ages has been the ways in which men and women differ. How do you think your gender affects how you see the world? Do you find that it's easier to talk with persons of the same gender? Deborah Tannen has written some fascinating books on the different communication styles of men and women.[4] You might want to check them out! What is your race? This question may be difficult for some of you. You may have a mixed heritage, or you may be Anglo, in which case you may not see yourself as being of a particular race. Typically, as Whites, we have the luxury of not having to think in terms of our race. (More on this later!) What is your religion, and how does this influence your beliefs about human difference? What is your ethnicity? For instance, are you German American (as I am), Irish American, Appalachian? How would you characterize yourself in terms of socioeconomic status? Indeed, human beings differ in a multitude of ways, and these differences all contribute to our assumptions about the world.

The next question, then, would be, how do you think your race, ethnicity, gender, socioeconomic status, sexual orientation, and religion have shaped who you are as an individual? What beliefs and values do you have as a result of your heritage and your class position in society? At this point, many of my students point out that there are other elements of human difference that also affect who they are as individuals. For instance, students who are considered overweight talk about how their weight has affected how they perceive themselves and how they relate to others. Students with varying physical challenges have certainly been influenced by those conditions. Age can also be an important variable. Certainly, there are multitudes of human differences that make us who we are.

In my letters to you, I will be focusing primarily (although not exclusively) on two of these dimensions: race/ethnicity and socioeconomic class.

At the beginning of my course in multicultural education, my students—who are primarily Anglo—often protest that we talk too much about race, and not enough about differences that affect them directly (such as weight and age). I then tell them that the primary reason that race and socioeconomic status are discussed so extensively is that they are the factors most directly related to educational failure in our country. Despite extensive efforts aimed at preventing dropouts, students of color still drop out of school in greater numbers than Anglo students. Consider these facts. According to recent data compiled by the National Center for Education Statistics, 13.8 percent of African American youth and 29.5 percent of Hispanic youth ages 16–24 were high-school dropouts, compared with 7.7 percent of White youth in this same age category. From October 1997 to October 1998, when the data were compiled, 5.2 percent of African American students and 9.4 percent of Hispanic students dropped out of school (compared with 3.9 percent of White students). Socioeconomic class also is highly correlated with educational underachievement. These same data reveal that young adults from the bottom 20 percent in terms of family income were four times more likely to drop out of high school than families from the top 20 percent.[5]

Even when income remains relatively constant across various racial groups, however, students of color still tend to lag behind. Consider, for example, the case of Shaker Heights, a relatively affluent, racially integrated suburb of Cleveland, where the schools have received national recognition for their attempts to maintain an education of high quality for both Blacks and Whites.[6] While African American students in Shaker Heights tend to outperform Black students elsewhere, nevertheless there is still an achievement gap between students of color and White students. In fact, about 95 percent of the students in the lower academic tracks in Shaker Heights are students of color. This situation is not atypical of school districts elsewhere. Therefore, as educators, I think we need to understand how schools have failed in their efforts to serve these students.

I should also mention here that various immigrant groups are not as severely affected by educational failure as are other "minority" groups. The reasons for this are somewhat complex and will be examined in a future letter. Did you notice that I put the word *minority* in quotes? The use of this word implies that certain populations are somehow outside of the American mainstream. The term "minority" can be problematic in a country that is ruled by the majority because it implies that certain groups have less power. Also, we need to be aware that within the next few decades, it is predicted that Whites will actually be the "minority" race in terms of numbers of persons in the United States. A quote that I like to share with my students is from an article written by Richard Figueroa and Eugene Garcia: "In 2026, we will have the exact inverse of student representation as we knew it in 1990 when White students made up 70 per cent of our enrolled K-12 student body."[7] Unfortunately, our teaching force is still overwhelmingly Anglo, which makes it imperative that White teachers learn how to address the educational needs of non-Anglo students.

Certainly, dealing with human differences such as age and physical challenges would be less controversial than talking about such hot topics as racism and classism. I might add that I will also be sending you letters on sexism and homophobia—two other hot topics! My students often want to retreat to "safer ground" by discussing their experiences with foreign students on campus, for instance. I've even known many faculty members who view global education as "doing" multicultural education. While experiences with individuals from other nations are invaluable and should certainly be encouraged, they do not directly relate to the issue of educational failure that we must address as a society. To deal with these issues, we cannot escape having serious dialogues about the racism and classism that still exist, and that continue to plague our educational institutions. Sexism can also influence academic success, as can one's sexual orientation. It is worth noting here that gay and lesbian students have the highest suicide rate among all adolescents, which is why we as teachers must be willing to talk openly about homosexuality.

Some of you may not feel comfortable talking about these topics. I would encourage you to take a moment to think about what is causing your discomfort. Is it because as a society we are just not accustomed to talking about such issues? Do you ever talk about race (or socioeconomic class, or homosexuality) with your friends or colleagues? Often I find that students are embarrassed by such topics and tend to try to hide their embarrassment by jokes or sarcasm when talking with their peers. Another common response is silence. That is, when we are uncomfortable with certain remarks about others we simply remain silent because we do not want to risk our relationship with the other person by offending him or her. Of course, our silence merely reinforces the sexist or racist inclinations of the other person. (I often tell my students that "we support oppression through our silence.")

I hope that by the time you have read all of my letters to you, you will feel more comfortable discussing the "hot topics" with others in an honest and direct way. I also hope that you will not remain silent!

Talk to you again soon,
Becky

otes

1.   Christine E. Sleeter, *Multicultural Education as Social Activism* (Albany: State University of New York Press, 1996).

2.   "Multicultural Education as Anti-Racist Education: An Interview with Enid Lee." In *Rethinking Our Classrooms: Teaching for Equity and Justice* (Milwaukee, WI: Rethinking Schools, 1994). Also see G. Pritchy Smith, "Who Shall Have the Moral Courage to Heal Racism in America?" *Multicultural Education*, vol. 5, Spring 1998, pp. 4–10.

3.   James A. Banks, *An Introduction to Multicultural Education* (Boston: Allyn and Bacon, 1994); and James A. Banks, *Educating Citizens in a Multicultural Society* (New York: Teachers College Press, 1997).

4.   See, for example, Deborah Tannen, *You Just Don't Understand: Women and Men in Conversation* (New York: Ballantine Books, 1990).

5.   Phillip Kaufman, Jin Y. Kwon, Steve Klein, and Christopher D. Chapman, *Dropout Rates in the United States: 1998* (Washington, DC: U.S. Department of Education National Center for Education Statistics, Report #2000–022, 1999). The figures for American Indian youth may be even higher. Current data from the U.S. Bureau of Census reported by The Education Trust, Inc. indicate that of every 100 Native

American kindergartners, only 58 will graduate from high school. See *Achievement in America* (Washington, DC: The Education Trust, Inc., 1998).

6.   See, for example, John W. McWhorter, "Explaining the Black Education Gap," *The Wilson Quarterly*, vol. 24, Summer 2000, pp. 72–94; and Mano Singham, "The Canary in the Mine: The Achievement Gap Between Black and White Students," *Phi Delta Kappan*, vol. 80, no. 1, September 1998, pp. 9–15.

7.   Richard A. Figueroa and Eugene Garcia, "Issues in Testing Students from Culturally and Linguistically Diverse Backgrounds," *Multicultural Education*, vol. 2, Fall 1994, p. 11.

Part Two

Straight Talk about Biases

Letter Three

Confronting Racism

Dear Readers,

I must confess that I am experiencing a bit of anxiety as I begin this letter to you. My anxiety stems not from the topic of racism, but rather from the fact that I'm afraid that I will not be able to discuss it adequately in one short letter. Indeed, numerous volumes have been written about the subject of racism in the past several decades, and yet racism still persists. It has been my experience in working with Anglo teachers and students that most do not feel that they are racist. To a certain extent, this is true. Most do not harbor an internal hatred of persons of color, nor do they practice overtly racist acts. Many have friends who are from another racial background and thus they feel that they are not prejudiced. So, if you are Anglo, many of you may be thinking something like "Oh, here we go again. I'm tired of hearing about racism. Besides, I'm not racist. Can't we just skip this letter and move on to something else?"

My experiences with students of color, on the other hand, are another matter altogether. Having been forced to live within a racialized society all of their lives, many are angry and resentful. They see their White peers, many of whom honestly believe that racism is a thing of the past, as being essentially naive and ignorant. They also complain that they feel that they are always put in the position of having to educate Whites. "Why don't they try to educate themselves?" they complain. And they claim that when they try to educate Whites, their Anglo peers often fail to hear what they are saying, and tend to trivialize or dismiss their experiences with racism as being insignificant or even wrong—as not representing instances of racism at all.

In my multicultural education course, we spend a good part of the semester struggling with the concept of racism. The reason that we do this is that I believe strongly that you cannot deal with human difference until you understand yourself. And confronting our own culture as Whites—and as persons of color—is an essential first step. Typically, my Anglo students go through various stages in this struggle. First, they deny any association with racism. "I treat everyone the same," they say; or "I just don't see color." If you are reading this letter as a White person and have not thought much about racism, then you will probably relate to what I am saying here.

Then, the difficult work begins. We begin to explore the notion of "White privilege" through videos and various readings. This is tough work, for most of my Anglo students have never even thought about their race. For them, as for most Whites, "whiteness" is regarded as "normal" or "natural" in our society, and everyone else is seen as different. Generally, at first, my students deny the reality of White privilege. They point out the ways in which they believe persons of color are "privileged" through affirmative action, and they sense that affirmative action programs have taken away some of their own power. They are angry with me for asking them to think through the ways in which Whites have exercised power throughout U.S. history (both nationally and globally) in order to maintain a privileged status. They do not want to admit that they may be inadvertently contributing to this system by remaining silent on issues related to racism. Another frequent response is one of guilt, and an attempt to absolve oneself of it: "My ancestors may have contributed to a racist system, but what does that have to do with me? That was then, and now is now." Fortunately, by the end of the semester, most of my Anglo students (although not all), have taken a more productive stance and have begun to acknowledge that *all* of us have been negatively influenced by a racist system—Blacks and Whites alike. It takes a while to get to this stage however, which is the source of my anxiety that I mentioned at the start of this letter to you.

Before I proceed, I need to talk a bit about what I mean by the term "racism." What comes to mind when you hear this term? Do you picture burning crosses? Racial slurs? Perhaps even beatings and lynchings? Certainly, this is racism at its worst, and if this is the only perspective we have of racism, then indeed most of us would not be considered "racist." We might even be tempted to believe that racism has diminished in recent years.

Of course, many of you may be thinking, "Oh, racism is more than that. It also involves discrimination in housing, employment opportunities, educational opportunities, etc." Again, if this is the only perspective we have of racism, we (primarily Whites) might be tempted to believe that racism has been virtually eliminated. After all, don't we have laws that protect people's civil rights? And what about affirmative action? Of course, persons of color will tell you that our society still has a long way to go before they can live without fear, and before their civil rights are realized. Yet, often Whites do not want to hear this. Hence, we remain polarized along racial lines, and I believe we will continue to remain so until Whites begin the hard task of looking at their own racist assumptions.

Bob Blauner, in his aptly titled chapter "Talking Past Each Other: Black and White Languages of Race," looks at the history of the term "racism" and tells us that "For twenty years European-Americans have tended to feel that systematic racial inequities marked an earlier era, not our own."[1] He writes that until the 1960s, the term "racism" was not commonly used. In the 1950s and early 1960s, the focus was on racial attitudes and behavior expressed through prejudice and discrimination, that is, hostile feelings and stereotypes projected toward persons of color and the subsequent actions meant to harm them. By the mid-1960s, however, seeing racism simply as individual attitudes and actions was perceived as too limited to explain the system of racial bias in society. With the publication in 1967 of *Black Power* by Stokely Carmichael and Charles Hamilton, "institutional racism" became recognized as a more subtle yet pervasive and fundamental form of racism. Blauner writes that "Racism, in this view, was built into society and scarcely required prejudicial attitudes to maintain racial oppression."[2] In his research in the 1970s on Black and White attitudes toward racism, Blauner found that Whites tended to adhere to an individual perspective of racism ("I don't personally practice discrimination; therefore I'm not racist"), whereas Blacks considered the more recently recognized meanings of racism to be more basic. Blacks still felt that racism "pervaded American life, indeed, had become more insidious because the subtle forms were harder to combat than old-fashioned exclusion and persecution."[3]

Before we go any further, I think it's important to emphasize again one of the sentences quoted above: "Racism, in this view, was built into society and scarcely required prejudicial attitudes to maintain racial oppression." How do you react to this statement? For me, it is quite startling. So, does this mean that I can try to eliminate individual prejudice, yet racism will still persist? Absolutely. Of course, this does not mean that we shouldn't attempt to overcome prejudice. But what I would like to explore with you further is the idea that racism goes beyond individual prejudice and acts of discrimination; it has become a part of the very fabric of our society. And as teachers, I believe that we have a responsibility to create a *better* society—one where there is more hope, more compassion, more human understanding.

When I am teaching about racism, I like to use the scheme developed by James Jones and expanded upon by Janet Helms in her theory of racial identity.[4] This scheme helps me to conceptualize racism in all of its many forms—not just as individual prejudice. Jones suggests that there are actually three forms of racism—individual, institutional, and cultural. Individual racism is what we popularly tend to think of when we hear the term "racism," that is, the inferior treatment of persons of color based upon a belief that Whites are a superior race. Individual racism often takes quite overt forms, but it can also include more subtle prejudicial attitudes and actions. Helms writes that individual racism consists of "personal attitudes, beliefs, and behaviors designed to convince oneself of the superiority of Whites and the inferiority of non-White racial groups."[5] Therefore, when Whites say "I treat everyone the same—I don't see color," they are attempting to deny individually racist tendencies. What such persons fail to recognize, however, is that when you ignore someone's race, you also refuse to acknowledge the significance of that race. That is, you do not see their race or the contributions of that race as being valuable; in essence, you are denying an important part of their identity. (I will have more to say about this later!)

The second form of racism identified by Jones is institutional racism. According to Helms, institutional racism means "social policies, laws, and regulations whose purpose is to maintain the economic and social advantages of Whites over non-Whites."[6] If we were to think about it, we could come up with several examples of institutional racism. For instance, segregation policies designed to provide students of color with an inferior education were a manifestation of institutionalized racism, as were Jim Crow laws. Even today, however, institutionalized racism exists, although it can be more subtle. For instance, regulations designed to keep persons of color from participating fully in an organization or institution are evidence of this form of racism. These regulations can be overt (e.g., strict requirements for membership in a club), or subtle (e.g., hiring requirements that make it difficult for persons of color to attain employment).

In schools, the practice of tracking can be considered to be an example of institutionalized racism, since the tests, cultural knowledge, language, and so on required for placement are generally based upon White, middle- and upper-class norms. Consequently, "minority" populations continue to be underrepresented in the higher academic tracks in our schools. The criteria for placement are thought to be "neutral," but in reality they are biased in favor of Whites who are generally from middle- or upper-class homes. We will explore this phenomenon further in another letter. The use of textbooks and other curriculum materials that present only the perspectives and histories of the White race is another example of institutional racism, since this practice ignores or marginalizes the contributions of other races and can reinforce a sense of inferiority/superiority.

At this point, you may be thinking that racism is actually more complex than you had originally thought. If you are White, you may never have considered tracking or a monocultural curriculum to be instances of racism. At the same time, you may be denying my assertion that these are instances of racism by thinking something like "tracking is fair; persons who are in the upper tracks earned the right to be there." Without going into this issue in depth in this letter, I can assure you that there is a great deal of evidence to the contrary. (I'll be sharing a story of tracking as early as first grade in my next letter to you.) You may also be saying to yourself, as many Whites do, something like "I see the point you are trying to make, but haven't Whites done everything that has been of significance in this country? So why should we learn about the histories of others?"

My first reply to this statement is that if you have gone through a monocultural curriculum yourself (as I have), how would you have learned about the contributions of others in order to make this assumption? (The very fact that you have thus far been able to ignore the contributions of non-Whites can be considered an example of "White privilege.") My second reply would be to look at the evidence. Did you know that the first open-heart surgery was performed by an African American surgeon, Daniel Hale Williams, in 1893? Did you know that an African American, Charles Richard Drew, is responsible for developing the system of storing blood plasma and for the introduction of blood banks? Did you know that the process of using carbon filaments in electric light bulbs was developed not by Thomas Edison, but by a Black man who worked with him, Lewis Howard Latimer? Did you know that one of the pioneers in the field of space science is Franklin Chang-Diaz, who was the first Hispanic American in space? Did you know that Ely Parker, a Seneca Indian, drafted the terms of surrender for the Civil War? Did you know that the gas mask that has saved countless lives was invented by an African American named Garrett A. Morgan? Did you know that the first person to plant the American flag at the North Pole was Matthew A. Henson, an African American explorer? Did you know that Navajo Indians created a secret code that their "code talkers" used to transmit messages during World War II, a tactic that saved numerous American lives?

If you did not know these things, then you are probably not alone. Indeed, our nation is rich with the scientific insights and the artistic and literary achievements of persons of color, yet these contributions are not always recognized. It is also important to note that our nation was literally built on the backs of no-wage and low-wage labor—the labor of persons whose names may be unknown to us but whose sacrifices nevertheless contributed significantly to making this nation what it is today.

What supports individual and institutional racism, however, is the third form identified by Jones—cultural racism. For me, cultural racism is the most pervasive, and also the most subtle, form of racism. Helms defines it as "societal beliefs and customs that promote the assumption that the products of White culture (e.g., language, traditions, appearance) are superior to those of non-White cultures."[7] When I first introduce the notion of cultural racism to my students, I bring in popular magazines like *People*,

Seventeen, Newsweek, and *Women's Day*. I ask them to look at the images in the photographs and to try to determine the messages that are being reinforced. (You might try doing this exercise yourself!) Invariably the students begin to acknowledge that the images of beauty being portrayed are largely Anglo—small nose and mouth, straight (non-kinky) hair, lightish skin. Even when "token" non-White models are included, they tend to "look White." When you consider that we are literally bombarded with such messages on a daily basis from the time we are born, it becomes clear that we are essentially conditioned to perceive the world in a certain way—one that celebrates "whiteness" over other cultural forms.

Our assumptions about language, too, are also based upon a racist (as well as classist) ideology in that the superiority of the standard linguistic form is generally taken for granted. Yet when one considers that according to linguists, all language forms are equally complex and legitimate, we must ask why Standard English has been able to achieve such prominence. The answer lies in the fact that it is the language spoken by those in power. (This is true not only in the United States, but in other countries as well; the "standard" to which citizens aspire is the language spoken by those who have the most power and privilege in that particular society.) Did you ever consider why the Black vernacular is not the language of choice in our schools and in society, particularly given the fact that it tends to be more efficient than Standard English (e.g., "two cent" versus "two cents")? Or why Appalachian English is generally devalued? I often tell my Kentucky students that if Appalachia had achieved power over the northern capitalist states, we would all be speaking a mountain dialect! Most parents from marginalized populations know that the standard discourse is the "language of power," which is why they insist that their children learn Standard English, and also why the introduction of Ebonics into California schools generated so much controversy.

The overall effect of individual, institutional, and cultural racism is a system that supports the privilege of Whites over other races. In all honesty, most Whites I know are not *consciously* racist. Neither was I; and before I began to study racism and all of its forms, I truly believed that I was not racist. In fact, I believe that most Whites try very hard NOT to be racist, by taking a "colorblind" stance, which is why it can be very disconcerting to them to learn about the various forms that racism takes in our society. Personally, I now recognize that racism is embedded in our society, and that while most Whites would perhaps consciously choose otherwise, we *unconsciously* support a system of racism through our silence and inaction. In other words, I believe that Whites are socialized to be racist. (This is a rather bold statement, I know, but think about it for a moment.) That is, Whites are socialized to see "White" as "right"—to believe that White norms in terms of beauty, language, traditions, and so on are superior to those of persons of color, and that everyone else wants to be like "us." Jones and Carter argue that "As long as the only standards of cultural acceptability continue to be those models of European heritage and upper-class white Americans, visible racial/ethnic groups will always be seen as inferior unless they adopt the cultural ways thought to be better."[8]

Cultural racism can be a difficult concept to grasp, so let's talk about it a bit more. Perhaps the most blatant example of cultural racism in our society was the establishment of boarding schools for Indian children, which reached prominence in the late 1800s.[9] These schools were explicitly designed to assimilate Native American children by removing them from their families at a very young age and stripping them of their Native culture, language, and values. In fact, generally, Native youths were not even allowed to return to their families during the summer months but instead were placed in the homes of European Americans, where they learned about Anglo ways and also provided a source of cheap labor. In her article on the history of Native American women, Deirdre Almeida writes that "This formal education system contributed enormously to the breakdown of Native families, including women's traditional roles, and led to the development of many of the social ills that still affect Native nations today, such as dysfunctional families and substance abuse."[10] While schools that serve American Indian youth today are not as overtly racist and often strive to be more culturally relevant, Native youths are still faced with tremendous obstacles in their desire to remain Indian while simultaneously learning how to maneuver in a White world.[11]

This struggle is not unlike that faced by other marginalized populations, who attempt to affirm their group's cultural values and norms in a White-dominated society. Consider, for instance, the emergence of Black beauty pageants and other cultural events. Indeed, many Whites may resist the essentially segregationist approach inherent in this trend, yet given the reality of cultural racism, such events are crucial in establishing Black notions of beauty and culture and thus in developing a sense of pride in being a person of color in this nation.[12]

Individual, institutional, and cultural racism all contribute to a system that is designed to maintain the privileged status of Whites and the consequent inferior status of persons of color. In what is now a frequently cited monograph on White privilege, Peggy McIntosh suggests that racial privilege is like an "invisible knapsack" containing assets that we (Whites) can use to our advantage.[13] I have already alluded to some of these assets. For instance, as Whites, we can choose not to learn about the histories and contributions of persons of color. We can also choose not to learn other languages and dialects. In other words, we will not be disadvantaged in our society if we do not learn these things. Indeed, we can choose not to listen when persons of color talk about racism, or we can choose not to take them seriously. These are all assets that Whites can enjoy because of the dominance of their race.

To help you think more about the issue of White privilege, I have developed the following checklist. Some of these ideas are related to the list of assets presented in McIntosh's paper, while others are my own. I invite you to take a moment to complete this exercise. I encourage you then to think about the impact that these benefits have had on our lives as individuals and as a society.

Checklist of White Privileges

_____ I can always be sure that when I go to vote for my representatives, someone with my skin color will be running for office.

_____ I can always be sure that when I read the newspaper or turn on a television news broadcast, someone with my skin color will be shown in a position of authority.

_____ I know that in school, I will learn about the history of persons with my skin color.

_____ I know that in school, I will read books written by persons with my skin color.

_____ I know that in school, I will always be able to find teachers and administrators who are of my race.

_____ I know that in school, I will never be made to feel that the way I speak is wrong.

_____ In know that in school, I will never have to worry that my teacher may not like me because of my race.

_____ I know that in school, if I am placed in a lower academic track or lower achievement group, it will not have anything to do with my race.

_____ I never have to worry whether my skin color will be a factor in purchasing or renting a place to live.

_____ I never have to worry whether my skin color will be a factor in where I will be seated in a restaurant, or how I will be treated.

_____ I never have to worry that my children will be devalued because of their skin color.

_____ I never have to worry that my children will be treated poorly, discriminated against, or called names because of their skin color.

_____ When I go into a store, I know that I will not be ignored, mistrusted, or questioned because of my skin color.

_____ I know that I will always be able to find hair products that are appropriate for my type of hair.

_____ I know that I will always be able to find hose, band-aids, makeup, and other products that match my skin color.

_____ When I attend a meeting, I do not have to worry about representing my entire race.

_____ When I take a test, I do not have to worry that my poor performance may be perceived to be a negative reflection on my race.

_____ When I am hired for a job, I can be sure that it was because of my qualifications and not because they needed someone of my race to fill a quota.

_____ When someone compliments me, I can be sure that it is because of my performance and not because someone wants to prove that he or she is not racist.

_____ I can always be sure that someone from my race will be represented in a beauty pageant.

_____ When information or materials arrive at my institution relating to multicultural programs and issues, I don't have to worry that they will always be sent to me to review.

_____ I can pretty much be sure that when I am asked to serve on a committee or board, it is because I am valued for my expertise and not because they needed someone of my color to represent my race.

_____ I can limit my participation on committees and boards because there are already several individuals from my race who serve on them.

_____ I do not feel that I must always represent my race favorably and be a role model for others of my race to follow. While I may feel a responsibility to be a model that others can emulate, I do not feel the need to do this because of my race.

_____ When I get up in the morning, I do not have to worry that something negative might occur that day as a result of my race.

_____ I can be fairly certain that no one will write an article or book that tries to prove the biological inferiority of my race.

_____ I can be fairly certain that the standardized tests that I must take are not biased against my race.

_____ I do not have to worry about offending someone or being put on the defensive when I try to explain why an experience or statement might be construed as racist.

_____ When people of another race want to be my friends, I do not have to worry that they may be using our friendship to show others how open-minded they are.

_____ In meetings or other public forums, I do not have to worry about being ignored or dismissed because of my race.

_____ I do not have memories of negative experiences that occurred because I am of a particular race.

_____ When I am stopped by a police officer, I know that he or she will not be influenced by my race.

_____ I can be sure that the justice system will not be biased against me because of my race.

_____ I do not feel that it is my duty to teach others about racism.

_____ I can choose when and where I want to think about and respond to racism, or I can choose not to think about it at all.

As you tally your score, recognize that the lower the number of check marks you made, the more you have been negatively affected by White privilege. The higher the number, the more you have been positively affected by White privilege. I must admit that my own score is quite high. My White race, coupled with my relatively high socioeconomic class, has given me a number of benefits over the years. The only time I can recall when my race worked against me is when I applied for a teaching position in a public school system in North Carolina nearly two decades ago. At that time, schools were required to fill hiring quotas in order to continue receiving federal funds. While this situation affected me personally (I never did get a teaching job and was forced to take a job as a secretary), I was able to acknowledge that hiring teachers of color was important for the children in that district. It was also important in a society that purported to support an ideology of justice, fairness, and equality. We still have a long way to go in balancing the scales.

Like Peggy McIntosh, as I began to develop this checklist, I was amazed at how many assets I was able to come up with in such a short period of time. There are undoubtedly many that I have left out. If you are a person of color, these assets probably seem quite obvious to you. (It has been my experience that most students of color agree with them, and can add several of their own.) If you are Anglo, however, chances are you have never really thought much about the benefits of being White in this country. I would encourage you to be honest in your responses and to think about them carefully, for we (Whites) do tend to see the world very differently from the way persons of color see it. I often remind my college students that places such as "Whites only" restaurants, theaters, water fountains, and bathrooms existed in my own lifetime, and while such overt discrimination may not be as evident today, *we are still living with its legacy.* In other words, White benefits and the negative impact of these benefits on persons of color have had a cumulative effect over time.

It's also important to state here that many of the benefits on this list come from experiences that have been shared with me by my Black friends, and their willingness to share has helped me, as a White person, to see the world through a Black lens. For instance, from a White perspective, having a policeman stop you late at night to request a sobriety test after driving a bit erratically from fatigue may seem like standard procedure. Yet after hundreds of years of discriminatory treatment, the same event will be construed quite differently by persons of color. In fact, this particular experience actually occurred to a friend of mine who is a high-ranking administrator in the public school system. Another friend was worried about her son's new dreadlocks because she was afraid that he would be stopped by the police, and indeed he was, shortly thereafter. Yet another friend shared with me once the fact that he never sat in a restaurant with his back to the door. "It's just something you learn never to do as an African American child," he told me.

In her work on White privilege, McIntosh writes that we tend to see the benefits of "whiteness" as "neutral, normal, and universally available to everybody." She goes on to explain that "Whether through the curriculum or in the newspaper, the television, the economic system, or the general look of people in the streets, we received daily signals and indications that my people counted, and that others *either didn't exist or must be trying, not very successfully, to be like people of my race*."[14] Such is the elusive nature of cultural racism; the standards upon which we judge others are seen as "neutral" and even "normal" because we have been conditioned to accept them as such. As I grew up in my insulated White community, I never really thought about how difficult it must be for a child who came from a different cultural and linguistic background to acquire *my* language and *my* culture; indeed, I never really had to think about it much.

I recall a time in my childhood (I think I was about seven) when my church sponsored a "missions project" to bring African American children from the inner city into our White suburbs during the summer so that they might learn how to "be like people of my race." I shudder now at the culturally racist assumptions that were inherent in this project—not unlike the Indian boarding school concept a hundred years before. My main recollection of these two weeks spent with Rose and Margaret, my temporary Black sisters, was how knowledgeable and "streetwise" they were when compared to my sheltered White suburban naiveté. While this experience at least taught me something about my own privilege as a White child growing up in an upper-middle-class White community, for Rose and Margaret it probably merely intensified and reinforced their anger and resentment at living in a racialized society that works for the benefit of some (me) and not others (them). In fact, I have found that Whites are often surprised and dismayed at this anger, which is often (justifiably, I think) directed at them. I think that this reaction stems from the fact that most Whites do not recognize or acknowledge the pervasiveness of racism in society, and therefore are hurt when persons of color accuse them of being racist.

Yet over the years, I have come to realize that essentially racism IS a system of White privilege. This system is maintained in a lot of different ways, for example, through individual acts of discrimination, through procedures and policies that are designed to perpetuate the power of Whites, and through the (often unconscious) acceptance of White norms, values, and standards of behavior. *If you are White in our society, then you have benefited—and you continue to benefit—from this privilege.* "But what about affirmative action?" you might ask. Affirmative action is an attempt to counteract this system of privilege. (And isn't it interesting that we as Whites are so quick to say this policy is "unfair" when our own privilege that we have enjoyed for so long is being challenged?) Perhaps the reason that affirmative action is such a contested issue is that it serves as a constant reminder of our White privilege—a fact that we would prefer to deny.

When my White students begin to confront the reality of White privilege, I often find that the typical response is one of guilt. Guilt is not necessarily a negative reaction, but it can lead to a negative response if we continuously feel that we must justify our privilege. I think it's important to recognize here that we did not *create* this system of privilege; at the same time, however, we reinforce it through our inaction. Guilt will persist—and can actually *reinforce* a system of privilege—through our continuous need to defend and justify our privilege. (That is, in order to stop feeling guilty,

I have found that Whites often try to convince themselves that they have really earned the benefits they have acquired as a result of being White.) At the same time, guilt can lead to positive action if we use it as a catalyst to create a more just and equitable society. For many of my students, once they understand the benefits of being White in this nation, they become committed to educating others about racism.

For Whites, the fight against racism must begin with an understanding of "whiteness" and what that means in a society grounded in White privilege.[15] For persons of color, the struggle often becomes one of developing a positive racial identity. Because "being Black" or "being Brown" is often viewed in our society as having a negative connotation, students of color often go through several stages in their own identity formation, from denying the reality of their racial identity, to immersing themselves in a Black/Brown culture, and finally to internalizing a positive and personally relevant racial identity. According to Janet Helms, while in the stage of immersion, persons often act in stereotypical ways in an effort to "act Black," and there can be generalized anger both toward Whites and toward other persons of color who have not yet reached this level of development (or who have gone beyond it).[16] In their anti-racism course, Louise Derman-Sparks and Carol Brunson Phillips find evidence of these various stages among their students. They report that their students of color often move from an acceptance or denial of society's negative view of their racial group, through a reexamination of their own racial identity, and eventually toward a commitment to work toward societal transformation. In the final stage of growth, they are able to make connections with other forms of oppression (e.g., class oppression, anti-Semitism, etc.) and forge relationships with members of other oppressed groups: "understanding that the common experience of oppression stems from the same source—institutional racism—helps students of color overcome negative feelings about members of other racial groups."[17] Further, they develop a deeper understanding of how a system of racism has adversely affected Whites, and begin to reexamine their own role in societal change.

In one short letter to you, I cannot possibly address all of the thoughts and assumptions that you undoubtedly have about racism. All that I can do is to invite you to think about this topic some more, and to keep an open mind and heart. I would also advise that you look for instances of racism in your daily life and not be afraid to discuss them with others. For example, it is not unusual for my Anglo students to bring up statements that peers have made in their classes or dorms and to say something like "a month ago I would not have thought this to be racist, but now I see that it is." More important, however, is the need to challenge those who make such comments to think about their own racial assumptions, and some of my students are able to get to this stage.

At this point, I feel that I must apologize to my readers of color, for I acknowledge that this letter has been primarily addressed to White readers. This is because I have come to believe that racism fundamentally ought to be a concern of *Whites*, for until we as Whites begin to acknowledge the ways that we unconsciously (and sometimes even consciously) support a system of White privilege, then racism will not be eliminated. With this acknowledgment comes the need to *act* in some way. For if we continue to remain silent, then in essence we are endorsing a racist system.

Part of this action, for me, has been to educate other Whites about racism and the ways in which we contribute to it. In doing this, it is not my intent to place a "guilt trip" on other Whites, but rather to acknowledge that we have all been miseducated. We have been socialized to accept a system of White privilege, and therefore we must begin the tedious journey of deconstructing this system through questioning the norms and values associated with it. This is not an easy journey. At times, I still find myself feeling guilty because of the privileges that I continue to enjoy as a result of my skin color. I also find myself feeling angry at the monocultural education that I received, which resulted in tremendous ignorance about non-White populations—an ignorance which I probably will never be able to overcome. And, while I find this to be difficult to admit, I often find myself admiring the moral strength, fortitude, and sheer perseverance of persons of color who have had to struggle against great odds to achieve what I have achieved with relative ease as a result of my privileged status.

Yet at the same time, an acknowledgment of my whiteness has given me a sense of commitment and urgency to work to overcome this disease known as racism—a malady that negatively affects not only persons of color, but Anglos as well. (For, as Peggy McIntosh suggests, and my own experience confirms, dominated persons often acquire qualities that members of the dominating group may never acquire, and Anglos can seem ignorant, naive, and even foolish in comparison.) Education has a huge role to play in this effort, for it is only through education that we can reverse the miseducation of the past and present. This will require us to confront the issue of racism in our schools and classrooms by having students read about it, write about it, talk about it. In other words, we can no longer pretend that racism does not exist or that it does not affect us directly. It does—even when a school is primarily Anglo—because it affects us and divides us *as a society*. Will you have the courage to teach an anti-racist pedagogy in your classroom?

Until next time,
Becky

Notes

1. Bob Blauner, "Talking Past Each Other: Black and White Languages of Race," in Fred L. Pincus and Howard J. Ehrlich, eds., *Race and Ethnic Conflict*, 2nd ed. (Boulder, CO: Westview, 1999), p. 31.

2. Ibid., p. 33.

3. Ibid., p. 34. This is not to say that racial prejudice is no longer a major problem in our educational institutions. For instance, Peter Nien-chu Kiang documents the frequency of racial harassment and violence toward Asian Pacific American (APA) students. In one survey, 54 percent of APA students reported that they had been called names or harassed, and 24 percent reported that they had been physically attacked in school. See "'We Could Shape It': Organizing for Asian Pacific American Student Empowerment," in Valerie Ooka Pang and Li-Rong Lilly Cheng, eds., *Struggling to Be Heard: The Unmet Needs of Asian Pacific American Children* (Albany: State University of New York Press, 1998), pp. 243–264.

4. James M. Jones and Robert T. Carter, "Racism and White Racial Identity: Merging

Realities," in Benjamin P. Bowser and Raymond G. Hunt, eds., *Impacts of Racism on White Americans,* 2nd ed.. (Thousand Oaks, CA: Sage Publications, 1996), pp. 1–23; Janet E. Helms, ed., *Black and White Racial Identity: Theory, Research, and Practice* (Westport, CT: Praeger, 1993).

5. Helms, *Black and White Racial Identity*, p. 49.

6. Ibid., p. 49.

7. Ibid., p. 49.

8. Jones and Carter, "Racism and White Racial Identity," pp. 17–18.

9. See, for example, Deirdre A. Almeida, "The Hidden Half: A History of Native American Women's Education, *Harvard Educational Review*, vol. 67, no. 4, Winter 1997, pp. 757–771; and Ardy Bowker, *Sisters in the Blood: The Education of Women in Native America* (Newton, MA: Women's Educational Equity Act Publishing Center, 1993).

10. Almeida, "Hidden Half," p. 762.

11. For an interesting ethnographic study of the dual identities required of American Indian youth, see Alan Peshkin, *Places of Memory* (Mahwah, NJ: Lawrence Erlbaum, 1997).

12. Consider, for instance, the Afrocentric movement, which is an effort to reconstruct an African culture among African Americans in this country and to make Blacks conscious of the many ways in which they have been dominated by the White culture. One of the goals of Afrocentricity is to help persons of African descent to view the world from an African, versus a European, perspective. See Molefi Kete Asante, *Afrocentricity* (Trenton, NJ: Africa World Press, Inc., 1988).

13. Peggy McIntosh, *White Privilege and Male Privilege: A Personal Account of Coming to See Correspondences Through Work in Women's Studies* (Wellesley, MA: Center for Research on Women, Working Paper Series, no. 189, 1988), pp. 1–2. Also see my article entitled "Overcoming Cultural Racism: The Promise of Multicultural Eduation," *Multicultural Perspectives*, vol. 2, no. 3, 2000, pp. 8–14.

14. McIntosh, "White Privilege and Male Privilege," pp. 10–11.

15. For interesting discussions of this topic, see Bowser and Hunt, eds., *Impacts of Racism on White Americans*; Ruth Frankenberg, *White Women, Race Matters: The Social*

Construction of Whiteness (Minneapolis: University of Minnesota Press, 1993); George Henderson, *Our Souls to Keep: Black/White Relations in America* (Yarmouth, ME: Intercultural Press, 1999); Paul Kivel, *Uprooting Racism: How White People Can Work for Racial Justice* (Gabriola Island, British Columbia: New Society Publishers, 1996); and Alice McIntyre, *Making Meaning of Whiteness: Exploring Racial Identity With White Teachers* (Albany: State University of New York Press, 1997).

16. Helms, *Black and White Racial Identity.*

17. Louise Derman-Sparks and Carol Brunson Phillips, *Teaching/Learning Anti-Racism: A Developmental Approach* (New York: Teachers College Press, 1997), pp. 120–121.

Letter Four

Confronting Classism

Dear Readers,

When you think of poverty, what comes to mind? Deteriorating inner cities? Shacks and outhouses in Appalachia? Women sitting idle as they collect their welfare checks? It has been my experience that few topics engender stronger opinions than the topic of poverty. Many of my students believe that persons in poverty deserve their lot, that they intentionally have babies so that they can collect higher welfare checks (and therefore add to the national debt), and that their children will inherit this "culture of poverty"[1] and require government assistance themselves. If you, too, have these perceptions, then perhaps the following data will surprise you. In a March, 1995 special report in *Phi Delta Kappan* on the American family, Stephanie Coontz provides the following statistics:

- Aid to Families with Dependent Children (AFDC) accounts for only 1 percent of all federal expenditures and at the time of the report the percentage had been declining, rather than increasing, in proportion to other spending;
- The typical woman on AFDC has 1.9 children, and the longer she stays on welfare the *less* likely she is to have more children;
- In the United States, mothers living in states with higher AFDC payments return to work more quickly than those in states with lower payments; and
- Despite all the rhetoric about a self-perpetuating cycle of dependency, only 19 percent of black daughters and 26 percent of white daughters of highly dependent welfare families become highly dependent on welfare themselves.[2]

Coontz goes on to state that 75 percent of social welfare spending goes to those who are not poor, in the form of Social Security, various subsidies (e.g., housing and agriculture), and corporate bail-outs. In fact, during the 1950s and 1960s, subsidized suburban housing and new roads for commuting to suburban areas, paid for out of governmental funds, contributed significantly to the economic decay of our inner cities. States Coontz: "Federal housing support for suburbia exacerbated segregation and hastened the decay of the urban ghettos.... Some observers have called this pattern socialism for the rich and private enterprise for the poor."[3]

It's evident that misperceptions about welfare recipients contributed to our current system of welfare reform, which was intended to move individuals off of the welfare rolls. The primary purpose of the Personal Responsibility and Work Opportunities Reconciliation Act (PRWORA), which was signed into law in 1996, was to move people from welfare to work, so that they would no longer be a burden to society. Many would suggest that welfare reform thus far has been a great success; but if we dig a bit deeper, it becomes evident that PRWORA has not been the panacea that many thought it would be. For instance, consider the following statistics:[4]

- Most former welfare recipients who find work are working at jobs that pay between $5.50 and $7.00 per hour. The median monthly salary is $1,149, which is below the official poverty level for a family of three.
- Data from the Department of Health and Human Services suggest that only 21.7 percent of welfare recipients leave the rolls because they got a job. The majority—56 percent—leave for unknown reasons.
- A General Accounting Office report on former welfare recipients in seven states reveals that in five of those states, their average earnings were below the poverty level.
- A national study has shown that one-fourth of former welfare recipients have moved because they couldn't pay their rent.
- Less than one-fourth of those moving from welfare to work are covered by health benefits.

It's important to acknowledge that welfare reform will not eliminate poverty in our nation without other structural changes. While there may be some merit to the new system (certainly achieving enablement rather than dependency is a worthy goal), most of the poor in our country are working poor. In fact, even before welfare reform, nearly two-thirds of poor families worked for wages, and "real" wages have been steadily declining for the last several decades. From 1973 to 1993, the average weekly inflation-adjusted earnings declined 19 percent, and from 1979 to 1993, the real value of the minimum wage decreased 24.9 percent.[5]

Indeed, more than half of those who fall into poverty do so as a result of changes in the labor market. What is equally disturbing is that the typical corporate CEO in 1990 made 135 times as much as his average employee.[6] Poverty is also highly correlated with race and gender: In 1994, a full 44 percent of female-headed households with children lived below the official poverty level, and the problem is particularly acute among women of color.[7] Poverty rates for African Americans have grown steadily, even as high school graduation rates for this same population have risen. Thus, poverty not only reflects socioeconomic class divisions, but it is also tied to the continuing racism and sexism in our society.

Unfortunately, our children are often the ones that must suffer the most. Here are a few more statistics that might surprise you. Did you know that one in five children live in poverty in our country? That according to data compiled by the Children's Defense Fund, nearly one-third of children in young families headed by a high-school graduate and more than a quarter of children in White young families were poor in 1990?[8] If you're like most people, you might tend to disregard the data, failing to see the names and faces behind the statistics. Or, you might be tempted to believe that real poverty and oppression does not exist in a nation where there is so much affluence. I recently spoke with a former principal from a large urban school district, who told me that going into some of her students' homes was like "going into a third world country." Some of the families she visited lived in shacks with dirt floors and no indoor plumbing. I have also known students who have lived in old abandoned school buses or in temporary shelters because that was all that their families could afford. I believe that Coontz makes an important point when she says that "it is hard to convince people to plan very well for the future when they don't expect to have one."[9] Schools are generally thought to be an important means for overcoming poverty. Let's take a look at how socioeconomic class affects a student's experiences with schooling.

About 10 years ago, when I first began research for my dissertation study in eastern Kentucky schools, I recall taking a tour of one of the elementary schools in which I would be spending a lot of time over the course of the year. As we were walking down the hall, the principal showed me one first-grade classroom and told me "this is the class for the higher achievers." Across the hall was the classroom of the first-grade teacher I had chosen to study; her children were referred to as the "low achievers." I still remain appalled that children are labeled at such an early age. These were six-year-old children, who had only been in school for a year. How could one possibly know which children were the "high achievers" and which were the "low achievers"? I asked the teacher I was working with how these determinations were made, and she told me they were largely based upon the recommendations of the kindergarten teacher. As the weeks progressed, I also learned that the "high achievers" were the children of teachers and other professionals. The "low achievers" came from the "hills and hollows"; that is, their parents tended to be poor, many were receiving government assistance, and some were temporarily living with their mothers at a local shelter for women who were experiencing abuse. (The children who arrived from this home were automatically placed in the "low achievers" group.)

Fortunately for these children, their teacher was dedicated to assuring their success. She was a gifted teacher who exerted tremendous energy in educating them and who believed with all of her heart that they could succeed. And by the end of the year, most of them had succeeded. Unfortunately, however, most children who come from impoverished homes are not this lucky. In fact, poverty has consistently been linked to a lack of educational achievement. In their review of research that examined factors associated with "at-risk" student populations, Edward Vacha and T. F. McLaughlin found that "the single most consistent factor characterizing at-risk students is social class. Social class is a powerful determinant of school success, and, as a consequence, at-risk students are disproportionately drawn from families from low socioeconomic status."[10]

We often like to blame the educational system or—even more commonly—to "blame the victim" for lack of achievement in school. Certainly, there are poor teachers and poor educational conditions that should not be tolerated, especially in this nation of unprecedented wealth. (Indeed, David Berliner has pointed out that the United States ranks ninth among 16 industrialized nations in per-pupil spending for students in grades K-12, "spending 14% less than Germany, 30% less than Japan, and 51% less than Switzerland."[11]) And, of course, there are students who resist being educated. (This is actually a much more complex phenomenon than it might appear, and I'll say more about it later.) But poor teachers and poor schools are only a part of the problem, although they're the part that legislators and the general public like to focus on because this enables us to avoid acknowledging the tremendous economic disparities in our nation. That is, while it is certainly important that we have high-quality teacher preparation programs and that schools are adequately funded, the crux of the problem is poverty, which leads to hopelessness and despair among our youth.

One of the most powerful books that I have read is Jay MacLeod's *Ain't No Makin' It*.[12] In this book, MacLeod reports on his research with two groups of male teens who live in the inner city. One group, which he refers to as the "Hallway Hangers," is largely White, while the other group—"the Brothers"—is Black. Through the book, the reader gets to know these adolescents as individuals and learns about the struggles that they must face on a daily basis. It is interesting that the Brothers tend to be more successful in school, largely because they and their parents still buy into the American dream. While the Brothers believe that race was a barrier to their parents' success, they do not believe that the same will be true for them. Thus, they tend to work hard in school and conform to its rules, yet the academic performance of most of them is only mediocre.

The Hallway Hangers, on the other hand, consider their chances for success to be remote, so they largely dismiss the idea that education can lead to personal upward mobility. Further, they find that as a result of their social status, they are devalued in school and are placed in the lowest educational tracks. They are not seen as "college material," or even as future productive citizens. This perception leads to oppositional behavior that in the long run undermines their chances for breaking out of the system of poverty: "The subculture of the Hallway Hangers must be understood as an attempt by its members to insulate themselves from these negative judgments and to provide a context in which some semblance of self-respect and dignity can be maintained."[13] That is, the counterculture of groups such as the Hallway Hangers functions to provide a sense of worth and belonging, which serves to counteract the sense of exclusion that they experience in school (and in society in general).

MacLeod suggests that, as educators, we ought to look beyond the hardened exterior of adolescents such as the Hallway Hangers, and appreciate their resiliency and intelligence:

> The Hallway Hangers are not living a fantasy. The world of the street exists—it is the unfortunate underside of the American economic system, the inevitable shadow accompanying a society that is not as open as it advertises. Moreover, the Hallway Hangers *are* physically hard, emotionally durable, and boldly enterprising. Those of us who are supposed to be succeeding by conventional standards need only venture into their world for the briefest moment to feel as though our badges of success are about as substantive and "real" in that environment as the emperor's new clothes.[14]

What MacLeod is suggesting here is that it takes a certain amount of intelligence and entrepreneurship just to survive in situations of poverty—a point that is thoroughly documented as he follows the daily lives of these students. This idea is in stark contrast to the ideology presented in books such as *The Bell Curve*, in which the assumption is made that the poor remain poor because of their low intelligence.[15] Such explanations, while they may have a great deal of popular appeal, fail to consider the daily life experiences of individuals in poverty who must continuously use their creative energies just to survive. They also ignore the complexities of schooling and the fact that some students and their parents actively *resist* the norms of an institution in which they are made to feel inferior and insignificant. Thus, academic underachievement is often not the result of low cognitive functioning, as some would have us believe, but rather is the result of a system that tends to reject and/or marginalize anyone who does not conform to a middle-class ideal.

Explanations of poverty based upon limited cognitive functioning also ignore the harsh reality of life for poor persons, many of whom long ago stopped believing in the American dream. Put simply, America has "worked" for some of its citizens, but not for others. In the second edition of his book, MacLeod looks at the lives of the Brothers and Hallway Hangers eight years after his original study. He found that despite their desire to live a so-called "normal" life, the Hallway Hangers had been in and out of prison, many were using drugs, and only one had a steady job, working in a warehouse. Most had held jobs, but they were generally low-paying and often seasonal, in what MacLeod refers to as the "secondary labor market," where "wages are lower, raises are infrequent, training is minimal, advancement is rare, and turnover is high."[16]

As for the Brothers, who had higher aspirations, most were stuck in low-level jobs. One member of the group, Derek, graduated near the top of his class and then entered the navy. Frustrated when they inexplicably cut off his pay for two months and unable to provide for his wife and child, he went AWOL and ended up in a military prison. At the time of the study, he was working the night shift at an airport making $7.50 per hour. Another Brother, who was employed as a delivery van driver and had always vowed to "stay out of trouble," turned to selling crack cocaine after a police officer planted marijuana on him and he ended up in jail. Many of the Brothers reported that they would like to go back to school, but lacked the financial means to do so. One group member, Craig, did graduate from college in good academic standing, and after spending more than a year seeking employment, he landed a stable job. Yet his annual salary was barely one-third of the national median for men.

What does all of this mean for educators? How are we to interpret MacLeod's findings? I think the first thing that needs to be said here is that schools are not isolated institutions. They tend to reflect the larger society, and our society is stratified along economic lines. In fact, the economic disparities between the haves and the have-nots are actually increasing rather than decreasing, and by some estimates, one out of every four individuals is currently living in poverty in the United States.[17] Also, it is important to be aware of what is occurring in our economy. In his recent article, entitled "Profits Without People," Clinton Boutwell examines current job trends, and notes that in 1994, two-thirds of all newly created jobs were low-wage and carried no benefits.[18] He also states that at least a quarter of our employees are part-time, temporary, or contract workers. Put simply, Boutwell claims that corporate America is not living up to its bargain with American workers or with its schools. In effect, we are becoming overeducated; schools are producing more highly qualified workers than are required in today's economy, which will have the ultimate effect of lowering wages even further:

> [C]orporate America has been insistent in its demand that the education system produce a world-class work force....Thus the education system is developing an ever-growing supply of workers with high-performance abilities. But that supply of well-qualified graduates (along with those employees displaced from their current jobs) will overwhelm the available demand for such workers. Millions of American college and high school students are being prepared for high-performance jobs that may never exist.[19]

Boutwell also projects that in the future, only 20 percent of university graduates will be able to find the well-paying, challenging jobs for which they were trained. I don't know about you, but I find these ideas rather disconcerting. Given the fact that high-quality jobs are simply not available, even for the highly educated, is it any wonder that young people such as the Hallway Hangers live with a sense of hopelessness? (Indeed, this hopelessness is quickly encroaching on the middle class.) Yet, we tend to want to believe that we all have an equal chance to succeed in our society if we only work hard enough. In fact, theorists have come up with a name for this belief. It's called the "myth of meritocracy." While of course hard work is important, it simply isn't true that everyone has an equal chance to succeed (hence, the notion that it's a "myth").

Let's talk about the "myth of meritocracy" for a moment. One of the activities that I ask my students to do is to think about the various behaviors and "cultural possessions" that can help us to get ahead. What are some of the things that you might put on this list? If you wanted to land a high-quality job, for instance, what would you need to have? Typically, my students will come up with things like having the "right connections," speaking "proper" English, knowing how to "dress for success," and knowing the proper etiquette for job interviews. (One student of mine even said that knowing how to play golf would be a definite asset!) We call these things part of our "cultural capital."[20] This is a form of "capital" that we acquire through membership in a particular culture, and that we can draw upon and use to our advantage. Persons who come from a lower-class background have different "cultural capital." They may be (and often are) quite resourceful, yet they do not have the "right" cultural capital for acquiring high-status jobs. That is, they generally do not have connections with executives or managers; they often do not speak "proper" English; they lack the knowledge and/or the means to "dress for success"; and they generally cannot afford the cost of golf lessons!

Here, we might use the analogy of running a race. The person who has a higher financial status is given the inside lane, has been able to afford the best instruction and conditioning equipment, has had adequate time to train, and has numerous spectators in the stands rooting for him and believing that he can win. The person of lower financial status, however, is on the outside lane, has had limited access to training equipment, has been forced to balance training time with a job, and has very few spectators who think that he even has a chance of winning. If you were putting money on this race, who would you bet on to win? Yet isn't this essentially what we do to many of our poor children? Certainly, this was the case in the elementary school in Appalachia that I visited. The children were already being seen as "low achievers" simply because of their socioeconomic status. (I'll say a bit more about low teacher expectations in another letter.)

At this point, you might be protesting, "but schools are the Great Equalizers, aren't they? I still think that if students just study hard, learn Standard English, do their homework and essentially conform to what is being asked of them, then they can succeed." To a certain extent, you may be right, for education obviously *does* help us to achieve our goals. But in reality, things are just not this simple.

One of the theorists whose work I refer to a lot is James Paul Gee. Actually, Gee is a sociolinguist who looks at language use within social contexts. Gee suggests (and I agree) that we all have several different ways of speaking or "being in the world"—what he calls "discourses."[21] We each have a primary discourse, or the discourse of our family and community, and over time through our interaction in various social institutions, we also acquire a number of secondary discourses. These discourses are essentially "identity kits." So, as a teacher, I have acquired the discourse of "teacher," complete with an understanding of how to speak, dress, and act like a teacher. To acquire this discourse, I had to play the part of teacher for a while. That is, I couldn't just learn how to "be a teacher" by reading it in a textbook. I had to participate in the social context and learn from veteran teachers.

Our primary discourse comes to us naturally; it is the discourse that we grew up with and hence we are comfortable with it. When we enter a social situation where others are interacting in a different discourse, we tend to feel somewhat out of place. For instance, I recall sitting in a hotel room a few years ago with three highly educated African American women who were interacting in a discourse quite different from my own. While they were speaking Standard English, the *ways* in which they spoke—the words they used, the timing of their responses, their nonverbal cues, and so on—were distinctly unlike my ways of using language, and I found that I simply could not "get it." Hence, I was largely excluded from the conversation, although I am sure that the exclusion was not intentional on their part. In order to learn this discourse, I would have to be immersed in it for a long period of time. For these women, however, it was a very natural way of interacting; in fact, having to interact using a "White" discourse style is unnatural for them, even though they have learned to do it quite well. That is, the academic (and typically White) discourse is one of probably many secondary discourses that they have mastered.

Having said all of this about discourses, think about the children in our classrooms. Some come to school with a primary discourse that essentially matches that of the school. They interact easily with their teachers. They sense a good "fit" between school and home. Children with a different primary discourse may sense that they do not "fit" within the educational institution, just as I felt somewhat alienated in the conversation in that hotel room. In fact, they will often get the feeling that their discourse is not as highly valued as the discourse of the school—that it is considered to be inferior. Indeed, several researchers have documented this "lack of fit" between the language and literacies used in the home and those of the school.[22] It is not that children come to school with *deficient* language patterns and ways of taking from texts; they are merely *different*. Because our language is an essential part of our identity, it is a very small jump for children to perceive that they themselves are inferior—that they have nothing of value to contribute to this institution we call "school." When their self-worth is challenged and sometimes even assaulted on a daily basis, is it any wonder that some students and their parents come to resent, and therefore eventually to resist, the process of schooling?

I must regress a bit here to explain that I am not suggesting that we should abdicate our responsibility to teach Standard English to our students. The standard vernacular is the "dominant discourse" in our society; it is the "language of power"—part of the cultural capital we need in order to "get ahead" in life. Certainly, we would be doing our students a real disservice not to teach it to them. At the same time, however, we need to introduce the dominant discourse in ways that respect our children's home language. This is a critical point. One of my students put it this way: "So, what we need to teach our kids is that sometimes, in certain circumstances, they need to 'dress up' their language." Precisely! We all need to acquire various secondary discourses. For instance, in order to be successful in a job interview, I must learn the discourse of "interviewee." To be successful in my current job, I had to acquire the discourse of "professor." That is, I had to learn how to "dress up" my language so that I can interact effectively in various academic settings. Another important point, however, is that I did not learn these secondary discourses by reading about them from a book or by completing grammar exercises. I had to be immersed in the social context in which the discourse was used. I had to practice being in the situation of "interviewee," not only learning how to speak, but also how to dress, what kinds of nonverbal cues to avoid, when to show up for the interview, and so on. Our children will also learn these secondary discourses when they are asked to use them in meaningful situations and when their primary discourse is simultaneously respected and affirmed.[23]

Hopefully by now you are beginning to recognize that perhaps schools haven't always been the Great Equalizers that we'd like them to be. Language is just one element of our "cultural capital" that can affect a student's chances for success in school. Students and parents from lower-income environments are often treated differently, too. I often present this scenario to my students: As a teacher, if a parent walked into your classroom speaking a nonstandard discourse, dressed rather shabbily, and with unkempt hair, what would be your first reaction? Inevitably they honestly admit that they would probably consider this parent to be relatively ignorant and uneducated. It has been my experience that teachers also generally feel that such parents just "don't care about their children's education" and that they suffer from character flaws that prohibit them from taking an active role in their child's schooling. Vacha and McLaughlin point out that "It is very important to distinguish between cultural capital and values. Most of the evidence available indicates that parents from all social classes attempt to instill in their children remarkably similar values, and they do not differ in regard to their desire for their children to succeed in school."[24] Yet, given such perceptions on the part of educators, is it any wonder that parents are often reluctant to become involved in their children's education?

I think it is also important to ask ourselves how often we as educators are willing to "walk that extra mile" and take the time to develop genuine, mutual relationships with parents from lower-income communities. Occasionally this occurs, but it is still far too rare. Typically our lower-income parents will not come to us. Simply put, they do not often feel welcome in our schools. Hence, *we* need to go to *them*. It takes a lot of effort on the part of educators, yet if we fail to make this effort, the result often will be miscommunication. I recall a time when I was in the home of a low-income parent with whom I had become friends, and she showed me a letter she had received from her children's school. The letter was very formal in tone and she asked that I read it so that I might confirm what she thought the letter was saying—that her twin boys were being referred for special education. Understandably, she felt angry, frustrated, and powerless over a decision that was to affect her children's future yet had been made without her input. In essence, the school was treating her as if she were ignorant and therefore unqualified to know what was best for her own children. Her anger was compounded by the fact that school personnel never bothered to talk with her face-to-face about this decision but chose to inform her through an impersonal letter.

There is another important point to be learned from this story. Statistics bear out the fact that lower-class children (and also minority children) are disproportionately represented in our special education programs. We must ask ourselves why this is so. Probably the reasons for this phenomenon are complex, and certainly poverty can have a negative impact on a child's readiness for school. Indeed, richness of experience in the early years of life can also affect a child's cognitive development. Yet, as I indicated to you earlier, this is only a small part of the puzzle. As in the case of the Appalachian elementary school, children are often labeled at a very young age as being "special education material." As educators, we must be conscious of the ways in which social class affects our perceptions of the children we teach. It has been my experience that children from lower-income communities are often quite intelligent; they are simply not viewed as such because they do not always conform to the expectations of the school. Consequently, teachers never recognize their abilities.

Before I close this letter to you, I challenge you to think about the reality of poverty in our nation, the ways it affects the children that we teach, and the role of schools in addressing it. Unfortunately, our society is not as equitable as we might like it to be, and not everyone has an equal chance of achieving upward mobility. Even school funding in the United States reflects this inequity, in that schools in poor districts tend to receive less money per student than schools in wealthy districts.[25] The subtle message here is that poor students are not "worth as much" as middle- or upper-class students. Like the Hallway Hangers in MacLeod's study, many of our young people enter our schools with tremendous despair and hopelessness—victims of a society that has largely given up on them, that tells them their lives are of little worth and their plight is the result of their own ignorance and lack of perseverance. Certainly, it is easy to "blame the victim": "They just don't care about learning." "Their parents don't value education." "These students are lazy and unmotivated." As I have suggested throughout this letter, responses such as these can be *the results of* a system of schooling that tends to devalue and denigrate one's family and culture; they generally are not the *sources* of educational failure. Yet by placing the blame on students and their parents, we absolve ourselves of any responsibility to deal with the issue and to examine how schools might actually be contributing to students' underachievement, and, hence, perpetuating a cycle of poverty.

I often ask my students, "Who in your classroom needs your advocacy?" I ask you to think about this question carefully. Students from upper- and middle-class environments generally have lots of advocates. The world tends to "work" for them; doors open for them; they have connections that will help to assure their success. (Indeed, these are the students who generally "buy into the system" and thus tend to be relatively easy to teach.) Many of our students, however, have very few advocates. These are the students that need us the most. They need to know that we believe in them, that we respect them, that we support them, and above all, *that we will not allow them to fail*. It's not easy to be the kind of educator that cares so much about her students that she simply will not allow failure; it takes a tremendous amount of energy and commitment. Yet these are the teachers that can truly make a difference in students' lives. I challenge you to become that kind of teacher.

Courage,
Becky

P.S. It's also critical that the curriculum be relevant to the lives of these students. I'll talk more about this in a future letter.

Notes

1. The term "culture of poverty" was first coined in the 1960s to describe the values, behaviors, and characteristics thought to be associated with persons in poverty. Thus, poverty was no longer thought to be merely a matter of economic status; it was also thought to involve various (undesirable) social traits.

2. Stephanie Coontz, "The American Family and the Nostalgia Trap," *Phi Delta Kappan*, March 1995, pp. K1–K20.

3. Ibid., p. K6.

4. Reported in the Fall 2000 issue of *ColorLines*. See Gary Delgado, "Racing the Welfare Debate," *ColorLines*, vol. 3, no. 3, Fall 2000, pp. 13–17.

5. Herbert J. Gans, "Fighting the Biases Embedded in Social Concepts of the Poor," in Chester Hartman, ed., *Double Exposure: Poverty and Race in America* (Armonk, NY: M. E. Sharpe, 1997), pp. 146–147.

6. Coontz, "American Family," pp. K9–K11.

7. See, for example, Sonia M. Pérez and Denise De La Rosa Salazar, "Economic, Labor Force, and Social Implications of Latino and Educational Population Trends," in Antonia Darder, Rodolfo D. Torres, and Henry Gutiérrez, eds., *Latinos and Education: A Critical Reader* (New York: Routledge, 1997), pp. 45–79; and the statistical appendix in Fred L. Pincus and Howard J. Ehrlich, eds., *Race and Ethnic Conflict: Contending Views on Prejudice, Discrimination, and Ethnoviolence*, 2nd ed. (Boulder, CO: Westview, 1999), pp. 461–464.

8. Patrick Shannon, *Reading Poverty* (Portsmouth, NH: Heinemann, 1998), pp. 46–48.

9. Coontz, "American Family," p. K9.

10. Edward F. Vacha and T. F. McLaughlin, "The Social Structural, Family, School, and Personal Characteristics of At-Risk Students: Policy Recommendations for School Personnel." *Journal of Education*, vol. 74, no. 3, 1992, pp. 9–25.

11. David C. Berliner, "Mythology and the American System of Education," *Phi Delta Kappan*, April 1993, p. 637.

12. Jay MacLeod, *Ain't No Makin' It: Aspirations and Attainment in a Low-Income Neighborhood*, 2nd ed. (Boulder, CO: Westview Press, 1995).

13. Ibid., p. 117.

14. Ibid., p. 118.

15. Richard Herrnstein and Charles Murray, *The Bell Curve: Intelligence and Class Structure in American Life* (New York: The Free Press, 1994). For a thorough critique of this book, see Joe L. Kincheloe, Shirley R. Steinberg, and Aaron D. Gresson III, eds., *Measured Lies: The Bell Curve Examined* (New York: St. Martin's Press, 1997).

16. MacLeod, *Ain't No Makin' It*, p. 169.

17. J. Schwartz and T. Volgey, *The Forgotten Americans* (New York: W. W. Norton, 1992). Cited in Shannon, *Reading Poverty*, p. 44.

18. Clinton E. Boutwell, "Profits Without People," *Phi Delta Kappan*, October 1997, pp. 104–111.

19. Ibid., p. 109. Also see Gerald W. Bracey, *Setting the Record Straight: Responses to Misconceptions About Public Education in the United States* (Alexandria, VA: Association for Supervision and Curriculum Development, 1997). Bracey writes that "Currently, about 30 percent of college graduates take jobs that require no college. As more and more students go to college and as more and more low-paying, low-skill jobs are created, this problem will only increase" (p. 164).

20. Peter McLaren defines cultural capital as "ways of talking, acting, modes of style, moving, socializing, forms of knowledge, language practices, and values." See Peter McLaren, *Life in Schools: An Introduction to Critical Pedagogy in the Foundations of Education* (White Plains, NY: Longman, 1989), p. 190.

21. James Paul Gee, *Social Linguistics and Literacies: Ideology in Discourses* (London: The Falmer Press, 1990).

22. See, for example, Shirley Brice Heath, *Ways With Words: Language, Life, and Work in Communities and Classrooms* (Cambridge: Cambridge University Press, 1983); Denny Taylor and Catherine Dorsey-Gaines, *Growing Up Literate: Learning From*

Inner-City Families (Portsmouth, NH: Heinemann, 1991); and Gordon Wells, *The Meaning Makers: Children Learning Language and Using Language to Learn* (Portsmouth, NH: Heinemann, 1986).

23. I examine literacy and language issues in greater depth in my book, *Literacy as a Moral Imperative: Facing the Challenges of a Pluralistic Society* (Lanham, MD: Rowman and Littlefield, 1999).

24. Vacha and McLaughlin, "Social Structural, Family, School, and Personal Characteristics," p. 12. Also see Nancy Feyl Chavkin, ed., *Families and Schools in a Pluralistic Society* (Albany: State University of New York Press, 1993). In his chapter, "Benefits and Barriers to Parent Involvement: From Portugal to Boston to Liverpool," Don Davies reports on interviews he conducted with low-income parents in three cities. He notes that while most teachers felt that their students' parents were apathetic, the parents had a different opinion: "Low-income parents did not consider themselves hard to reach. They said they would come to the school when asked for a good reason, but by and large they did not come on their own, and many—perhaps most—carried bad memories of schools and talked about being intimidated by teachers and administrators. Many said they simply don't like to go to a school" (*Families and Schools*, p. 208).

25. In a June 11, 1993 article in the *Washington Post*, Iris Rotberg reports that "In Sweden, per-pupil expenditures in low-income schools are two to three times higher than in affluent schools. These ratios are quite common in the United States—only here, rich children are the winners." Cited in Gerald W. Bracey, "The Third Bracey Report on the Condition of Public Education," *Phi Delta Kappan*, October 1993, pp. 104–117.

Letter Five

Confronting Sexism

Dear Readers,

A couple of weeks ago I came across an old high-school yearbook from the late 1960s. Next to each senior's picture was a statement about what he or she hoped to accomplish in life. I think the responses are quite revealing about the legacy of sexism in our society. Here's what was written next to the boys' pictures on the first four pages:

Howard: Might go into accounting...
Thomas: Helps us with psychiatry...
Harold: Set his sights to be a top mathematician...
Robert: Hopes to be a mighty, tough football player...
Philip: Intends to be a writer...
Michael: May add up to an accountant...
Gary: Wants to tinker with hot rods...
Leslie: Has intentions of serving Uncle Sam...
David: May figure out to be an engineer...
Kenneth: Has designs on getting a BFA...
William: Will operate vending machines...
Joseph: Aiming for an engineering degree...

Now, here are the girls' responses on those same four pages:

Susan: Has hopes of being a teacher of Phys. Ed....
Susan: Will have her own restaurant...
Judy: Intends to be a secretary...
Pamela: Going to Purdue...
Candace: Wants to be a nurse...

Peg: Finish school, get a job, and travel…
Cheryl: Couple of years of fun, and then…
Jeanne: Will specialize in scenic design…
Arlyn: Will be a secretary…
Linda: Might teach the future W.H.S.'ers…
Sharon: Will go to college and then…
Linda: Go into beautician's work…
Cheryl: Aims to teach Algebra…
Susan: Intends to fly the skies as a stewardess…
Nancy: May become a secretary…
Diane: Will be a professional surfer…
Deborah: Go into home economics…
Linda: Hopes are in being a housewife…

Because my home community was largely middle/upper-class and White, it is not surprising that many of the graduating seniors intended to pursue a higher degree (including the girls). What strikes me so much about these lists, however, is that the boys generally had quite definite career goals, whereas several of the girls did not. Also, it's interesting that their selected careers are quite stereotypical. That is, most of the women chose careers like those of nurse, secretary, beautician, teacher, and housewife, whereas the men chose higher-paying careers, such as engineering and accounting.

For many of you who have graduated in more recent years, this list may seem a bit unreal. But for those of you who were young women during the 1960s and 1970s, as I was, it probably does not seem strange at all. Certainly, we have come a long way in overcoming the gender stereotypes of the past and in providing more opportunities for women. Yet we are not there yet. Research shows that women are still significantly underrepresented in higher-level management and administrative positions, and still earn about 68 cents for every dollar earned by men. In fact, men make more than women even in professions that historically have been dominated by women, such as teaching. In addition, even in the new millennium, it is not hard to find instances of gender bias in classrooms and in society.

For instance, recently I visited the classroom of a male upper elementary teacher who is in his first year of teaching. I found it interesting that he addressed the boys in his classroom as "sir," and the girls as "hon" or "honey." In our conversations after my observation, I asked him about this obvious discrepancy. He informed me that at the beginning of the year, he felt that the girls were intimidated by his presence as a male teacher and therefore he decided to use a more personal style in his interactions with them. He also stated that he did not use this term with all the girls—"only the ones who would not take it as being condescending."

In defense of this teacher, I believe he was honestly trying to bridge the "power gap" that exists between teachers and students. (After all, as teachers, we *do* have power over our students, although we may not always think that we do!) In addition, I did not notice any other instances of gender discrimination in his classroom. The girls were called on as often as the boys and were provided with a great deal of positive teacher time and attention. Instructional groups were mixed by gender. The girls seemed to talk at least as much as the boys in the groups—perhaps even more. And it was evident that the teacher had high expectations for both girls and boys.

Nevertheless, I continue to be disturbed by the condescending way in which he addressed many of his female students. For me, it represents the subtleness of the sexism that exists in our society—a sexism that, like racism and classism, often goes unnoticed but which can have detrimental effects on students. Indeed, many of you who are reading this book may have the same response as this teacher. When I talk to students about sexism, many of my students (both males and females) state that they do not believe sexism exists in today's society. Many women also tell me they are not offended when someone calls them "honey."

So, what's the big deal? Perhaps we need to consider some facts:

- Men continue to be substantially overrepresented in high-paying areas, such as mathematics, science, and engineering;
- Sexual harassment in schools is a major problem, and few schools effectively enforce sexual harassment policies;
- Boys continue to outperform girls on high-stakes testing, such as the SAT;

- Although the gap has begun to narrow, boys continue to outperform girls in science and math, as measured by the National Assessment of Education Progress (NAEP);
- Women continue to earn significantly less than their male counterparts, even in professions that have been traditionally female. In fact, women with four years of college earn only slightly more than men who have only completed elementary school;
- Women are underrepresented in administrative positions at all educational institutions, elementary through college;
- In the classroom, research shows that female students typically get less attention, praise, encouragement, or criticism than their male counterparts. Often, they are simply ignored.[1]

It's important to point out that discrimination based upon gender is not just a problem for women. Young boys in our society are taught to withhold their emotions and to be "macho," which can hinder the development of meaningful relationships. Boys are also taught to be more aggressive than girls, which leads to more negative interactions with teachers. It has also been found that when boys and girls break rules, the boys are more likely to be penalized.[2] Finally, sexual harassment is not just a problem faced by women. A recent survey of students in grades 8 through 11 indicates that 10 percent of male students report that they have been sexually harassed by teachers and staff (compared to 25 percent of women students).[3]

Yet despite all of this, when asked what they think their lives would be like if they woke up one day as the other sex, most boys report that they would find life as a girl to be disgusting and appalling. Myra and David Sadker, who collected essays from almost 1,100 children in grades 5 and 6, report that "[f]orty-two percent of the girls found many good things to say about being male," while 95 percent of the boys "found no advantage at all to being female." In fact, 16 percent of the male respondents talked about "fantasy escapes from their female bodies, with suicide the most frequent getaway selection."[4]

Like racism and classism, sexism is based upon power relations in our society. In their book *Changing Multiculturalism*, Joe Kincheloe and Shirley

Steinberg examine the system of patriarchy, which they define as "the gender arrangement in which men form the dominant social group."[5] This patriarchal system is reinforced in schools and in society in a variety of ways, which, like the forces that maintain race and class privilege, often remain invisible to us. That is, we have become so accustomed to living in a society that endorses a system of male dominance that in most cases we do not even recognize instances when it is reinforced. For example, did you know that most television commercials use male voices, even when the products they advertise are primarily for women? It is felt that the male voice holds more authority and will therefore sell more products. Consider, too, the popular images of females; in movies and fiction, they are often portrayed as objects to be used for the sexual pleasure of men—or, just as damaging, as persons easily influenced by the so-called superior intelligence and savvy of males.

When I discuss such things with my students, they often think that I am overreacting. Indeed, many of you who are reading this letter may feel the same way. Yet consider the effects of several years of such subtle subjugation, where men are portrayed as being in charge and in control, and women are portrayed as constantly deferring to men. I'm reminded of films such as *The Horse Whisperer*, a popular movie of a few years back that was nominated for several awards. At the beginning of this film, the lead female character is portrayed as a strong, intelligent, and sophisticated business-woman, yet by the end of the film, after having fallen "head over heels" in love with her wise and omniscient horse trainer (Robert Redford), she behaves more like a child—she is uncertain, vulnerable, and unable to make decisions without the help of a man. Indeed, when you begin to view films, cartoons, commercials, and other media forms through a critical lens, you will find that evidence of sexism (and racism and classism) abounds. The problem is that we have become oblivious to it; or, perhaps, we choose to overlook it because it's easier just to accept the status quo.

Kincheloe and Steinberg argue that male dominance is maintained in part by the feelings of many women that they are less rational and more emotional than men, and therefore their ways of knowing about and understanding the world are inferior to men's. Such thinking produces a false dichotomy between men and women, in which men are viewed as objective and rational thinkers, whereas females are viewed as emotional and intuitive. According to Kincheloe and Steinberg,

> The false dichotomy perpetuates an unjust system that exempts men from nurturing, service types of work while holding women responsible for such unpaid forms of domestic toil. It is essential for educators and cultural workers to understand these patriarchal dynamics, for it is these forces that work to hide a young woman's abilities from her teachers, her potential employers and, most importantly, herself.[6]

Our patriarchal system has had devastating effects on women in our society, both emotionally and physically. For instance, two-thirds of those in poverty over the age of 65 are women; four out of five single-parent families are headed by women, and most of these are poor; one in six wives are beaten by their husbands. A system of patriarchy has negative effects on men, too, in that they are taught to believe that they must always be strong and in control; hence they often feel they must continually prove their strength and abilities. The need to fulfill this stereotypic role takes its toll: Males commit suicide two to three times more often than females and account for more than 90 percent of drug- and alcohol-related arrests.[7] It is important to point out that race and class intersect with gender in that these and other social problems are generally intensified for persons of color. For instance, single women of color are the most impoverished group in our society.

The struggle to end this system of patriarchy has a long history in the United States, and it has had the support of women and men alike. In fact, early efforts for women's rights emerged out of the anti-slavery movement in the 1840s, and was endorsed by abolitionists such as William Lloyd Garrison and Frederick Douglass.[8] After the Civil War, White and Black women joined forces to fight for the right to vote. Leaders such as Carrie Chapman Catt, Ida B. Wells-Barnett, Susan B. Anthony, and Abigail Scott Duniway were able to persevere and, in 1920, women's right to vote was finally granted through the ratification of the Nineteenth Amendment. (By the way, did you recognize the names of these famous women suffragists?)

The struggle for women's rights did not end there, however. In 1923, the Equal Rights Amendment (ERA) was introduced into the U.S. Congress, and was brought forth every year thereafter until it was finally passed by Congress on March 22, 1972. Very simply, the ERA reads as follows:

> Section I: Equality of rights under the law shall not be denied or abridged by the United States or by any state on account of sex.
> Section II: The Congress shall have the power to enforce, by appropriate legislation, the provisions of this article.
> Section III: This article shall take effect two years after the date of ratification.

Unfortunately, after a fight that lasted nearly 50 years, the ERA failed to be ratified by the required number of states and therefore never became a part of the U.S. Constitution. It may be a surprise to some of you to learn that to this very day, women are still not guaranteed equal rights under the Constitution. Many of those who opposed the ERA were women who fervently believed that its passage would contribute to the destruction of the family. (Indeed, similar arguments for denying women's rights can be heard today. The rationale behind such arguments seems to be that strong families can exist only if women remain inferior to men.) I can remember the ERA's defeat vividly; many of us wore ERA pins and necklaces to indicate our support of the movement. Yet despite the ERA's defeat, I believe that because of the movement many citizens became much more aware of the ways in which women have been discriminated against in our society, and this awareness has led to more freedom of choice for women.

During this same time, however, other measures were passed that have helped to assure education equity based on gender. These include Title IX of the Education Amendments of 1972, which prohibits sex discrimination in educational institutions that receive federal assistance, and the Women's Educational Equity Act (WEEA), which provides funding for research, materials, and training to help eliminate gender bias. Despite these hopeful signs, however, Myra and David Sadker note that "Complaints were lodged, paperwork piled up, delays were common, and penalities became a new mythology.... Between 1972 and 1991, no school lost a single dollar of federal funds because of sex discrimination."[9] Perhaps this is an indication of just how far we have to go to eliminate sexism in our educational institutions.

How does sexism become manifested in schools? As institutions that are designed to socialize students to accept the norms of society, schools generally mirror the power relationships of the larger society. As with racism and classism, however, the ways in which sexism is reinforced are often invisible; we become conditioned to "not seeing" instances of sexism as they occur. Let's begin with preschool classrooms. Research shows that preschool teachers interact with children differently based upon their gender, and that they guide children toward certain toys and activities that are consistent with stereotypical gender perceptions. Preschool teachers are generally gentler with girls than with boys, and they direct them toward less aggressive play. Boys are encouraged to engage in activities like climbing, sand play, and construction—all activities that develop spatial and scientific skills.[10] The next time you are in a preschool classroom, you might look for these gender patterns.

What happens when these children reach school age? Myra and David Sadker, who have conducted extensive research on gender bias in schools and classrooms, have found the following characteristics.[11] Some of these findings might surprise you, while others, perhaps, are consistent with your own schooling experience. First, male students tend to dominate discussions. For instance, boys call out more than girls, and they get significantly more attention from teachers. Bright boys are often cast in the role of "stars"; they are listened to and respected. Low-achieving boys also receive more teacher attention, but it is typically negative in nature. Research has revealed that boys talk more and longer than girls, they ask more questions, and they interrupt more often. In fact, one interesting research finding is that boys not only monopolize classroom conversations, but they also monopolize classroom space and school space, such as computer centers, playgrounds, and lunchroom tables. (The next time you are visiting an elementary classroom, I encourage you to see for yourself if this is true.)

Girls, on the other hand, are reinforced for their passivity. Girls often get better grades than boys, and are generally quieter; hence the sense is that they are doing well. When the Sadkers analyzed computer data on classroom trends, the following patterns emerged: White boys received the greatest amount of teacher time and attention, followed by male students of color and

White females, with females of color receiving the least amount of teacher attention. The researchers claim that "the smart girl is the student who is the least likely to be recognized."[12] These patterns seem to be exacerbated as students move up through the elementary grades, with Black girls becoming the most invisible group.

I would challenge you to think about the ramifications of this data. One of the questions I occasionally pose to my students is this: Have you ever felt invisible in a classroom? I recall the response of one somewhat shy young woman in my multicultural education class, who stated that she felt invisible in one of the other college classes she was taking that same semester. "The professor does not even know my name," she told us, "and he never makes eye contact, nor does he call on me even when my hand is raised." She talked at some length about how the professor's reaction made her feel. She confessed that she did not try as hard in his class as in others, and probably did not perform as well as she was capable of performing because of her lack of motivation.

Over time, such reactions can have devastating effects on students' achievement and self-esteem. The Sadkers have also analyzed videotapes of the kinds of feedback that students receive from teachers, and have found that girls receive more general responses from teachers for their efforts (such as "okay"), whereas boys receive clearer feedback on their academic performance (in the form of helping, correcting, and providing specific praise). In other words, the responses that teachers tend to give to girls are not particularly helpful because they do not provide enough information. Like the beginning male teacher that I talked about earlier in this letter to you, often teachers believe they are being kind because they fear that girls might become upset if they are given negative feedback about their performance. What such teachers fail to recognize, however, is that specific feedback is necessary for improving student learning.

In addition, it has been found that teachers are less likely to provide explanations and directions to girls on how to complete a particular task, but rather will end up doing the task for them. For instance, a teacher might show a male student how to perform a particular task on the computer, but will end up doing it for a girl. Teachers may believe that they are being supportive by helping girls in this way. But consider the messages that underlie these actions. The subtle message being conveyed to boys is: I know you are capable of doing this; you just need to be taught how. The subtle message being conveyed to girls is: I really don't think you are capable of completing this task; therefore, I'll do it for you.

One of the results of such differential treatment between boys and girls is that girls' achievement suffers. Susan Hoy Crawford points out that "Females are the only group in America to enter school ahead but leave behind. That this decline has received so little national attention is evidence of the pervasiveness of sexism in education."[13] In addition, girls attribute their success to hard work, whereas boys attribute their success to ability. In other words, when boys achieve, they tend to believe it is because they are smart. When girls achieve, however, they tend to believe it is because they worked hard. For instance, after doing poorly on an algebra exam, it is not unusual to hear a young woman say "I've never been good at math." A young man, on the other hand, will more likely say "I just didn't study hard enough." Particularly between elementary and middle school, girls lose faith in their own abilities, and their sense of individual competence continues to decline throughout high school. Myra and David Sadker refer to this process as the "short circuit syndrome"; after experiencing years of being interrupted in their attempts to do things on their own, and having others "take over," girls begin to question their own capabilities. Unfortunately, teachers often reinforce these perceptions. In a recent study, first-grade teachers were asked to identify their best and worst math students. "These teachers tended to choose boys more often than girls as their most successful math students, even when achievement test scores indicated that in many cases girls achieved at a higher level than boys."[14]

I wonder if any of you have experienced this phenomenon of "short-circuiting"? As a woman, I have experienced it often. Even today, all I have to do is to make a comment about something not working properly, and my husband steps in and takes over. For instance, I might say something like "the e-mail system is certainly slow today," and he will chase me out of the chair and try to fix the problem. Of course, those of us who are astute are conscious of these gender dynamics, and may even use this phenomenon to our advantage. For young girls, however, the process often is not a conscious one, and it can have serious long-term consequences.

For instance, it has been found that short-circuiting has a negative effect on girls' self-esteem. While girls in the lower and middle elementary grades have high self-esteem, by middle school their level of self-esteem has plummeted. In elementary school, 67 percent of boys and 60 percent of girls are satisfied with the way they are; by high school, 46 percent and only 29 percent of girls say they are happy with the way they are.[15] Hispanic girls seem to be the most vulnerable; they experience a full 38-point drop on the self-esteem scale (from 68 percent in elementary school to 30 percent in high school). Interestingly, African American males and females both exhibit high levels of self-esteem, and African-American girls' sense of self-worth actually seems to increase from elementary school to high school.[16]

In an effort to become more popular, many adolescent girls deliberately downplay their intelligence and may even use creative tactics so that they do not appear to be "too smart." Some of the women reading this letter may be able to relate to this discussion on a personal level, as I can. When I was in high school, I did not attempt to hide the fact that I was a good student. I studied hard, made good grades, and volunteered often in class. I was in the National Honor Society and even spoke at my high-school graduation. At the same time, while I had many male "friends," I rarely got asked to go out on a date. The most popular girls with the local guys, it seemed, were those who tried hard to appear vulnerable and not-too-smart. In college I was somehow able to overcome the "nerd" image; perhaps this was because, like most young women, I began to underestimate my abilities.

Despite all of the research on gender equity, it is disheartening to learn that textbooks and curriculum materials continue to reinforce gender stereotypes. While recent studies have shown some improvement, we still have a long way to go. For instance, children's books still contain stereotypical images of boys and girls, with boys being more active and creative and girls being more passive, dependent, and submissive. In textbooks, the contributions of women are often merely "added" to the text, either in separate text boxes or as supplements at the ends of chapters. This is an example of what educational theorist Michael Apple calls "mentioning," whereby the voices and experiences of women and persons of color are included, but only in a superficial way.[17] That is, the information is isolated from the main text, creating the sense that it is less important or even superfluous.

And then, of course, there is the issue of language. Some of you may be thinking, "Oh no. Here we go again with all of that 'politically correct' stuff." I agree that language issues can sometimes get distorted and perhaps even overemphasized to the exclusion of substantive reform. At the same time, however, language *does* make a difference in how we perceive the world. I wonder, for example, if you have ever considered all of the different ways in which our language equates women with chickens!

> Reporting on "The Chickenization of Women," author Anne-Jeanne D'Arcy notes that women are frequently referred to as poultry. Young women are chicks, married women cluck at hen parties. They egg men on. Mothers watch their broods. Child rearing ends with the empty nest syndrome. Husbands at home are henpecked by their wives.[18]

Similarly, as Janice Streitmatter points out, when we speak of women's sexuality we tend to use words that associate them with animals (fox, dog, chick), whereas the terms referring to men imply dominance (dude, stud, hunk).[19] Streitmatter goes on to declare that there are 220 terms in our language describing sexually promiscuous women, while there are only 22 such words for men.

Of course, one of the most obvious examples of sexism in our language—and the example that is most often discussed—is the use of *he* and *man* to refer to both genders. Many people may find recommendations to eliminate this bias in our language to be trivial and unnecessary. Yet research has clearly demonstrated that children and adults alike visualize *only* males when presented with these generic terms. Hence, because of such language bias, women become excluded from the texts that they read. If you need more convincing, I invite you to try a little experiment. The next time you are reading a textbook (say, a history text), change all of the generic male terms to generic female ones (so, *he* becomes *she*, *men* becomes *women*, *mankind* becomes *womankind*). Does it make a difference in your perceptions? I know that it does for me. In fact, I never realized how women's voices have been subtly excluded until I began using this technique. (You might also try this with your students.)

Theresa McCormick points out that our language is not innately sexist; rather, using words such as "he" and "man" generically to refer to both men and women was a practice imposed by male usage authorities and grammarians during the eighteenth century.[20] Thus, as I discussed in a previous letter, language use is never neutral; rather, what is considered to be appropriate usage is determined by those who have the power to make such decisions. Hence, we *do* have a choice as to the words that we use. So, we have a choice as to whether to call office workers "girls" or "women"; we have a choice as to whether to refer to doctors, lawyers, and engineers in our writing as "he" or "she"; and we have a choice as to whether to address our students as "honey" or "Ma'am." Often it is just a matter of becoming conscious of our sexist (and racist) language.

Before I close this letter to you, it's important to address a critical issue relating to gender bias in schools—sexual harassment. A report recently published by the National Coalition for Women and Girls in Education provides the following statistics, which I think you will agree are quite startling. These statistics were compiled by the American Association of University Women (AAUW) Educational Foundation in a 1993 survey of over 1,600 students in grades 8 through 11. Behaviors that were considered to fall into the category of sexual harassment include the following: making sexual comments, jokes, gestures, or looks; giving you sexual pictures, photographs, illustrations, messages, or notes; writing sexual graffiti about you on bathroom walls, in locker rooms, and so on; spreading sexual rumors about you; saying you are gay or lesbian; spying on you as you dress or shower; touching you, grabbing you, or pulling on your clothing in a sexual way; intentionally brushing up against you in a sexual way; blocking your way or cornering you in a sexual way; forcing you to kiss him or her, or to do something sexual other than kissing. Here are the results:

- Eighty-one percent of the individuals surveyed reported that they had experienced sexual harassment.

- Seventy-nine percent reported that they were targeted by a fellow student.
- Girls experiened sexual harassment at a higher rate than boys (85 percent versus 76 percent).[21]

The AAUW study is not an anomaly; other teen surveys report similar statistics. And in a study conducted by *Seventeen* magazine, more than one-third of the girls (39 percent) said that they were harassed every single day.[22]

Sexual harassment can have a debilitating effect on students' learning. For instance, 33 percent of the girls who suffered harassment (and 12 percent of the boys) reported that they did not want to attend school; 32 percent of the girls (and 13 percent of the boys) reported that they did not want to talk as much in class; 28 percent of the girls (and 13 percent of the boys) said that they found it harder to pay attention in school. Clearly, sexual harassment has a more profound effect on girls than on boys; nevertheless, when approximately one out of three girls and one out of ten boys report that sexual harassment impairs their ability to learn, it seems evident that we have a major problem.

Unfortunately, when students complain to adults about sexual harassment, they often get very little support. Rather than addressing it head-on through education and the enforcement of rules, educators and other adults often choose to ignore the problem—or worse still, they "blame the victim." In a special *Phi Delta Kappan* report on sexual harassment in schools, author Elaine Yaffe cites many reasons for the inaction of educators and parents. Many simply don't want to "rock the boat" or cannot agree on what constitutes harassment. Others just view it as "natural" behavior, that is, "teens will be teens." Still others believe that if they confront sexual harassment in their schools, they will actually be creating a problem by "putting ideas in students' heads." Yaffe declares that "It is difficult to get people to accept that this behavior is a first cousin of other forms of harassment, such as racial and religious harassment, that we have outlawed for a long time."[23]

Just as racial harassment is an outgrowth of racism, sexual harassment is an outgrowth of gender bias in our educational institutions and in society.

In fact, it is perhaps one of the most blatant indications of the gender stereotyping that continues to pervade our classrooms and hallways. Susan Smith states that "It is generally believed that power, not sexual attraction, is the impetus for sexual harassment."[24] Hence, harassment is embedded in a patriarchal society where there is an ongoing struggle for power and recognition.

You should know that there are laws that protect students from sexual harassment, and in recent years courts have used Title IX to collect money for victims. As educators, it is important that we take students' accusations seriously, and that we do everything in our power to stop such harassment from occurring. This means insisting that students interact with one another in a mutually respectful way, and teaching them how to stand up for themselves in situations where they might be made to feel uncomfortable. We need to have honest discussions with students about what is appropriate, respectful behavior and what is not. In fact, students *want* us to have such conversations. But, of course, our conversations will never be effective unless we also communicate through our actions that we respect and value *all* of our students and that we are serious about gender equity.

Until next time,
Becky

Notes

1. See the American Association of University Women's report, entitled *How Schools Shortchange Girls: A Study of Major Findings on Girls and Education* (Washington, DC: AAUW Educational Foundation, 1992); National Coalition for Women and Girls in Education, *Title IX at 25: Report Card on Gender Equity* (Washington, DC: National Women's Law Center, 1997); Donna M. Gollnick and Philip C. Chinn, *Multicultural Education in a Pluralistic Society* (Columbus, OH: Merrill Publishing Company, 1990); and Iram Valentin, *Title IX: A Brief History* (Newton, MA: Women's Educational Equity Act Equity Resource Center, 1997).

2. Myra and David Sadker, *Failing at Fairness: How Our Schools Cheat Girls* (New

York: Simon and Schuster, 1994).

3. American Association of University Women, *Hostile Hallways* (Washington, DC: AAUW Educational Foundation, 1993), pp. 10–11.

4. Sadker and Sadker, *Failing at Fairness*, pp. 83–84.

5. Joe L. Kincheloe and Shirley R. Steinberg, *Changing Multiculturalism* (Bristol, PA: Open University Press, 1997), p. 137. Also see Kathleen Weiler, *Women Teaching for Change: Gender, Class and Power* (South Hadley, MA: Bergin and Garvey, 1988).

6. Kincheloe and Steinberg, *Changing Multiculturalism*, p. 140.

7. Sadker and Sadker, *Failing at Fairness*, p. 221.

8. Theresa Mickey McCormick, *Creating a Nonsexist Classroom: A Multicultural Approach* (New York: Teachers College Press, 1994).

9. Sadker and Sadker, *Failing at Fairness*, p. 36.

10. McCormick, *Creating a Nonsexist Classroom*; Linda Measor and Patricia J. Sykes, *Gender and Schools* (New York: Cassell, 1992); Janice Streitmatter, *Toward Gender Equity in the Classroom: Everyday Teachers' Beliefs and Practices* (Albany: State University of New York Press, 1994).

11. Sadker and Sadker, *Failing at Fairness*. Barbara Houston argues that such participation patterns may be linked to gender differences in linguistic styles. She also notes that teachers have a difficult time measuring fairness: "When teachers feel they are being fair, or even showing favoritism to girls, the empirical evidence shows otherwise." Barbara Houston, "Gender Freedom and the Subtleties of Sexist Education," in Ann Diller, Barbara Houston, Kathryn Pauly Morgan, and Maryann Ayim, eds., *The Gender Question in Education: Theory, Pedagogy, and Politics* (Boulder, CO: Westview, 1996), pp. 50–63.

12. Sadker and Sadker, *Failing at Fairness*, p. 50.

13. Susan Hoy Crawford, *Beyond Dolls and Guns: 101 Ways to Help Children Avoid Gender Bias* (Portsmouth, NH: Heinemann, 1996), p. 175; Sadker and Sadker, *Failing at Fairness*, p. 78.

14. E. Fennema, P. Peterson, T. P. Carpenter, and C. A. Lubinski, "Teachers' Attributions

and Beliefs about Girls, Boys, and Mathematics," *Educational Studies in Mathematics*, vol. 21, pp. 55–69. Cited in Streitmatter, *Toward Gender Equity*, p. 71.

15. Crawford, *Beyond Dolls and Guns*, p. 180.

16. Sadker and Sadker, *Failing at Fairness*, pp. 78–79.

17. Michael W. Apple, *Official Knowledge: Democratic Education in a Conservative Age* (New York: Routledge, 1993).

18. Anne-Jeanne D'Arcy, "The Chickenization of Women," *NOW News*, February 1981. Cited in McCormick, *Creating a Nonsexist Classroom*, p. 79.

19. Streitmatter, *Toward Gender Equity*, p. 96. Also see Laurel Richardson and Verta Taylor, eds., *Feminist Frontiers II: Rethinking Sex, Gender, and Society* (New York: McGraw-Hill, 1989).

20. McCormick, *Creating the Nonsexist Classroom*, p. 79.

21. Data cited in National Coalition for Women and Girls in Education, *Title IX at 25: Report Card on Gender Equity*, p. 32. Also see Susan J. Smith, *Title IX and Sexual Harassment* (Newton, MA: Women's Educational Equity Act Equity Resource Center, 1998).

22. Elaine Yaffe, "Expensive, Illegal, and Wrong: Sexual Harassment in Our Schools," *Phi Delta Kappan* (special report), vol. 77, no. 3, 1995, pp. K1–K16.

23. Ibid., p. K11.

24. Smith, *Title IX and Sexual Harassment*, p. 2.

Letter Six

Confronting Homophobia

Dear Readers,

A few years ago, I was blessed to have Steven in my graduate philosophy of education course. Steven is an elementary teacher, and he is one of the most caring and compassionate human beings that I have ever met. He is also gay.

In this class (as you might imagine), we spend a great deal of time talking about our beliefs and perspectives associated with diversity. In an effort to encourage reflection, my students are required to write daily in their response journals. One day, Steven wrote the following entry in response to a piece written by Maria Arguelles,[1] an entry which he has agreed to allow me to share with you:

> Arguelles has written a marvelous article dealing with self-discovery through freedom of thought. She explains the process of her life as being controlled by family and society. Her life was being lived in order to please others instead of pleasing herself. Even her display of emotions was dominated by her family. The article touched my heart. I can certainly relate to it since my life was controlled by others.
>
> In the last year and through numerous hours of thought and ponderance, I was able to discover myself. After almost thirty years, I could come to terms with my homosexuality. This was the hardest task of my life, and one that I was determined not to accept. However, I am finally at peace with myself and happier than I have ever been. Please read the following with an open mind and heart.
>
> I was born into a loving family with a devoutly religious mother. She was wonderful. I held her, and the beliefs she held, dear and close to my heart. I loved the Lord and the Bible. I attended religious functions whenever possible, and even walked to church when no other family members attended. I learned all the rules and commandments for living, and tried my best to lead "a Christian life." The Christian Church I attended taught a simple acronym: JOY. It stood for J-Jesus

first—O-Others Second—Y-Yourself last. My mother would also remind me of this acronym when I failed to use its message in daily living. In retrospect, I truly did abide by J-O-Y. I became an individual who cared for others and their feelings more than my own.

I knew from a very early age that I had some type of special feelings for males. I remember as a first grader having a strong attraction to a fellow classmate. However, due to my religious background and my parents' discussions on "sissies," I felt like there was something very wrong with me. Thinking of Bible stories and the unacceptable behavior of homosexuals, I decided that being gay was a burden placed on me by God and that it was my Christian duty to cover up my homosexuality. It is difficult to understand, but I had a debilitating fear that someone would figure out I was gay. Also, since I had learned that it was the "worst sin," I felt it was necessary for me to be "extra good" in order to have any chance of entering heaven. I was a very caring, sensitive person to others. I found it particularly easy to be caring to younger children or older adults. I felt that the younger children were oblivious to sex roles, and I felt that older adults surely did not even know about homosexuality. I became a loner somewhat to family members and classmates, not that I wanted to be, but the terror of them discovering who I was caused me to withdraw.

I reached puberty during my sixth grade year. At that period of time, I became very attracted to males. I only had female friends because I could converse with them easily, and they were more like me—caring of others. During this time, I knew that I needed to begin showing an attitude toward girls in more of a puppy love concept. This became a very unhappy period in my life. I could not be honest with myself.

During the sixth grade, I met a girl that also was deeply caring for others. She basically was just like me; very religious, a perfectionist, a "good girl." She had extremely over-protective parents who made it very clear from the beginning that no kissing or any type of physical behavior would be tolerated by anyone dating their daughter. I was very willing to abide by their rules because I had no desire to be physical with her. From the fall of 1980 to March 30, 1991 (the date we married), I tried my best to only care for her and her family. I went along with anything that she wanted me to do or that she gave an opinion on. I only wanted to make her happy. My prayer was that God would help her to think enough of me to marry me. I knew if I was married, people would forget about my homosexuality. I could hide in marriage.

Our marriage was not even consummated until July of 1992. During our marriage, I was very unhappy, although I did make those around me happy. I became a workaholic. My wife and I became the parents of two children during the next four years. I loved my children very much, but I still wasn't happy. From January of 1996 until March of 1997 I became very depressed. I wanted to die so badly. I did not know who I was because my life had been an act. I felt like an actor in a never-ending play. I knew by dying that I could take my secret to the grave and all would be for the better. I wanted to commit suicide but lacked the courage to carry it out. I had been brought up with the belief that suicide was also a ticket to hell. I was in despair. My dad, realizing my frame of mind, set up an appointment for me with a counselor. Through the counselor, I was able to come to terms with my homosexuality and the realization that my children needed me alive and not dead. Upon deciding that suicide was not the step for me, I began to care more about myself.

The most difficult day of my life came the day I told my wife about my homosexuality. We both cried for several hours. I felt that I had ruined her life. We eventually separated in April of 1997. It was a very difficult period of time. I moved from [town X] to [town Y]. I continued to teach in [town X]. [Town X] is a small town, and rumors spread quickly. A week after moving, the rumor that I was "gay and living with a man," went through the town quickly. Being a fourth grade teacher in a small town scared me. I was so afraid of losing my job. Thus far, I have been spared any major controversy with faculty members, parents or students. I do not want to cause any controversy. I love teaching.

I know that I caused a lot of difficulties during the past year to my wife and family. I would rather have died than to have "come out." I lost several things that I had worked for, a family that stayed together, a home in a familiar community, and part of my reputation. I know that most society members feel like homosexuality is wrong. I don't debate with them. I feel like God made me a homosexual, and I am at peace with it. I am still very religious. God must have a reason for what my wife and I have gone through. I must be patient and wait for the answers. I am good at being patient.

As a father, teacher, and adult my job is to help children to grow up to be happy with life, career, family, and above all self. I know that I am a good person and role model. I hope that one day society will be more accepting of homosexuals.

I, like Arguelles, found self-discovery through years of denying myself. Being honest and accepting of yourself is the key to life.

I was deeply moved by Steven's life story. On the last night of class, he asked if he could read his autobiography, and of course I said yes. Most of my students found Steven's story to be quite powerful and were very supportive of his decision to "come out." A few, however, remained silent, and some expressed negative reactions to me privately at the end of class.

It has been my experience that nothing leads to more heated debate than the issue of homosexuality. A few years ago I served as an advisor to a group of freshman students. We met with the other 150 or so freshmen who were enrolled in the Freshman Experience course once a week and then had a small-group discussion session. One week we invited several gay and lesbian individuals to speak to the large group. The response of the students was interesting. While a couple of negative, homophobic comments were audible during the presentation, most students were at least tolerant and listened patiently. The students in my particular advisory group, much to their credit, were respectful and expressed regret at the homophobic comments and reactions. Nevertheless, in the small-group session that followed a day or so later, their anti-gay/lesbian biases were strong and immediate, and went something like this:

> With all of the issues dealing with diversity, why did we have to focus on *that* issue? Why not talk about physical differences? (Interpretation: Let's please talk about something "safe.")

> I was so upset that this college would invite homosexuals to speak to us that I called my parents. (Interpretation: Why would a Baptist college invite such obvious sinners to campus?)

> What they are doing is wrong. They choose to be that way. It's a sin, and that's all there is to it. (Interpretation: Homosexuals choose to sin.)

I informed my students that there is a great deal of research that suggests that homosexuality is biological, and challenged them to think about why people would choose this lifestyle given the oppressive treatment that they receive as a result. Nevertheless, there was nothing that I could do or say to change their opinions. As with other issues, I told them that while I disagreed with their beliefs, I did not have the right to change those beliefs. I only had a right—and an obligation—to present another perspective and hence to get them to think through their own assumptions. At the same time, equitable education gives everyone a voice, so they also had a right to challenge *my* beliefs and assumptions. Indeed, this is what "critical" multicultural education is all about.

I made a conscious decision to include a letter in this book on homosex-uality. I recognize that I may be "sticking my neck out" by talking about such a volatile issue. Indeed, homosexuality engenders such strong reactions that some of my readers might dismiss much of what I say in this book because I have included a letter on gay and lesbian experiences. If you find yourself having strong reactions to what I am saying here, I encourage you to try to keep an open mind. While I may not agree with your perspective, I agree with *your right* to disagree. Another problem with addressing homosexuality is that some potential advocates of multicultural education end up being opposed to the "multicultural movement" because some of us choose to include sexual orientation in our discussions of human difference.

So, given all of this, why do you think I felt that it was important to address the issue of homosexuality? Mainly, it is because of all of the "Stevens" who are out there in our classrooms, who desperately need us to understand what they must endure on a daily basis. Gays and lesbians often share stories of instances when they have been teased or ostracized, when they have had their cars tampered with, when they have been denied jobs, even when they have been beaten. Recently a report was released by the Human Rights Watch documenting the harassment that lesbian, gay, bisexual and transgender (LGBT) youth experience regularly in schools. Of the 140 youth interviewed, nearly all reported that "name-calling, written notes, obscene or suggestive cartoons and graffiti containing anti-gay epithets were part of their everyday experience."[2]

Whatever your beliefs about homosexuality, as educators I believe that it is important that we acknowledge that real students are experiencing real problems based upon merely the *perception* that they might be gay. They are called names; they are harassed in hallways and parking lots; they are attacked in restrooms. Incredibly, just like those who perform overt racist acts against persons of color, many students feel justified in their negative treatment of homosexuals. (For instance, a high-school social studies teacher told me recently that one of her students had been informed by his preacher that because homosexuality is a sin, he was justified in using the term "faggot"!)

One of the most disturbing things to me is the homophobic bias among

teachers and educational staff. In a 1993 survey conducted by the Massachusetts Governor's Commission on Gay and Lesbian Youth, over half (53
percent) of the students reported that they had heard homophobic comments
made by school staff.[3] Here are some other startling statistics: 97 percent of
the time, teachers do not intervene in the homophobic incidents that occur
in their school; 80 percent of prospective teachers report negative attitudes
toward gays and lesbians; and two-thirds of guidance counselors have
negative feelings toward gay and lesbian individuals.[4] So, in an institution
that is supposed to be a safe place for all learners, our gay and lesbian youth
continue to experience isolation and fear.

As a current or future educator, you should be aware that the incidence
of suicide attempts by homosexual teens is significantly higher than among
heterosexual youth.[5] Further, homosexual young people are dropping out of
school in large numbers because of the homophobia that they experience in
our educational institutions.[6] Boys are the most likely to be targets of
homophobic behavior, which can begin as early as first grade. Our lesbian
and gay young people are suffering in our schools, while most teachers and
administrators choose to look the other way.

How do you feel about homosexuality? How will you respond to a
student who comes to you and tells you that he is gay (or that she is lesbian)?
Will you be an advocate for that student, protecting his right to safety and
decency and affirming him as an individual? Or will you retreat in silence,
afraid of becoming too involved?

In "What Do We Say When We Hear 'Faggot'?" Lenore Gordon states
that "Teaching children to be critical of oppression is teaching true morality,
and teachers have the right, indeed the obligation, to alert their students to
all forms of oppression. Educating children not to be homophobic is one way
to show the difference between oppression and nonoppressive behavior."[7]
She goes on to argue that "if adults criticize other forms of name calling but
ignore antigay remarks, children are quick to conclude that homophobia is
acceptable because gay men and lesbians deserve to be oppressed."[8] Do you
agree with Ms. Gordon? Will you be the kind of teacher who will confront
homophobia in your classroom and school, or will you remain silent? I
encourage you to think about this issue and to sort through your feelings

about homosexuality.

Ms. Gordon chooses to confront homophobia directly in her elementary classroom by discussing name-calling in general. She explains that there are two types of name-calling, one that is unrelated to a particular group, and one that is group-biased and implies negativity toward a particular group. She then shares the history of the term "faggot" with her students:

> I explain that a faggot, literally, is a stick used for kindling. I also explain that gay people used to be burned in medieval times simply for being gay, and they had to wear a bundle of sticks on their shirts to indicate that they were about to be burned. [9]

The students then explore what the terms "gay man" and "lesbian" mean to them, and why it is insulting to be called names. Students are also asked to imagine how they would feel if they are called names as they walk with a close friend of the same sex, and to suggest some possible responses to those who verbally attack them.

I wonder if you were as appalled as I was to learn that at one time, homosexuals were burned at the stake. In fact, Gordon states that at times, gay men were used as kindling in the burning of accused witches! I continue to be amazed at men's (and women's) inhumanity toward others.

As a teacher, what messages will you send to the gay and lesbian students in your classroom? For instance, how will you react when a student comes to you in confidence and confesses that he is gay? Will you refuse to believe it? Will you try to change him? Will you suggest that he seek counseling? I have known well-meaning teachers who have taken these approaches. Even if your advice is given out of genuine care for the student, consider that the message you are sending to the student is that he is not acceptable to you, and will never be acceptable unless he changes his sexual orientation.

It's important to note that many national education organizations, such as the American Federation of Teachers, the National Education Association, and the Association for Supervision and Curriculum Development, have embraced an anti-bias stance and are encouraging their members to be proactive in combating homophobia in our schools. In fact, in "Challenges for Educators: Lesbian, Gay, and Bisexual Families," James Sears informs us that "Though some teachers, administrators, and guidance counselors are reluctant to discuss homosexuality in schools, every major professional educational association has adopted resolutions calling upon schools to address this topic."[10] We can begin by making sure that the school district in which we teach has specific antiharassment policies that prohibit any form of homophobic hostility or discrimination. We can also include relevant information on gays and lesbians in our curriculum and in our everyday teaching practices.

Perhaps you will be willing to be proactive on this issue; perhaps you will not. Regardless of personal beliefs about homosexuality, however, as teachers we must value and affirm the unique identities of each and every student we teach. Steven continued to deny his own identity because he had not been accepted for *just who he is*. The messages of nonacceptance he continually received from those around him caused him to live a lie. Is this what we want for our students? Or do we want our students to become confident, self-assured, caring individuals who are able to recognize and use their unique gifts for the benefit of themselves and others? I encourage you to think about these issues carefully.

One of the first things that we all can do is to educate ourselves. Often I have found that homophobia is largely the result of ignorance. In addition to educating ourselves in order to dispel our own anti-gay biases and stereotypes, there are other positive steps that we can take to ameliorate the plight of gay and lesbian youth.[11] These include being aware that the gay student is often uncomfortable, invisible, and isolated, showing the student that he is accepted and valued, and treating "sexual orientation" as you would any other human variation—as not "bad" but merely "different." Further, when you hear a homophobic remark, try to use it as an opportunity to educate others by asking questions, for example, "Where did you learn that term?" In other words, don't be afraid to confront homophobia among your students and colleagues.

Perhaps our greatest challenge as multicultural educators is to fight against homophobia, just as we must continue to fight against racism, classism, and sexism. It will not be easy. Indeed, it seems that homosexuality is the "marginalized" issue in multicultural education. Where will you stand? Will you remain silent and hence tacitly support homophobia in our society, or will you join in the struggle and try to make a difference?

Peace and Courage,
Becky

Notes

1. Maria Arguelles, "Inside/Out Learning," in Erskine S. Dottin and Lynne D. Miller, eds., *Teaching as Enhancing Human Effectiveness* (Lanham, MD: University Press of America, 1994), pp. 26–31.

2. Reported in Joe Kosciw, "Classroom Abuses," *Respect*, Summer 2001, p. 5.

3. *Making Schools Safe for Gay and Lesbian Youth: Breaking the Silence in Schools and in Families* (Boston: The Massachusetts Governor's Commission on Gay and Lesbian Youth, 1993).

4. D. Moritz, "Making Schools Safe for Gay and Lesbian Youth: A Gateway to Diversity and Multiculturalism," paper presented at the 8th Annual Conference of the National Association for Multicultural Education, October 7–11, 1998, St. Louis, Missouri. Also see Bennett L. Singer and David Deschamps, eds., *Gay and Lesbian Stats* (New York: The New Press, 1994).

5. Lesbian and gay young people are two to three times more likely to attempt suicide than their heterosexual peers, and account for up to 30 percent of all completed suicides among youth. See Singer and Deschamps, *Gay and Lesbian Stats*. Also see Gary Remafedi, *Death by Denial: Studies of Suicide in Gay and Lesbian Teenagers* (Boston: Alyson, 1994).

6. It is estimated that 28 percent of gay youth drop out of school, in comparison with 11 percent of non-gay youth. Moritz, "Making Schools Safe."

7. Lenore Gordon, "What Do We Say When We Hear 'Faggot'?" In David Levine, Robert Lowe, Bob Peterson, and Rita Tenorio, eds., *Rethinking Schools: An Agenda for*

Change (New York: The New Press, 1995), pp. 40–41.

8. Ibid., p. 41.

9. Ibid., p. 42.

10. James T. Sears, "Challenges for Educators: Lesbian, Gay, and Bisexual Families," in Carl A. Grant, ed., *Educating for Diversity: An Anthology of Multicultural Voices* (Boston: Allyn and Bacon, 1995), p. 286.

11. Moritz, "Making Schools Safe." Also see Eric Rofes, "Opening Up the Classroom Closet: Responding to the Educational Needs of Gay and Lesbian Youth," *Harvard Educational Review*, vol. 59, November 1989, pp. 444–453.

Part Three

Straight Talk about School Failure

Letter Seven

Marginalization

Dear Readers,

Hopefully, by now, you are beginning to see that multicultural education is not just a matter of teaching a multicultural curriculum. Rather, a school that is truly multicultural and equitable is committed to addressing the needs of all of its students. This includes making a thorough examination of the school's learning environment and an honest assessment of the ways in which some students may feel alienated, ignored, or even degraded because of their cultural and/or socioeconomic backgrounds or sexual orientations. In this letter to you, I will explore one aspect of the learning environment that can lead to student resistance to learning: marginalization.

This morning my son, who is a senior in high school, went to school early so that he might attend a meeting of the Fellowship of Christian Athletes (FCA). Several years ago, when he first joined this club, I told him that I had difficulty with the name of this organization because I thought it excluded students who might have strong religious convictions but not be Christians. He protested rather vehemently, and countered that all students were welcome to join the club even if they were not Christians; the club did not discriminate based upon religion. Perhaps this is true, but at the same time, I doubt that students of Jewish, Muslim, or other faiths would choose to associate themselves with a Christian organization.

This is just one example of "marginalization"; it is a practice that tends to tell some students that they are not quite as significant as others, and hence they are "pushed to the margins"—they are forced to remain outside the mainstream culture within the school. We marginalize students when we tell them (in subtle and not-so-subtle ways) that their cultural knowledge, language, and ways of "being in the world" are less important than ours.

Rather than viewing their cultural differences as rich learning opportunities, we expect conformity. Thus, in essence, we deny them their voice.

Generally, when students are a definite minority in a school (for example, when there are only one or two of a particular heritage), they tend to remain silent, and to "blend in" as best they can with the majority culture. I recall a graduate student who shared her feelings of marginalization growing up as the only Jewish child in her school. Because she never openly expressed the sense of alienation that she felt, most of her teachers and peers were simply not aware of it. Marginalization occurs, however, even when a certain population of students (such as African American or Hispanic students) make up the majority, simply because of the dominance of the Anglo culture in schools.

If you are a person of color, you probably will be able to relate quite easily to what I am saying here. Undoubtedly you have had to sit through many classes where White history, language, and experiences were presented while yours were ignored (or even demeaned). If you are a White person, however, particularly if you are of an upper- or middle-class background, you may have more difficulty relating to the concept of marginalization. For you, the White (and perhaps male, Christian, and upper-class) perspective has probably always appeared "normal," whereas the perspectives of those from diverse backgrounds have appeared "different." Indeed, this is one way that marginalization occurs. That is, whiteness is seen as the neutral or "unmarked" category, and other categories become "marked" as "different" in relation to it. Thus, everything is viewed (generally unconsciously) through a White lens. So, the "real" history and culture belongs to Whites (and often male, middle/upper-class Whites); the history and cultural experiences of those who do not fit into this category are viewed as different, and often deficient or inferior.[1]

At the outset, it is important to recognize that what is taught in schools is not neutral; it always represents someone's interests, values, and experiences. Often, we do not want to admit this. We'd like to think that what is being taught is "value-free" and "objective." But the reality is that the curriculum represents a particular version (or versions) of what is deemed important to know. Consider, for example, the ongoing controversies in many communities over which textbooks to use and which literature to incorporate in English classrooms. Has this ever happened in your community? Has there ever been a particular group of people who insisted that a particular book not be used, or that a particular perspective be taught in the classroom (such as Creationism)? Throughout history, the curriculum has always been contested as various groups vie for inclusion, whether it be corporate America or the Christian Right. The winners in this contest are generally the dominant groups who wield the most political, economic, and cultural power. Often, the power is exercised not through an actual protest, but rather through what is deleted from what we teach. That is, teachers will say "I would be afraid to teach about ___," simply because they fear reprisals by parents and/or administrators.

In *Official Knowledge*, Michael Apple maintains that textbooks represent a "selective tradition": "someone's selection, someone's vision of legitimate knowledge and culture, one that in the process of enfranchising one group's cultural capital disenfranchises another's."[2] Think about the concept of "disenfranchisement" for a moment. What does this mean to you? Technically, it means to deny the rights of citizenship, especially the right to vote. In this context, however, Apple is referring to the process of depriving a particular group of privilege and power, while simultaneously enhancing the privilege and power of another group. We do this, he suggests, through maintaining a curriculum that reinforces the knowledge and culture of a particular population while simultaneously omitting the knowledge and culture of other populations. Most multicultural educators refer to this type of curriculum as "monocultural"—a curriculum that presents the knowledge and experiences of only one group (typically White and upper/middle-class, and often male).

At this point, you may be protesting, "but haven't textbooks changed in recent years? Most of the textbooks that I have used included information about diverse populations." To a certain extent, you would be right. Apple goes on to state that curricula aren't imposed, but rather negotiated, as non-dominant groups struggle to be heard. What tends to occur through this process of conflict and negotiation is that the knowledge and perspectives of dominated groups are included but become marginalized. That is, textbooks essentially remain as they are, but isolated elements of the history and culture of dominated groups are "mentioned" throughout. There is no substantive change in the basic ideology of the texts, and no substantial elaboration of the experiences of persons of color, women, and other dominated groups. Indeed, what tend to be included are those individuals and historical experiences that support the status quo; those who dared to challenge the dominant social and economic system are rarely studied in depth. What we tend to have, then, are monocultural texts—texts that basically present a single perspective. (Take a look at a current U.S. history textbook, and you will probably find "boxes" that highlight certain events relating to the experiences of subordinated populations. You might then contrast this text with a book like Howard Zinn's *A People's History of the United States 1492-Present*, which looks at history from the perspective of marginalized populations.[3] There's a big difference!)

There are other ways in which we marginalize the voices of non-dominant groups, however. Even when we study their experiences, it is often as "tourists" would study another country. That is, we treat those experiences as if they are not a part of the American narrative—as if we are visiting a foreign country. Have you ever attended a "culture fair"? This is perhaps the prototype of a "tourist" approach. We learn about different foods, dances, and traditions, but we never have to talk about the difficult issues like our experiences with persons who differ from ourselves, or the inherent contradictions between our professed ideology of freedom and justice and the lived realities of persons of color. The tourist approach is evident when students learn about how populations such as American Indians lived and dressed, but they never see Native Americans as an integral part of American history, or as an important part of our present and future. The tourist approach is also evident when we attend exhibits and learn about Chinese artifacts, but we never confront the exploitation of Chinese labor through much of our history, or the sanctioning of discrimination through the Chinese Exclusion Act, or the continuing racial discrimination that Chinese American (and other Asian American) students face daily in our schools.

In an excellent article on how to teach American history from a multicultural perspective, John Wills and Hugh Mehan argue that we often teach our nation's history using a tourist approach.[4] Do you see how this approach can actually end up doing damage by reinforcing stereotypes about other populations? We do not need this kind of information in order to deal with current issues, which is why we study American history in the first place. Rather, as Wills and Mehan argue, what we need to know is how various populations related to one another throughout history, and how those relationships affect what is occurring today. They call this the "sociological approach" to teaching history. For instance, rather than just learning facts and information, this approach might have us ask questions such as these: What were the human relationships involved in this particular period in our history? How was history being shaped as various groups came together and interacted? How did these interactions change the outlook and way of life of the various players? When you think about it, human history is more about *relationships* than events; that is, it is about how relationships caused and shaped events in our past. If we look at history this way, then it will lead to questions such as how the institution of slavery affects what is happening in our nation today, and how the taking of land by Europeans relates to current issues.

Wills and Mehan also argue that we tend to "add on" the contributions of non-dominant groups after the main story has been told. This is similar to what Apple refers to as "mentioning." In these ways, women and persons of color are never seen as primary actors on the historical stage, but are always viewed as "the Other." It's an easy step, then, to see persons of color and other marginalized populations as being somehow "outside the American mainstream"—as not being "true Americans." (Consider my earlier remarks concerning whiteness being viewed as "unmarked" and "normative.")

One other thing that tends to happen, the authors suggest, is that history is often taught as a series of discontinuous events. Think about your own American history classes for a moment. It has been my experience that this is true: First we study the colonial period, next the Revolutionary War, and so on. Was this the case in your own study of American history? Was the process of colonization ever connected to the later exploitation of persons of color? (For instance, colonization was actually extended throughout our history as Europeans took land from other populations, such as American

Indians and Mexicans.) Was slavery ever connected to the Civil Rights Movement? Was industrialization ever connected to current labor struggles or to the subjugation of women? When we don't make these connections with our students, then history cannot really help us to make choices for the present and future. In advocating a sociological approach to teaching history, Wills and Mehan argue as follows:

> History is made in interaction. If history is to provide any lessons for the present, then students need to examine and understand these relations in the past.... With this conception of history in mind, the criteria for including diverse groups becomes more clear. Women and people of color must be visible in specific historical events to be visible in history. Furthermore, they must appear as active participants, that is, social actors who made sense of their circumstances and orient their actions to others around them.[5]

The authors suggest that American history be taught around the organizational theme of the continuing struggle for civil rights. I don't know about you, but I find this idea intriguing. How might a history course look if civil rights was the focus? We might start with religious persecution and that persecution's connection to the decision of Europeans to establish communities in a foreign land. We might study the roles of women in the emerging economy, and the ways their roles have changed over time. We might also have students examine the Constitution and Bill of Rights and the ways in which these documents have served as a vision of what our society might become. Of course, the relationship between Europeans and native populations—from the initial encounters between these two populations through the present day—would be an important study. We might also explore the idea of religious freedom and the historical and current relationships between Christians, Jews, Muslims, and other religious groups. Black-White relationships in society would be examined through an historical lens, as would current immigration policies. Can you see how this way of studying American history might help to inform us on current issues? Contrary to what some would argue, we do not need to be able to rattle off a bunch of facts and dates; rather, we need to be able to understand the historical basis for the problems we face today.

I have digressed a bit from the topic of marginalization. The main point I am trying to make, however, is that when we do not consider history in this way, we tend to view all non-European populations as "the Other"—as living in the margins of our history rather than as being central players. The relationships between Europeans and other populations (Africans, American Indians, Chinese, Japanese, etc.) have *everything* to do with our history. In fact, these relationships shaped our history, from Columbus' expedition, through the Mexican-American War, the Civil War, the period of industrialization, up to the present day. Can you see how persons of color, women, and various immigrant groups have always been central players in our history? Can you see how current relationships between African Americans, Asian Americans, Native Americans, European Americans, and other populations have been shaped by the relationships we have had in the past? Yet when we teach a monocultural curriculum—one that focuses primarily on the contributions of Whites (and males) to the exclusion of others—our perspectives become skewed. In addition, we essentially tell marginalized populations that they "don't count"—that they weren't important in shaping our history.

At this point, you might be wondering what all of this has to do with educational failure. In my multicultural education class, I ask students to read a chapter by Herbert Kohl in which he shares his experiences as a visitor to a public school classroom. All of the students in this junior high classroom are Hispanic, and they are studying the Mexican-American War. As in most American history textbooks, this era in our history is being presented from an Anglo perspective. In the midst of the lesson, the students are essentially refusing to learn, and in frustration, the teacher introduces Kohl as a visiting teacher and leaves the room. In the ensuing conversation, the students express their resentment of what they are learning and the fact that their own historical perspective is being denied them:

> The class launched into a serious and sophisticated discussion of the way in which racism manifests itself in their everyday lives at school. It amounted to nothing less than full-blown and cooperative not-learning. They accepted the failing grades it produced in exchange for the passive defense of their personal and cultural integrity.[6]

In an effort to maintain a sense of pride and self-worth, the students in this classroom actively resisted the formal curriculum through their refusal to learn. Kohl goes on to state that "Until we learn to distinguish not-learning from failure and respect the truth behind this massive rejection of schooling by students from poor and oppressed communities, it will not be possible to solve the major problems of education in the United States today." Unfortunately, far too many educational institutions place more emphasis on teaching the standard curriculum than on meeting the needs of their students. When that curriculum distorts, ignores, or even denigrates the cultural knowledge and experiences of many of our students, why should we be surprised when they rebel?

Other students' resistance may be more subtle. For instance, Arlette Ingram Willis writes about the experiences of her young African American son, Jake, as he struggles to come up with writing topics that his primarily Anglo classmates can relate to.[7] In an article published in the *Harvard Educational Review*, she describes a conversation she has with Jake about his choice of a topic for the upcoming Young Authors Contest. When she suggests that he write about his experiences at the barbershop, he replies, "They won't understand." What he is really saying here is that his classmates won't understand the African American cultural context in which this event occurs. Willis asks:

> Where, I wonder, has he gotten the idea of a "White" audience—that is, the sense that his classmates and others who read his writing will not appreciate what he has to share? When did his concept of a "White" audience arise? My questions persist: How long has Jake known, intuitively perhaps, that his school literacy experiences have been tempered through a mainstream lens? Will Jake continue to resist "writing for a white audience?" When do culturally and linguistically diverse children learn that they must choose between selfhood and accommodation?[8]

I think it's time for us to acknowledge that we continue to marginalize students in our schools, and that such marginalization can have detrimental effects on the academic engagement and achievement of various student populations. Consider, for example, the school calendar and the holidays that we choose to celebrate; the songs that we choose to perform; the literature that we ask students to read; the events that we ask students to study. In the same article, Willis shares an experience of her oldest son, who was told that he could not mention the concept of race when writing for a national essay contest on the topic, "What it means to be an American." For an African American student, who must deal with his own racial identity on a continuous basis, this proved to be a difficult task; he lost interest in the assignment and completed it only for a grade.

Such marginalization has had devastating consequences on the education of underrepresented student populations. A well-known educational theorist, John Ogbu, has examined why some populations of students succeed, and some fail.[9] For instance, why do many immigrant students tend to do well in school, while African American, Native American, and Hispanic American students tend to be underachievers? Ogbu suggests that immigrant or "voluntary" minorities—those who come to this country voluntarily—have very different responses to schooling from the responses of those he refers to as "castelike" or nonvoluntary minorities. For immigrant minorities, their experiences with American schools are often an improvement over their experiences in their home countries. For instance, in some countries individuals must pay for their education, whereas in the United States it is free. Also, immigrants tend to have faith in the American dream and believe that hard work and perseverance in school will lead to economic gains. Finally, they often have the option of returning to their homeland if things don't work out here.

Nonvoluntary minorities, on the other hand, acquired their minority status against their will (for example, through slavery or conquest). Hence, they have very different perspectives on education. Historically, because of institutional racism, they have been denied jobs for which they were qualified. In addition, students of color have been disproportionately assigned to special education tracks and have been seen as less competent than their Anglo peers. For instance, Ogbu cites a study of twenty California school districts where Black students comprised about 27.5 percent of the student population but 62 percent of those designated as educable mentally retarded.

What is the effect of these racist practices on students of color? Ogbu suggests that these students and their parents tend to mistrust the educational institution and the values espoused by it. This mistrust of White schools has evolved over time and has its roots in the discriminatory treatment Blacks have experienced in schools: "History has left Blacks with a feeling that whites and their institutions cannot be trusted to benefit Blacks equitably." In addition, as Ogbu points out,

> disaffection and mistrust also abound because Blacks see inferior education perpetuated through many subtle devices they suspected the schools of using (e.g. biased testing, misclassification, tracking, biased textbooks, biased counseling, etc.), and because they doubt that these schools understand Black children and their needs.[10]

What tends to occur, then, is that while the parents of nonvoluntary minority students emphasize the importance of getting a good education, at the same time they tell their children that they will need to be "twice as good" as their White peers in order to get a good job. Children of color receive messages on a regular basis, both at home and through the media and their daily experiences, that the connection between school and job success is not as strong for Blacks as for Whites. Hence, they tend to doubt the value of schooling for their own future success. They also see cultural and institutional racism at work within the school—through tracking, a monocultural curriculum, biased teachers—which fans the flames of mistrust and disillusionment. Schooling becomes equated with "whiteness." That is, it is perceived that the educational institution works for the benefit of Whites.

Let's consider the evidence for a moment. Whites are found in disproportionate numbers in the upper academic tracks. Tests tend to be biased in favor of White achievement. Teachers—the vast majority of whom are White—generally are culturally similar to White children and are often ignorant of or misunderstand non-White cultures. Students of color are referred for special education in substantially higher numbers than their White peers. And the curriculum typically centers around White cultural knowledge and achievements. In essence, schools have "worked" for most (though not all) White students; they have often not "worked" for non-White students. Is it any wonder, then, that students of color tend to mistrust the schools?

A similar dynamic seems to operate for Hispanic students. In a recent ethnographic study in a large Houston high school, researcher Angela Valenzuela examined the responses to schooling of recent immigrants from Mexico and U.S.-born Mexican students and found that recent arrivals tend to have generally positive responses to their educational experiences in the United States.[11] The longer students remain in the United States, however, the stronger their resistance to schooling becomes. Valenzuela attributes this resistance to what she refers to as "subtractive schooling"—a process that systematically erodes students' integrity and cultural knowledge. Essentially, the students in Valenzuela's study reported that they are made to feel insignificant within a bureaucratic system that devalues them both as Mexicans and as individuals. Also contributing to students' resistance is what they perceive to be detached, uncaring relationships with teachers—relationships that are essentially incompatible with the more reciprocal and nurturing relationships within the Hispanic community. (I'll be discussing the topic of cultural incompatibility in greater depth in a future letter.) The result of these schooling practices is an extremely high rate of educational failure; more than 70 percent of the school's ninth graders never graduate.

At this point, some of you may still be thinking "I don't really buy any of this. After all, research shows that Asian children and White children are just smarter. That's why they experience a higher level of success in school." First, I must tell you that there is absolutely no scientific basis for this assumption. In my opinion, books such as the recently popular *Bell Curve*, which claims moral and genetic superiority based upon race and class, do great damage by perpetuating racism in this nation. In essence, they tell a White audience what they want to hear, and they do it in a way that appears "scientific."[12] Yet you should know that *The Bell Curve* (and other similar studies) have been refuted by numerous scholars from both the education and scientific communities.[13] In fact, scientists even deny the legitimacy of using "race" as a separate category. In other words, we are all so biologically similar that "race" is not even a useful way of categorizing human difference.[14] Nevertheless, we continue to use this category for making erroneous assumptions that justify and perpetuate racism. Joe Kincheloe and Shirley Steinberg ask the following questions:

> [W]hat does it mean that Karen scored low on her IQ test: is she genetically predisposed to low intelligence?; is English not her first language? has she been raised in an economically disadvantaged environment with little overlap between her cultural experiences and those rewarded by schools and standardized tests?... Herrnstein and Murray let us know that when the smoke clears an *objective* scientific analysis will produce only one correct answer: Blacks and Latinos are intellectually and morally inferior to Whites. Only through significant ideological manipulations of data could such a conclusion even be suggested.[15]

It seems that when entire populations are categorized as "the Other"—as somehow outside the American mainstream—then it becomes tempting (and convenient) to label and to victimize, rather than to take a close look at the ways in which our schooling processes and practices actually *cause* failure. Women and persons of color are an integral part of our past, our present, and our future, and to cast them as "the Other" is both divisive and destructive. To put it another way, we are all part of the American fabric, and we will either sink or swim together. The problems in our inner cities, in the mountains of Appalachia, or on the Texas borders are not the problems of a few, but *our* problems that must be examined and solved collectively. Marginalization is always divisive; it establishes criteria that separate the "insiders" from the "outsiders" along cultural and class lines. A multicultural education, on the other hand, is inclusive; it acknowledges the legitimacy of the experiences and contributions of all people and recognizes our common destiny as a nation.

Sometimes, marginalization actually occurs in very concrete ways, such as the use of physical space. A couple of years ago I overheard a conversation between two of my colleagues who had just been out to visit a local high school. They were discussing the fact that the low-track biology class (all African American students) was holding its classes in the boiler room because there was no other space left in the school. They had no equipment or materials for the study of biology. I presented this scenario to the students in my multicultural education class and asked them to consider the following questions: What message is the school giving to these students? Is it really important to the school that they learn biology? Of course, the answers to these questions are obvious. The school was telling them, in a not-so-subtle way, that they really did not expect them to excel in biology, nor did they care if they learned it. The next question, however, was a bit more challenging: If you were the teacher of this biology class, what would you do? Many of my students answered that they would just make the best of a bad situation. If this would be your response, then I suggest that it's just not good enough. By remaining silent and essentially accepting the situation, then you, too, would be telling your students that they just "don't count." While it is perhaps true that the situation could not be changed, nevertheless we could show our students that we cared by writing letters to the school board, protesting to the administration, and getting parents involved. We need to be advocates for our students by recognizing inequity when it occurs and leading them in the fight against it, for only then will students of color begin to trust the educational institution. It seems that if we are not willing to intervene actively to promote equitable learning situations for our students, then we merely contribute to the mistrust.

Before I close this letter to you, I must tell you about one other unfortunate consequence of marginalization in schools. When schools are perceived by students of color as being "White" institutions, then there is a tendency on the part of these students to resist "acting White" by refusing to learn, or by intentionally underachieving. In other words, because "whiteness" is equated with schooling, academic success is viewed as "joining the opposing camp"—yet another example of the divisive results of marginalization (versus inclusion). Recently Laurence Steinberg, B. Bradford Brown, and Sanford M. Dornbusch conducted an investigation to determine why some students achieve in school, and others fail.[16] After analyzing data that they gathered from 20,000 high-school students over a three-year period, the researchers concluded that peer influence is a primary indicator of academic success or failure. They argue that: "In many minority peer groups, scholastic success is equated with 'selling out' one's cultural identity, as some sort of surrender to the control of White, middle-class America." And, further, because peer groups in schools tend to be segregated along racial lines, it is often difficult for high-achieving students of color to find a support system. That is, the groups that value and respect academic success tend to be dominated by White students, making it difficult for students of color to join:

> The sad truth is that many students, and many Black students in particular, are forced to choose between doing well in school and having friends.... Thus, while just as many Black students as White students aspire toward membership in the "brain" crowd, membership in this group is more open to White than to Black students.[17]

The researchers also found that the aspirations of parents of Black and Latino youth for their children are being "undone" by peer pressure that tends to devalue educational achievement in the effort not to appear "White."

These findings are supported by other investigations. For example, in her study of high-achieving students of color, Signithia Fordham found that academically successful Black students often feel a need to distance themselves from their African American peers.[18] "The organizational structure of the school rewards racelessness in students and thus reinforces the notion that it is a quality necessary for success in the larger society."[19]

Thus, our students of color typically find that they must choose between academic success or the support of their peers. Many poor students face a similar problem. For example, in Appalachia, the phrase "gettin' above your raisin'" is sometimes used to describe those students who have high academic aspirations. In a society that is still marked by racism and classism, the decision to excel academically and risk appearing "White" or "middle-class" can be an extremely difficult one, and it is not hard to understand why some students choose community over academic achievement.

Counteracting these perceptions will be very difficult. Where do we start? It seems to me that, at the very least, we must begin to value the cultural knowledge and experiences of historically marginalized populations in our schools. Students of color have a rich literary, scholarly, and cultural tradition, yet when we ignore these accomplishments or perceive them as insignificant, we marginalize entire populations and reinforce the equation of academics with "whiteness." Thus, as I have suggested throughout this letter, we must transform the curriculum so that it represents our collective voice as a nation and incorporates *all* of our human experience.

Beyond this, however, I think it's important to believe in our students. Do we really think that all of our students can achieve at high levels? Do we *see* our students of color as "academic"? Or are we led to believe that some students are just not as intelligent as others, by the way they talk, the way they dress, the community they live in, or even their race? I'll have more to say about teacher expectation in my next letter.

Educational failure is the direct result of marginalization in our schools. I would like to leave you with one final thought: Can our society really afford to fail so many of our future citizens?

Until next time,
Becky

Notes

1. See Ruth Frankenberg, *White Women, Race Matters: The Social Construction of Whiteness* (Minneapolis: University of Minnesota Press, 1993). Also see Alice McIntyre, *Making Meaning of Whiteness: Exploring Racial Identity With White Teachers* (Albany: State University of New York Press, 1997); and Rebecca Powell, "Confronting White Hegemony: Implications for Multicultural Education," *Multicultural Education*, Winter 1996, pp. 12–15.

2. Michael W. Apple, *Official Knowledge: Democratic Education in a Conservative Age* (New York: Routledge, 1993), p. 49.

3. Howard Zinn, *A People's History of the United States: 1492–Present* (New York: HarperCollins, 1995). Also see Ronald Takaki, *A Different Mirror: A History of Multicultural America* (Boston: Little, Brown and Company, 1993).

4. John Wills and Hugh Mehan, "Recognizing Diversity within a Common Historical Narrative: The Challenge to Teaching History and Social Studies," *Multicultural Education*, Fall 1996, pp. 4–11.

5. Ibid., p. 8.

6. Herbert Kohl, "I Won't Learn From You! Confronting Student Resistance," in Bill
    Bigelow, Linda Christensen, Stan Karp, Barbara Miner, and Bob Peterson, eds.,
    Rethinking Our Classrooms: Teaching for Equity and Justice (Milwaukee, WI:
    Rethinking Schools, 1994), p. 135.

7. Arlette Ingram Willis, "Reading the World of School Literacy: Contextualizing the
    Experience of a Young African American Male," *Harvard Educational Review*, vol.
    5, Spring 1995, pp. 30–49.

8. Ibid., p. 135.

9. John U. Ogbu, "Literacy and Schooling in Subordinate Cultures: The Case of Black
    Americans," in Kofi Lomotey, ed., *Going to School: The African-American Experience*
    (Albany: State University of New York Press, 1990), pp. 113–131.

10. Ibid., p. 127. It's important to note here that it is not a distrust of education and
    schooling but rather a distrust of traditionally White institutions that has led to such
    resistance. In fact, African Americans have always had a strong commitment toward
    education. Consider, for example, the numerous Black colleges and universities that
    have been established, often at great sacrifice. Indeed, throughout our history, Whites
    have only rarely been committed to providing educational opportunities for students of
    color.

11. Angela Valenzuela, *Subtractive Schooling: U.S.-Mexican Youth and the Politics of
    Caring* (Albany: State University of New York Press, 1999).

12. Richard J. Herrnstein and Charles Murray, *The Bell Curve: Intelligence and Class
    Structure in American Life* (New York: The Free Press, 1994).

13. For an excellent, comprehensive resource, see Joe L. Kincheloe, Shirley R. Steinberg,
    and Aaron D. Gresson III, eds., *Measured Lies: The Bell Curve Examined* (New York:
    St. Martin's Press, 1996).

14. Paul Kivel, *Uprooting Racism: How White People Can Work for Racial Justice*
    (Gabriola Island, British Columbia: New Society Publishers, 1996).

15. Joe Kincheloe and Shirley Steinberg, "Who Said It Can't Happen Here?" in Kincheloe,
    Steinberg, and Gresson, *Measured Lies*, p. 6.

16. Laurence Steinberg, B. Bradford Brown, and Sanford M. Dornbusch, "Ethnicity and Adolescent Achievement," in Fred Schultz, ed., *Annual Editions: Multicultural Education 97/98* (Guilford, CT: Dushkin/McGraw-Hill, 1997), pp. 12–23.

17. Ibid., pp. 22–23.

18. Signithia Fordham, "Racelessness as a Factor in Black Students' School Success: Pragmatic Strategy or Pyrrhic Victory?" in Tamara Beauboeuf-Lafontant and D. Smith Augustine, eds., *Facing Racing in Education* (Cambridge, MA: Harvard Educational Review, 1996), pp. 209–243. Also see Ann Locke Davidson, *Making and Molding Identity in Schools* (Albany: State University of New York Press, 1996).

19. Fordham, "Racelessness," p. 238.

Letter Eight

Teacher Expectation

Dear Readers,

I wonder if there have ever been times in your own schooling experiences when you have felt that not much was expected of you? What did the teacher do (or not do) to make you feel this way? I can recollect many such experiences vividly. For instance, I recall the day when my college voice instructor informed me that he didn't have time in his schedule to teach me and that I would need to find another instructor. While he never stated it directly, he implied that he only had room for the "good" singers—those with professional potential. (I dropped the course.) I also remember a college religion class that was taught by a young and aspiring male professor. This professor encouraged discussion in his classes, but because I was somewhat intimidated by the confident and often articulate responses of some of the other students (most of whom I realize in retrospect were male), I recall remaining silent and feeling quite ignorant in this class. I also recall that the professor never intervened in this dynamic, nor did he ever do or say anything that would elevate my sense of competence. In essence, I believe he viewed me as I viewed myself: as merely an "average" student. (My final grade turned out to be "average," too.)

Then there was my high school social studies class, which was taught by one of the football coaches. I recall learning very little in his class because the teacher spent most of the period talking about athletics and other topics that had absolutely nothing to do with American history. (For the record, I have known many fine teachers who were also coaches!) Consider the messages that he sent to his students on a daily basis: (1) American history is essentially boring and insignificant; (2) as the teacher, I have the right to dominate this class by talking about anything I choose to talk about; and (3)

I do not respect you enough to teach you American history. *I suggest that when we fail to teach to the best of our ability, then we convey to our students that we do not feel they are worthy of our efforts.* (I invite you to think about this for a moment. Have you ever felt this way as a student?) Since the teacher didn't care about American history, neither did I.

There were many other classes in which I was made to feel inferior and incompetent (my high-school and college biology classes come to mind), but I think you get the picture. Fortunately, I have been able to overcome many of the feelings of inadequacy that I experienced in these and other classes throughout my school career. Yet I also had many instructors—male and female alike—who had high expectations for me and for the other students in their classes, and who managed to convey those expectations through insisting on quality work (and rewarding it). I also recall being called upon (often) in these classes, feeling free to ask questions when I did not understand a concept, and having teachers who took the time to explain things to me and to guide my thinking. At the same time, I attended school in a predominantly White, upper-middle-class suburb, and it was always expected that I would go to college. Many of our students are not that lucky. When race, class, and/or ethnicity enter into the equation, then things become more complicated.

In my multicultural class, I ask my students to read an article written by Ray Rist entitled "Student Social Class and Teacher Expectations: The Self-Fulfilling Prophecy in Ghetto Education."[1] In this article, Rist describes his research project documenting the ways in which teacher expectations work to lower the academic achievement of some students. He first takes his readers into a kindergarten classroom, where after only eight days of class, the students are seated at three separate tables based upon their perceived abilities. Those at table one get a great deal of teacher attention, whereas the children at tables two and three receive quantitatively less teacher attention. In fact, table one is located closer to the teacher and to the blackboard, while table three is located farther away from both, thereby assuring less interaction with the teacher. (Indeed, there are times when the children at table three cannot even see the board.) In addition, the attention given to the children at the various tables is qualitatively different; table three children receive substantially more criticism and negative feedback. What is so interesting—and also quite alarming—is that the children themselves begin responding in accordance with their designated labels. That is, the children at tables two and three perceive themselves to be inferior and begin acting out this perception. In fact, they even begin making derogatory remarks toward one another. The children at table one perceive themselves to be superior and contribute to the ostracism of the children at the other two tables. In other words, the children in this kindergarten classroom follow the teacher's lead and model her behavior, thereby mimicking her positive or negative treatment of them.

What is truly sad is that Rist found that when these children moved on to first and second grade, the same pattern was repeated and reinforced. The perceptions of the kindergarten teacher, which were formed during the first week of school and were based primarily upon superficial features such as language and dress (readiness test scores were unavailable), essentially determined a child's success or failure during the early elementary grades. So, early teacher expectations, which were determined largely upon factors associated with a child's socioeconomic class, became self-fulfilling prophecies: those who came from homes that were "more like the teacher's" were labeled as potentially high achievers and subsequently experienced higher levels of success than those from lower-class homes, who were not expected to do as well.

Many of my students become quite upset and angered by this article. "What a terrible thing to do to small children," they say. "Already, in kindergarten, these children were labeled as failures. And most of them will continue to be failures all the way through school." They also become disturbed at the ways in which the favored children began to act out their emerging sense of superiority. Other students in my class, however, deny that such labeling would ever occur in today's schools. "This article was published in 1970," they say. "I don't think such things would happen today." Even some of my colleagues question my use of an article that they perceive to be "outdated."

Perhaps they are right. Yet inevitably several of my teacher education students will begin to discuss classroom experiences they have witnessed in their fieldwork (a requirement in every methods class in our teacher education program) that clearly illustrate this self-fulfilling prophecy phenomenon at work. For instance, one student told us that a teacher she had observed the previous semester, just like the teacher in Rist's study, had actually seated his students in three distinct areas in the room based upon their achievement, with the lower-achieving students being placed farther from the teacher. Another said that a fifth-grade teacher she was observing that same semester simply handed out worksheets all day long and continuously ignored students' questions. Thus, he was sending a clear signal to them that he neither expected them to learn nor cared whether they learned. Others tell of classrooms where the teacher only calls on students who sit near the front of the room, or where students are permitted to sit in the back of the class and sleep. (This behavior is viewed as acceptable because, after all, "at least they don't bother the other students around them.")

Still other students can recall events from their middle-school and high-school years, where they were either placed in the high academic tracks and made to feel that they were "smarter" than the other students, or they were denied entrance into the higher achievement groups and felt that they had to prove that they were just as capable as anyone else. Indeed, just this past week, in a statewide meeting I attended to examine the achievement gap between Whites and students of color, the father of an African American high school student told us about his daughter's experiences when she enrolled in an advanced placement class against the teacher's advice. On the first day of class, the teacher announced to the other students that this student "didn't belong" in this class and would not be there long. She didn't even get the chance to prove herself; the teacher had labeled her as a failure before the class had even begun. To make matters worse, he made certain that she understood her status by humiliating her in front of her peers. Fortunately, this student had supportive parents who were able to counteract the damage that this teacher did to their daughter. Many of our students aren't that lucky.

In my fourth letter to you, I told about my experiences in a small elementary school in the mountains of eastern Kentucky where the classrooms were differentiated by perceived ability levels. Thus, there was a "high-achieving" first-grade classroom and a "low-achieving" first-grade classroom. It soon became evident that these designations were based upon socioeconomic class as determined by parents' occupation: the "teachers' kids" were in the high-achieving class; the "welfare recipients' kids" were in the low-achieving class. Luckily for the low-tracked children, their teacher believed in her students' abilities, and therefore most of them were able to succeed despite the negative labels placed upon them by the school. She expected them to succeed, and they did. I often wondered, however, about what happened to these children as they moved up through the grades.

If you have been through a teacher education program (or if you are currently enrolled in such a program) you have probably come across the study conducted by Robert Rosenthal and Lenore Jacobson in the late 1960s, which was subsequently published in their book, *Pygmalion in the Classroom.*[2] In this study, Rosenthal and Jacobson told teachers that they were able to use test data to identify children who are "late bloomers." Although the children so identified had actually been randomly selected, by the end of the year many of the identified children were performing at higher levels. The researchers attributed the children's academic gains to higher teacher expectations. This study generated a great deal of controversy after it was published, and similar studies have not always produced the same results. Other investigations, however—particularly those that do not try to manipulate teacher expectation through providing false data (which teachers may not always find credible)—have shown that teacher expectation can have pervasive effects on student learning.[3] That is, like the teachers and children in Rist's study, these data show that teachers tend to behave in certain ways toward students based upon their perceived abilities, and these expectations often come true—hence, they are self-fulfilling prophecies. It's important to realize, too, that it's not just the teacher's behavior that's the culprit here; *it's also the ways in which students respond to that behavior.* Some students may actually resist a teacher's negative expectation of them and work even harder to "prove her wrong," whereas others may develop a feeling of intellectual inferiority and will perform far below their capacity. Also, as we have seen, students themselves will often treat one another according to a teacher's perceptions. (How often have we heard students make negative comments about other students' abilities, such as, "Oh, he's just stupid"?)

Over time, students respond to these behaviors in a number of different ways. They may resist schooling, as we have seen, and may eventually drop out (which to me is the ultimate form of resistance). Or they may begin to think of themselves as less intelligent and therefore put in minimal effort. It's important that we realize that poor student performance can be the result of the expectations we hold for students, and not a lack of competence or ability.

To illustrate how pervasive such student responses can be, I turn to the recent work of Michelle Fine, a professor of psychology at the City University of New York.[4] Professor Fine met with students at Randolph County High School in Wedowee, Alabama, following a racial incident, in which the principal was so disturbed by the interracial dating in his school that he canceled the prom. (You might recall this incident because it received national attention.) Fine was interested in hearing the students' thoughts on why the upper and standard tracks in the school tended to be segregated along racial lines, particularly since students are allowed to choose the track they wish to be in. Yet, somewhat predictably, they tend to "choose" along racial lines. When Fine questioned the Black students about their reasons for choosing the standard over the advanced academic track, they replied, "Because I was scared," or "Because we thought it [advanced] was too hard." In contrast to this, a White student stated that "There are plenty of dumb white kids in my classes, but they would never go to the standard track," and claimed that if she ever told her guidance counselor that she would like to be in a standard track, her counselor would probably tell her "You're not going into the standard track. You're going to college."

This is a clear illustration of how students will internalize the expectations that teachers and educational institutions have of them. How tragic that, even when given the choice, the African American students opted for the standard, non-college-bound track because they just didn't feel that they were smart enough for the advanced track. Fine notes: "White racism here—and elsewhere—is so thoroughly institutionalized and embodied that young people, when given an opportunity, 'choose' their 'place,' and seemingly with little protest."[5] Like the students in Rist's study, these students began to believe that they couldn't succeed in the higher track, and thus, in a sense, they collaborated in their own underachievement. Of course, the school claimed racial innocence because, after all, the students "chose" their lot.

What has always baffled me is that, despite the fact that the ramifications of teacher expectations are quite well-known, educators continue to do damage to students based upon negative perceptions of students' abilities. In fact, I think this practice is much more widespread than we would like to admit. We would like to believe that our educational practices are "objective" and "scientific," based upon real empirical data such as test performance and student responses. And, to a certain extent, our decisions *are* based upon such data. Of course, as I have discussed in previous letters, such empirical data is not always valid, because students often resist learning for a variety of reasons. Also, test data can be culturally biased—a topic I will examine in depth in a future letter. Yet what is also troubling is that, when students begin to *perceive* that they are viewed as having lesser intelligence or ability—whether those perceptions are the result of race, class, or gender bias (or a combination of these)—then they will frequently perform according to those perceptions. And, unfortunately, such perceptions can be reinforced in ways that are often subtle and unconscious. ("Stereotype threat"—or the apprehension that one's performance will reinforce and confirm a negative stereotype—is also at work here. I'll have more to say about stereotype threat in a future letter.)

One way that such perceptions become reinforced is through ability grouping. Since grouping students by ability (either by placing them in separate in-class achievement groups or through a system of tracking) can have such pervasive and long-lasting effects on student achievement, I have decided to devote an entire letter to you on this topic. Suffice it to say, however, that students who are placed in lower-ability groups often respond in a variety of ways. For instance, they may decide simply to stop trying, in an attempt to avoid embarrassment. Thus, while their lack of effort will undoubtedly result in failure, at least they cannot blame their failure on a lack of ability. Or they may begin to care less about school and separate themselves from the whole process of schooling in an effort to avoid a situation that is psychologically painful to them. In other words, they may withdraw and become disengaged from learning, developing an "I don't care" attitude in an effort to "save face." Both of these responses are actually a form of resistance to a system that tells them that they are not as capable—and hence, not as valuable—as those who are in the top ability groups. (Consider, too, that when these students become parents themselves, they may continue to harbor negative feelings about school because of their own painful experiences there.)

There are other ways we convey our expectations to students, however, that may be much more obscure but nevertheless just as damaging. For instance, in my letter to you on sexism, I discussed the fact that teachers interact more with boys than with girls. Also, they tend to provide more explanations to boys on *how* to do something, whereas with girls, they will often do it for them. Consider for a moment the long-term effects of this behavior. The underlying assumption being conveyed to the girls is one of ineptness— "I really don't think you can do this, so I'll do it for you." Also, the more we call upon and interact with particular students, the more we show them that we value their opinions and knowledge. So, even our seating arrangements can make a difference, as it has been found that teachers tend to interact more with the students who are seated near the front of the room, while those in the far corners tend to be excluded.

In their extensive research in classrooms, Thomas L. Good and Jere E. Brophy identified several major differences in the ways that high achievers and low achievers are treated.[6] These include the following:

- Teachers do not wait as long for low achievers to answer a question.
- Teachers tend to provide answers for low achievers or call on someone else rather than giving clues or rephrasing questions.
- Teachers criticize low achievers more often for incorrect responses.
- Teachers praise low achievers less often.
- Teachers generally pay less attention to low achievers, call on them less often, and ask them easier questions.
- Teachers demand less from low achievers.

- If a grade is borderline, teachers tend to give high achievers but not low achievers the benefit of the doubt.
- Teachers' interactions with low achievers tend to be less friendly, and also less responsive in terms of nonverbal communication (e.g. eye contact, positive head nodding, etc.).
- Teachers tend to accept and use the ideas of low-achieving students less frequently than those of high achievers.

If you tend to skim over such lists, as I sometimes do, then I encourage you to take the time to read this one carefully. I think these teacher behaviors tell us a great deal about why some students eventually become disenchanted with school. When students become labeled as low achievers, then our behaviors as teachers (whether conscious or unconscious) can actually contribute to their lack of success. Indeed, this is one way that racism, classism, and sexism are reinforced in our educational institutions. For instance, I continue to be struck by the comments of an African American colleague, who told me that when she was in school her teachers rarely made eye contact with her, and she remembers to this day how insignificant she felt. Such behaviors—which may be interpreted by our students as reflections of race, class, ethnic, or gender bias—can communicate volumes to our students.

Consider, too, the messages that we send through our interactions with students. For instance, think about this typical classroom exchange:

Teacher: Marla, can you tell me what "demographic" means in this sentence?
Marla: (No response.)
Teacher: Do you know what "demographic" means?
Marla: (Shakes her head.)
Teacher: Okay. Who can help her?

What is being communicated to Marla here? First, I think it's commendable that the teacher calls on Marla, even though she probably did not have her hand raised. At least she is attempting to involve Marla in the lesson. Yet, when she is unable to give the proper answer, then the teacher essentially dismisses her and turns to the other students for "help." Seemingly, teachers do this to avoid embarrassing a student who does not know the answer. But while this response may appear innocent and perhaps even charitable, the message that is being conveyed to Marla is one of her perceived incompetence.

Let's take a look at another way that this teacher might have responded to Marla:

> Teacher: Marla, can you tell me what "demographic" means in this sentence?
> Marla: (No response.)
> Teacher: Do you know what "demographic" means?
> Marla: (Shakes her head.)
> Teacher: When you don't know the meaning of a word, what can you do?
> Marla: Look it up in the dictionary?
> Teacher: Okay, here's a dictionary. When you find the word, let me know and I'll get back to you. This word is important to understanding this passage, so we need to learn about it.

In this instance, the teacher is telling Marla that she believes in Marla's ability to find the correct answer. In fact, it has been recognized for a number of years now that this is simply what good teachers do; they "stay with" a student and provide assistance until the student is able to arrive at an appropriate response. They also teach students how to become independent learners. As teachers, when we do these things, we convey our high expectations to our students. In essence, we tell them that we believe that they are knowledgeable and capable individuals and that we take seriously our duty to teach them. In this example, the teacher is also sending the message to Marla that she has an important role to play in helping the class understand the passage.

On the other hand, when teachers allow students to "get by with" certain behaviors, they are sending the opposite message. For instance, when we allow students to turn in mediocre work, we essentially are telling them (albeit subtly and perhaps unconsciously) that we don't expect them to be able to do any better. When we permit them to sleep in the back of the room, we are sending the message that we don't really care whether they learn or not. And when we allow students to be invisible in our classroom—through never calling on them, never making eye contact, or failing to find alternate ways for shy students to respond—then we risk communicating the idea that very little is expected of them, and therefore they are free to remain silent.

Another way that we communicate low expectations is by allowing students with difficult home lives to "slide" in our classes. L. C. Clark, who is an elementary teacher in New York State, describes an incident that involved Jamie, one of her low-achieving math students.[7] Jamie would show up late to class, not turn in his homework, and generally just try to "get by." When she discussed this student with her principal, he stated that Jamie was undoubtedly having problems in class because of an incident in his home that involved the police. To this, Clark replies, "'How many times are we going to use the problems that happen at home to excuse ourselves from requiring Jamie to function as a learner in an academic setting?'"

I think Clark is making a critical point here. So often we tend to feel sorry for students because of difficulties they are experiencing in their lives, and we may feel that we are being charitable by allowing them to sleep in our classes, by assigning less homework, or even by ignoring certain actions or behaviors that will potentially lead to less learning. But, as Clark points out, generally the problems of dysfunctional families are not going to be solved quickly, so it's our job to make certain that students learn to take responsibility for their actions in school and that they don't fall behind academically. Clark writes:

> By adhering to a relativistic philosophy, educators in effect lock those considered to be "disadvantaged" or "at-risk" into the very situations from which education should free them.... I am not advocating such a rigid adherence to any standard that the humanity of a child be sacrificed. Rather, I am insisting that compassion be tempered with reason, so that a child deemed "at-risk" be allowed to fully develop and experience his or her power—intellectually, socially, and emotionally.[8]

It's difficult to stay on top of the "Jamies" in our classrooms. Certainly, it takes a lot of energy. They'll daydream, show up without a pencil, fail to do their homework, misbehave. But if we allow them to get by with such behaviors, we essentially send two messages: first, that they don't have to be accountable for their learning, and second, that we really don't care if they learn or not.

The gist of all of this is that we need to think about the messages we convey to students through our actions. And these actions don't necessarily have to occur only within the classroom. Consider just the fact that many of our students are forced to attend school in dilapidated buildings and overcrowded conditions. What message does this send to them? I recently had lunch with several colleagues at a national conference. A professor who is involved in a project in a large urban high school told us how appalled she was that the students and teachers were not even provided with the basic necessities for learning, such as science lab equipment and adequate textbooks. To this, an African American colleague who grew up in a large city in the South replied, "It's always been this way. You're describing my high school!" How sad it is that after 30 years, nothing has really changed. Of course, such schools are not only found in impoverished urban areas. In the late 1980s, I recall visiting a high school in eastern Kentucky where there were no soap or wastebaskets in the bathrooms because, I was told, the school simply couldn't afford them.

How can we expect students to learn at high levels when we send such clear messages to them that they don't count in our society? Like the students I mentioned in an earlier letter to you, those who were forced to sit through biology class in the school's boiler room, we tell students in so many subtle and not-so-subtle ways that we really don't care whether they learn. These students know that they are expendable—that they are being trained to be the future laborers and low-wage earners of our society. For if we truly saw them as the future leaders of our nation and world, wouldn't we provide the very best for them?

While facilities and the availability of materials and equipment may be largely beyond our control as teachers, the expectations we have for our students are not. At the same time, though, we're only human. It's impossible *not* to form expectations of our students. The important thing is that we continually monitor those expectations and that we keep an open mind. The problem arises when we tend, based upon our expectations, to look for certain behaviors, and not pay attention to other behaviors that would provide us with a different picture. It's basic human psychology that, inevitably, students will act in ways that confirm our expectations. For instance, if we feel that a student is a behavior problem, don't we tend to dwell on the student's negative behavior rather than look for the positive? If we believe that students are not very capable, don't we focus on the times when they don't know the answers to our questions rather than noticing the things that they *are* able to do well? So, we essentially "see what we look for" and therefore our original perceptions are continually reinforced. To put it another way, when we view our students as having deficits—in language, culture, behavior, or even intelligence—then we will act in ways that can actually *cause* them to become deficient.

I want to close this letter to you with a story about Manuel, a young Hispanic boy who attended an elementary school in a town in Mississippi.[9] Manuel was the first Hispanic child to attend this school, and he was an exceptional student. He was intelligent, highly motivated, and hardworking. Indeed, the teachers were all extremely impressed with Manuel's abilities and thought of him as an "ideal student." In the years that followed, several other Hispanic students enrolled at the school. None were as exceptional or as motivated as Manuel, yet despite language and cultural differences, they all became successful students. What helped these students to succeed, while so many other Hispanic students fare poorly in our public schools? Essentially, the teachers in this school *believed* that these students could learn at high levels, just like Manuel. They did not see the children's Mexican heritage as a barrier to learning; rather, they expected all Hispanic youngsters to perform as well as Manuel had performed, and therefore they treated them as intelligent and capable individuals.

For these teachers, Manuel became a role model for other Hispanic students. Think for a moment how our perceptions might change if we saw each child or young adult we teach as a future W.E.B. Du Bois, Martin Luther King, or Susan B. Anthony. Imagine going into your classroom tomorrow, looking at the faces of your students, and visualizing them as famous religious, political, or intellectual leaders. Would it change your image of the individuals you teach? Would it change your view of your role as an educator? Imagine how different our society might be if we prepared each one of our students for leadership! It's also important to stress that our students often do not visualize themselves as successful and competent individuals, so *it's up to us as educators to convince them of their own capacity for greatness.* As teachers, we *can* make a difference, if we only believe in our students, and help them to believe in themselves.

Keep the faith,
Becky

Notes

1. Ray Rist, "Student Social Class and Teacher Expectations: The Self-Fulfilling Prophecy in Ghetto Education," *Harvard Education Review*, vol. 40, 1970, pp. 411–451.

2. Robert Rosenthal and Lenore Jacobson, *Pygmalion in the Classroom: Teacher Expectation and Pupils' Intellectual Development* (New York: Holt, Rinehart and Winston, 1968).

3. See, for example, Kathleen Bennett, "Doing School in an Urban Appalachian First Grade," in Christine E. Sleeter, ed., *Empowerment Through Multicultural Education* (Albany: State University of New York Press, 1991), pp. 27–47; Steven A. Gelb and Donald T. Mizokawa, "Special Education and Social Structure: The Commonality of 'Exceptionality,'" *American Educational Research Journal*, vol. 23, 1986, pp. 543–557; Flora Ida Ortiz, "Hispanic-American Children's Experiences in Classrooms: A Comparison Between Hispanic and Non-Hispanic Children," in Lois Weis, ed., *Class, Race, and Gender in American Education* (Albany: State University of New York Press, 1988), pp. 63–86; Patrick Shannon, "Reading Instruction and Social Class," in *Becoming Political: Readings and Writings in the Politics of Literacy Education* (Portsmouth, NH: Heinemann, 1992), pp. 128–138; and George D. Spindler, "Beth-Anne—A Case Study of Culturally Defined Adjustment and Teacher Perceptions," in George D. Spindler, ed., *Education and Cultural Process: Toward an Anthropology of Education* (New York: Holt, Rinehart and Winston, 1974).

4. Michelle Fine, "Witnessing Whiteness," in Michelle Fine, Lois Weis, Linda C. Powell, and L. Mun Wong, eds., *Off White: Readings on Race, Power, and Society* (New York: Routledge, 1997), pp. 57–65.

5. Ibid., p. 59.

6. Thomas L. Good and Jere E. Brophy, *Looking in Classrooms* (New York: Harper and Row Publishers, 1987).

7. L. C. Clark, "Expectations and 'At-Risk' Children: One Teacher's Perspective," in Bill Bigelow, Linda Christensen, Stan Karp, Barbara Miner, and Bob Peterson, *Rethinking Our Classrooms: Teaching for Equity and Justice* (Milwaukee, WI: Rethinking Schools, 1994), pp. 126–128.

8. Ibid., p. 128.

9. I am indebted to Dr. Ray Melecio for sharing this story in his paper entitled "Hispanic Student Learning: It's Not All About Language," at the Equity Conference 2000, Lexington KY, May 17, 2000.

Letter Nine

Curriculum Differentiation

Dear Readers,

I have been blessed in having many friends of color who have taught me a lot about the experiences of growing up Black or Brown in this country. Two of these friends, both of whom have doctorates and are currently working as administrators at major universities in the United States, were at one time determined by a school to be below average in intelligence. One was told that she would be placed in a lower academic track, and one was actually referred for special education. If it had not been for the intervention of their parents, who refused to believe school personnel and fought to have their children placed in the higher tracks, they very well might have joined the ranks of those students of color who fail.

Unfortunately, many students are not this fortunate. Many parents trust the school to make the best decisions for their children. (After all, aren't we the "experts"?) This is particularly true of parents who may not be well-educated themselves, or who may not be familiar with the American educational system. What tends to occur with ability grouping is that students become stereotyped as "college material" or "not college material." Hence, individual differences often become overlooked as students become members of a particular category or class.

As professionals, it's important that we consider all the factors before we label children. In fact, I'm personally opposed to any labeling, whether it be "ADHD," "learning disabled," or "special education." Too often I have seen these labels take on "a life of their own," and children never seem to outgrow them. Have you ever noticed that we tend to use a "medical model" in labeling children? Think about the negative words we use: disability, treatment, diagnosis, remediation.[1] I suggest that an alternative is to look at what a child is able to do—that is, focus on his or her competence, rather than look for deficits. Then, gear your instruction toward the strengths! If my friends' teachers had focused on strengths rather than making negative and erroneous assumptions based on race and class identities, then they would have discovered that their students were highly intelligent and capable individuals with great academic potential. I wonder how many of our students have been lost to us forever because no one recognized their competence?

In my last letter to you, I talked about the pervasive effect that teachers' expectations can have on student achievement. In this letter, I want to examine ability grouping in more depth. From the outset, I think it's important to know some facts. In most schools, if you look at the lower academic tracks, you will find an overrepresentation of students of color and students from lower socioeconomic classes. In fact, if you are currently working in a school system, I invite you to do some research on your own. Do you find that your upper tracks are composed of students from professional families, whereas your low-track students come from poorer environments? Are the numbers of students of color in the upper tracks consistent with the percentage of students of color in your school, or are students of color disproportionately represented in the lower tracks? I hope by now you are realizing that inequity in ability grouping is generally not the result of students' innate abilities; rather, it is linked to the prevailing presence of racism and classism in our society and students' responses to these forces. That is, what we teach in school and the judgments we make about students and parents are generally based upon White, upper-class norms. Because schools are reflections of society, educational institutions tend to perpetuate the hierarchical relationships found in the larger community.

This is not a simple, direct process, however. As we have discussed, students and teachers can counteract this "social reproduction" in various ways. Schools have the potential to transform the inequities that are found in the larger society—which is a major reason why I chose to write this book. But, for such a transformation to occur, it's important first to understand how the process of reproduction works so that we can counteract it. In the last two letters, I talked about marginalization and teacher expectation. Both of these serve to recreate inequities in society; both, however, can be overcome. Now, let's talk about tracking.

Research shows that nearly every school uses some form of grouping by ability. If you talk to educators, most will claim that ability grouping is a convenient organizational structure for meeting the needs of individual students. It's also important to note that tracking, in and of itself, is not necessarily "bad." That is, there is evidence in the research that grouping students according to their achievement can be beneficial, *providing that the academic program remains rigorous for all tracks and that high expectations are maintained for all students.*

For instance, Linda Valli, in her study of a tracked Catholic high school, found that the tracking system there was successful because other elements in the school's culture mitigated the negative effects that often accompany ability grouping.[2] For instance, the teachers at Central Catholic showed students that they cared about them by maintaining high standards and showing an interest in them outside of the classroom. The school was teaching a central lesson: "that each student is worth the school's best effort at a suitable and challenging education and that each student in turn has an obligation to put forth his best effort to succeed."[3] Simply put, teachers did not allow students to "slide." In addition, the faculty and students had a shared history in that many of the faculty were graduates of the school, as were many of the students' relatives. In fact, administrators and faculty at the school saw themselves as part of the local community and took responsibility for enhancing it, and this sense of community contributed to a shared commitment and vision for success. (I'll say more about the importance of school-community relationships in a future letter.)

Finally, the teachers at Central Catholic believed in their students' abilities to achieve, and contrary to most tracked schools, they devoted more time and effort toward teaching those in the lower tracks than those in the more advanced tracks. The teacher-student ratio in these classes was smaller, and the best teachers were assigned to them. A great deal of effort was made to move students up, and in the senior year the lowest track (track IV) was eliminated. This was possible because the students in the lowest track were also required to complete rigorous courses in academic subjects. Valli notes that "At Central Catholic, the primary meaning of 'tracking' was not sending students along different paths, often with little guidance, but rather following and monitoring them, working hard to promote their best effort."[4]

This so-called "Catholic School Effect" has been found to be advantageous for lower-track students. Briefly put, it is felt that the limited resources of Catholic schools result in fewer tracks, and hence less curriculum differentiation, because students are forced to enroll in regular academic courses.[5] Although Central Catholic had a number of academic tracks, the "Catholic School Effect" was nevertheless operative because the school provided all students with a solid academic experience.

I think we can learn a great deal from this research. If every school made sure that all of its students were enrolled in a quality academic program, and if every teacher encouraged high-level student effort regardless of a student's placement, tracking might work as it is supposed to work. It would allow us to individualize instruction and would provide help to students who needed it. What tends to happen, though, is that tracking leads to qualitatively different educational experiences for students.

In *Affirming Diversity*, Sonia Nieto suggests that there are a number of negative outcomes of a tracking system.[6] First, students often are forced to choose their future occupations at a very young age, long before they ought to be making such decisions. Second, as I suggested in my last letter, students develop attitudes about their capabilities based upon the ability group they are in, either viewing themselves as smart and competent, or as dumb and incompetent. Third, tracking contributes to the learning gaps that already exist between students in high and low tracks. And fourth, students in lower tracks typically experience inferior instruction. Let's take a look at these negative consequences in greater depth.

I want to begin by looking at the "Catholic School Effect" more closely. One reason that teachers favor tracking, I think, is that it makes instruction manageable within a large, bureaucratic system. Consider that most secondary teachers in the public schools see anywhere from 100 to 150 students on a daily basis. Unless students remain in their classrooms for more than a single semester, it's simply impossible to know many of them on a personal level. Hence, tracking becomes a way of understanding the students that we teach. That is, it's a means for categorizing them: we assume that students in the higher tracks have plans to go to college; we likewise assume that students in lower tracks have different aspirations.

On the other hand, private schools generally serve a different clientele, where advanced education is often assumed; hence, academic tracks are favored for all students. Also, it is assumed that parents are supportive of their child's education and that they expect them to be academically challenged. R. W. Connell and co-researchers D. J. Ashenden, S. Kessler, and G. W. Dowsett summarize this position well:

> Most teachers don't know much about the kids' learning styles before they meet them in the classroom, and... most know very little indeed about their home backgrounds. The one big, indisputable fact they do know about them, and which naturally serves as an anchor for their thinking about them, is which school class they are in.[7]

Connell et al. suggest that teachers also acquire different perceptions of students' families through the system of tracking (or "streaming," as Connell calls it). That is, they construct images "of the 'good,' 'concerned,' or as academics have it, 'educationally supportive' families for the 'A' stream students, and of 'no-hoper' families for the 'G's and 'H's."[8] In other words, the various tracks actually become social categories, and the students assigned to them—along with their parents—acquire the reputation of being "that kind of student" and "that kind of family," whether the shoe fits or not.

I'm reminded of the story that Mike Rose shares in his book, *Lives on the Boundary*, of the time when his records were confused with another student of the same name and he ended up in the lower vocational track. Because Rose lived in a poor community, no one recognized the error. He might have stayed there for the rest of his school career, had it not been for a perceptive teacher who saw his potential and intervened. Rose discusses his placement:

> Neither I nor my parents realized what this meant. We had no sense that Business, Math, Typing, and English-Level D were dead ends. The current spate of reports on the schools criticizes parents for not involving themselves in the education of

their children. But how would someone like Tommy Rose, with his two years of Italian schooling, know what to ask? And what sort of pressure could an exhausted waitress apply? The error went undetected, and I remained in the vocational track for two years. What a place.[9]

In categorizing students through a system of tracking or "streaming," we essentially assign them labels, and these labels can become self-fulfilling prophecies. As I discussed in my last letter, there are many reasons for this phenomenon, not the least of which is teachers' expectations of students. But another important contributing factor is that students who are targeted for nonprofessional careers are sometimes placed in nonacademic tracks. Thus, even if they change their mind about their future careers, by the time they reach their junior year in high school they are already so far behind academically that there is no way they can catch up.

Let's take a more in-depth look at how this process works. Many of you who are reading this letter are undoubtedly currently enrolled in or have completed a course of study in a college or university. Who counseled you as you went through school? Did you have relatives who had gone to college before you who were able to give you advice on what college preparatory classes to take in high school? For many students, this is what happens. It's particularly true for those from professional homes, where it's expected that they will obtain one or more advanced degrees. In fact, this is part of the "cultural capital" that I talked about earlier; that is, some families just know how schooling "works" and what you need to do to get ahead.

Some students' families, however, lack the knowledge of what is needed to prepare for college. Because their own career opportunities were often limited, they may simply not know how to advise their children about career choices and what is needed to reach their goals. Thus, they leave it up to the school to do what is best for their children. For instance, Christine Sleeter and Carl Grant followed 24 students from working-class families over a seven-year period, from junior high school through high school and after graduation.[10] While 13 of the students had high career aspirations in eighth and ninth grades and planned to go to college, by the end of their senior year only 3 of the students were actually enrolled in a four-year college, and one dropped out after his freshman year. Here is what happened to the other 21 students: 3 entered a community college, 5 were planning to enroll in a vocational institution, 3 were considering joining the military (hoping to acquire money to attend college), 4 had graduated but had no definite career goals, and 6 never graduated.

While the students reported that money was a major obstacle to furthering their education, Sleeter and Grant place much of the blame for the students' ultimate career decisions on the school. They write that the school had a "laissez faire" attitude toward students, and many of them simply were not advised as to what courses to take. Those students who subsequently entered college received academic advice from friends and family members who had been to college; they received little advice from the school. Once they were enrolled in the appropriate courses, they were treated by their teachers as "college material." A second group of students—those who specifically thought they would take up a vocational occupation, for example, as a secretary or mechanic—were tracked into secretarial or autoshop courses in the tenth grade. Sleeter and Grant found that "little academic demand was placed on them in school." The same held true for the largest group of students, even though many had college aspirations. The researchers report:

> The other thirteen students—the largest group—floated through with only minimal demands made on them after tenth grade. Several thought they were going to college, others were unsure. Either way, it appeared that no one in the school seriously thought they were headed for college. The students assumed their needs were being taken care of and so did not seek advice on preparing for life after school. The school took steps mainly to help them fit into the blue-collar labor market.[11]

Because their parents were primarily familiar with blue- and pink-collar jobs, they generally trusted the school to make the appropriate decisions for their children. In fact, Sleeter and Grant report that the parents played only a minor role in helping their children fulfill their academic expectations. In addition, the students were never provided with information on college loans or scholarships. This proved to be a major disadvantage since most felt they could not afford college.

It seems that several factors are operating here. Some students were simply tracked into a vocation that they selected before they even entered high school. Thus they were intentionally denied the academic courses that would have given them other options later on. Other students, however, were never advised at all, and hence they chose to enroll in easier classes (for example, ceramics, office helper, chorus, gym, and job apprenticeships). Sleeter and Grant report that by their senior year, many of these students were bored with school and were bitter about their schooling experiences. They sensed that future education would also be boring, and that they had not been adequately prepared to pursue a higher degree. What is disconcerting is that no teacher or counselor intervened during their high-school years, assuming that they would become blue- or pink-collar workers.

Research has found that students in lower tracks are unlikely to be provided with the knowledge and skills that will enable them to move to a higher track. In essence, they experience a differentiated curriculum—a curriculum that has been "watered down"—with a more restricted range of topics and less in-depth coverage. In a comprehensive study of tracking practices at 25 schools, Jeannie Oakes examined the academic content in the various tracks, as well as the quality of instruction.[12] The findings are troubling. While we may think that all students have equivalent learning opportunities, the reality is that there are great differences between the various tracks in the kinds of knowledge that students have access to, and these differences can have a significant impact on students' futures. For example, Oakes reports that in the high-track English classes, students did a great deal of expository writing, studied the characteristics of literary genres, and analyzed literary elements. In short, they acquired knowledge that would be required in college. The lower-track classes, on the other hand, focused on acquiring basic reading skills, writing short paragraphs, and gaining functional literacy skills, such as those needed for completing job applications. Similar patterns were found in the math classes, where the curriculum in the low-track classes centered on basic computation and consumer math skills.

In addition, teachers had different goals for their students in the various tracks. When asked in interviews to name the five most important things that they wanted their students to learn in their class, teachers stated that they wanted their high-track students to learn to think critically, creatively, and analytically. They also wanted them to become independent learners, and to have confidence in themselves. In other words, teachers wanted their advanced students to engage in higher-level thinking and to be independent and self-reliant. Teachers typically had different goals for their lower-track students, however. For these students, they emphasized conformity: following the rules, getting along with others, improving their study habits, and conforming to classroom routines and expectations.

Oakes writes that apparently the teachers were successful in that they were able to instill these kinds of learning patterns in their students. When asked what they learned in their classes, students from high tracks stated that they learned how to solve hard problems, to have confidence in their abilities, to be able to speak in front of large groups of people, and to work independently. In contrast, students from low-track classes stated that they learned how to behave appropriately in class, to get their homework done, and to be quiet and follow the teacher's directions.

In analyzing these data, Oakes speculates that teachers perceive low-track students to be unmanageable, and therefore they tend to emphasize behavioral (versus academic) goals. The idea that there needs to be conformity to classroom rules of behavior before learning can occur is probably justified. Certainly, students aren't learning when they are out of control. It's also important to realize, however, that often students' behaviors are related to instructional factors, such as a boring or irrelevant curriculum, or the marginalization of their language and culture. Students' behaviors can also be misinterpreted, particularly if they come from cultural backgrounds that are considerably different from our own. Often the "cultural style" of certain student populations is inconsistent with White, middle-class norms, and that style is sometimes interpreted by White teachers as defiant and unruly. We'll look at what the research says about this in my next letter to you.

So student behavior—or perhaps the misinterpretation of it—is probably one reason why students end up in low-track classes. As I discussed in my former letters, there are probably many other reasons, and these reasons often have nothing to do with students' innate abilities. They may feel that their cultural knowledge is being devalued, so they resist the "official knowledge" of the school. Students of color may not wish to appear "too White," and thus they reject academic knowledge that is associated with a White institution. Or they may be victims of biased tests. Students' cultural and learning styles may be inconsistent with the individualistic and competitive style of the school—a topic that will be addressed in my next letter to you. Of course, students may simply be bored, and thus may refuse to conform. (Indeed, a common theme in the literature about students' perceptions of schooling is their general apathy and passivity toward what they are required to learn.)[13]

Whatever the reasons why students are placed in low-track classes, the fact remains that they often receive an inferior education there. Oakes also found significant differences in classroom climate—differences that can have a major impact on student learning. For instance, students in lower tracks perceived their teachers to be more punitive and critical (and indeed, more time is spent on discipline in low-track classes than in higher-track ones), whereas students in higher tracks perceived their teachers to be more concerned about them.[14] As I will discuss in my next letter, this finding has important implications for learning, particularly among diverse student populations whose cultural orientations are less individualistic and more community-based than those of the dominant culture. Essentially, when students feel that their teachers care about them, they tend to put forth more effort. Students in low-track classes, however, often stated that they felt excluded (or, to use the terminology of a previous letter, "marginalized"). Probably not surprisingly, then, students in high-track classes reported a higher degree of involvement in their learning, whereas low-track students reported a higher degree of nonengagement and apathy—often they simply didn't care whether they failed or not.[15]

All of these different experiences translate into very different academic outcomes for high- and low-track students. Track placement has also been found to effect a student's self-esteem, with students in lower tracks developing limited perceptions of their abilities, and students in higher tracks developing inflated perceptions. And, as research shows, students from lower socioeconomic groups and students of color tend to wind up in lower tracks in disproportionate numbers. Oakes writes:

> The view of schools as meritocratic institutions where, regardless of race or class, those students with the "right stuff" are given a neutral environment where they can rise to the top is called into question by our findings. Everywhere we turn we see the likelihood of in-school barriers to upward mobility for capable poor and minority students. The measures of talent seem clearly to work against them, resulting in their disproportionate placement in groups identified as slow. Once there, their achievement seems to be further inhibited by the type of knowledge they are exposed to and the quality of learning opportunities they are afforded.[16]

Consider that our school experiences will influence the ways we perceive educational institutions in general, so when our former experiences in school have been negative, then we'll tend to project these experiences onto our children. So often I hear my students say that the parents of the students they teach "just don't care about education." Study after study shows that this notion is simply false. While there may be a few isolated exceptions, parents from all walks of life *do* care about their child's education, and want their children to succeed.[17] What they resist is the process of schooling. As we have seen, it is a process that often tells their children that they are inferior, less capable, even dumb; that they are not "college material"; that "their kind" can never be doctors, lawyers, or engineers, but must be satisfied with their blue-collar status. In short, it is a process that dashes their dreams and aspirations and yet tries to convince them that the system is fair and equitable—that they earned their status because they are simply not as capable as their higher-achieving peers. Yet, somehow, students and their parents sense that the system is really not that equitable, and that schools have never really worked as they should for "their kind." Can we blame them, then, when they become disenchanted with our educational institutions and when they come to distrust the schools?

It does not have to be this way, however. Recently a number of schools throughout the United States have been involved in efforts to "detrack," and the results have been positive for most students.[18] For me, one of the most interesting outcomes of the heterogeneously grouped classes in these schools is that many of the teachers have begun to change their perceptions of lower-track students. That is, they come to realize that students who had formerly been labeled as "low ability" are actually much more capable than the teachers had previously believed. Detracking also leads teachers to change their teaching strategies, often engaging students in more active learning and providing more choices to students in order to accommodate a broader array of learning styles. Another interesting outcome of detracking (or "untracking," as it is sometimes referred to in the literature), is that the curriculum tends to become more multicultural. Of course, an obvious benefit of detracking is that all students take a common curriculum and therefore there is a greater chance that all students will be challenged academically.[19] (Consider how this relates to the "Catholic School Effect" I discussed earlier.)

At this point, many of you might be skeptical. Obviously, students *do* have different abilities. How, then, can a detracked program work? In their study of detracking, Jeannie Oakes and Amy Stuart Wells and their associates examined 10 middle and high schools which implemented tracking reforms.They found that the schools implemented various flexible structures that served as "safety nets" for students. For instance, some schools provided summer classes that helped to prepare students for a higher track. Some schools required students to enroll in back-up classes for extra instruction, or to enroll in a regular-track class at the same time that they were enrolled in an honors class. Other schools simply eliminated the lowest tracks and kept the regular and high tracks. In one case, the school schedule was altered so that the students could have a 25-minute tutorial period four days a week. One school proposed a year-round calendar with three-week intersessions to be used to provide extra help for those students who required it, but the school board voted against the plan.[20]

Unfortunately, even if educators are highly committed to providing equitable learning environments through detracking, there are many forces that work against it. First, Oakes, Wells, and associates suggest that teachers must get past the labels that we often give to students. The authors make a critical point: "Detracking does not work if the objective is to mix 'smart' and 'dumb.' Kids, in that case, will remain as labeled."[21] A major barrier to detracking, however, is the power of some parents, who feel that heterogeneous classes will have a negative effect on their children's learning.[22] While the research findings have been mixed, there is some evidence to support this concern.[23] Yet it should also be noted that often this resistance is rooted in race and class prejudice, in that some parents believe that certain students lower the academic standards for the entire school. Schools therefore will often back away from potentially transformative reforms because of a fear of "White flight." I encourage you to think about this for a moment. Often we tend to regard lower-class parents as "problem parents" because they may not be as involved in the school as we would like them to be. But it is often the elite and prejudicial attitudes of upper-class parents that stand in the way of reform efforts that would benefit all students.

Before I close this letter to you, I want to talk a bit about the notion of "equality." What do you think of when you hear this term? It seems that generally we tend to think of equality as the provision of equal opportunities and resources for every individual. It's evident from the data on tracking that very often schools are not equal institutions, because students in lower tracks typically receive *less*—less academic knowledge, less attention, lower expectations for success. Tracking, therefore, can reinforce inequality and end up perpetuating the inequalities that occur in the larger society. But, it doesn't have to be this way. A different notion of equality is one of "balancing the scales," so that those students who come to school with "less" actually receive *more*. Thus, if we are really serious about equality, we should allocate more time and resources to the students who have traditionally failed in our schools. Lowering class sizes, providing "safety nets" so that students don't fall through the cracks, and maintaining high academic standards for every student are good places to begin. I hope I've given you something to think about!

Imani,
Becky

Notes

1. I elaborate on the "medical model" of education in my book, *Literacy as a Moral Imperative: Facing the Challenges of a Pluralistic Society* (Lanham, MD: Rowman and Littlefield, 1999). Also see Mike Rose, *Lives on the Boundary* (New York: Penguin Books, 1989).

2. Linda Valli, "A Curriculum of Effort: Tracking Students in a Catholic High School," in Reba Page and Linda Valli, eds., *Curriculum Differentiation: Interpretive Studies in U.S. Secondary Schools* (Albany: State University of New York Press, 1990), pp. 45–65. Also see Margaret Camarena, "Following the Right Track: A Comparison of Tracking Practices in Public and Catholic High Schools," in the same volume; and Adam Gamoran, "Alternative Uses of Ability Grouping in Secondary Schools: Can We Bring High-Quality Instruction to Low-Ability Classrooms?" *American Journal of Education*, vol. 102, no. 1, November 1993, pp. 1–22.

3. Valli, "Curriculum of Effort," p. 51.

4. Ibid.

5. Kathleen Bennett deMarrais and Margaret D. LeCompte, *The Way Schools Work: A Sociological Analysis of Education* (New York: Longman, 1999).

6. Sonia Nieto, *Affirming Diversity: The Sociopolitical Context of Multicultural Education*, 3rd ed. (New York: Longman, 2000).

7. R. W. Connell, D. J. Ashenden, S. Kessler, and G. W. Dowsett, *Making the Difference: Schools, Families and Social Division* (Boston: George Allen and Unwin, 1982), p. 117.

8. Ibid., p. 117.

9. Rose, *Lives on the Boundary*, p. 24.

10. Christine E. Sleeter and Carl A. Grant, "Race, Class, Gender and Abandoned Dreams," in Christine E. Sleeter, *Multicultural Education as Social Activism* (Albany: State University of New York Press, 1996), pp. 155–180.

11. Sleeter and Grant, "Race, Class, Gender," p. 164. Also see Renee Smith-Maddox and

Anne Wheelock, "Untracking and Students' Futures: Closing the Gap Between Aspirations and Expectations," *Phi Delta Kappan*, vol. 77, no. 3, November 1995, pp. 222–228.

12. Jeannie Oakes, *Keeping Track: How Schools Structure Inequality* (New Haven, CT: Yale University Press, 1985).

13. See, for instance, Maxine Greene, *Landscapes of Learning* (New York: Teachers College Press, 1978); and Alfie Kohn, "Choice for Children: Why and How to Let Students Decide," *Phi Delta Kappan*, vol. 75, no. 1, September 1993, pp. 8–20.

14. Oakes, *Keeping Track*.

15. Ibid., pp. 113–136.

16. Ibid., p. 134.

17. See R. W. Connell et al., *Making the Difference*; also see Nancy Feyl Chavkin, ed., *Families and Schools in a Pluralistic Society* (Albany: State University of New York Press, 1993); and Denny Taylor and Catherine Dorsey-Gaines, *Growing Up Literate: Learning From Inner-City Families* (Portsmouth, NH: Heinemann, 1988).

18. See Robert Cooper, *Detracking in a Racially Mixed, Urban High School* (Baltimore, MD, and Washington, DC: Johns Hopkins University and Howard University, Center for Research on the Education of Students Placed At Risk, Report no. 12, April 1997); Barbara Miner, "Algebra for All: An Equation for Equity," in David Levine, Robert Lowe, Bob Peterson, and Rita Tenorio, eds., *Rethinking Schools: An Agenda for Change* (New York: The New Press, 1995), pp. 171–174; and Jeannie Oakes, Amy Stuart Wells, and associates, *Beyond the Technicalities of School Reform: Policy Lessons From Detracking Schools* (Los Angeles: UCLA Graduate School of Education and Information Studies, September 1996). I would also recommend the video *Off Track: Classroom Privilege for All*. It can be purchased through the Network of Educators on the Americas, P.O. Box 73038, Washington, DC, 20056–3038.

19. It's important to note that detracking structural reforms, in and of themselves, are not enough to effect positive change. Other policies must also be in place that will help to ensure quality instruction. For instance, in her study of four U.S. high schools, Linda McNeil found that in order to promote efficiency and to control student behavior, even teachers in high-track classes will fragment, omit, and simplify information. Thus she found that *all* students in some schools were denied the opportunity to think critically and to acquire important knowledge. See Linda M. McNeil, *Contradictions of Control:*

School Structure and School Knowledge (New York: Routledge, 1988). Also see Susan Hanson, "The College-Preparatory Curriculum Across Schools: Access to Similar Learning Opportunities?" in Reba Page and Linda Valli, eds., *Curriculum Differentiation: Interpretive Studies in U.S. Secondary Schools* (Albany: State University of New York Press, 1990), pp. 67–89.

20. Oakes, Wells, and associates, *Beyond the Technicalities of School Reform.*

21. Ibid., p. 18.

22. Ibid., pp. 24–30. For an interesting discussion of the power of upper-class parents and its damaging effects on schools, see Alfie Kohn, "Only for *My* Kid: How Privileged Parents Undermine School Reform," *Phi Delta Kappan*, vol. 79, no. 8, April 1998, pp. 569–577.

23. Literally hundreds of studies have been conducted on the effects of tracking and ability grouping. The research on the effects of detracking on high-achieving students has been mixed in its findings and is not definitive, although some data suggest that mixed ability groups can hinder the academic development of talented and gifted students and tend to boost the academic performance of low-achieving students. It's important to note, however, that a recent review of the investigations on ability grouping indicated that only a very few of the studies were well-designed and therefore their results may not be reliable. An analysis of the data from the few quality studies that were found is reported in Frederick Mosteller, Richard J. Light, and Jason A. Sachs, "Sustained Inquiry in Education: Lessons from Skill Grouping and Class Size," *Harvard Educational Review*, vol. 66, no. 4, Winter 1996, pp. 797–842. In analyzing the effects of tracking (or what they call "XYZ grouping"), the researchers concluded that "Results from the ten studies suggest that XYZ grouping seems modestly preferable to whole-class grouping for high-skill students. In contrast, medium- and low-skill students may learn a little more with whole-class instruction than with skills grouping. However, because of variability in the findings of these studies, they do not conclusively favor skill grouping for the high-skill students, nor do they favor whole-class instruction for the other skill levels. These data also indicate an urgent and troubling finding: the effects of XYZ grouping are not very well settled by these investigations" (pp. 806–807). Also see Robert E. Slavin, "Ability Grouping in the Middle Grades: Achievement Effects and Alternatives," *Elementary School Journal*, vol. 93, no. 5, May 1993, pp. 535–552; and Robert E. Slavin, "Achievement Effects of Ability Grouping in Secondary Schools: A Best-Evidence Synthesis," *Review of Educational Research*, vol. 60, pp. 471–499.

Letter Ten

Cultural Incompatibility

Dear Readers,

A couple of years ago I had a student in my multicultural class who felt strongly that we didn't need to study the influence of culture on students' learning. Instead, she believed that the role of teacher preparation programs was to present research-based methods for teaching reading, writing, science, math, and so forth. She felt that once she learned these, she would be able to teach effectively any population of students in any setting.

Hopefully, by the end of the semester she had begun to realize that good teaching is much more complex than simply knowing how to impart information effectively. Unfortunately, however, I think that even some professors of education (as well as many teachers, administrators, and policymakers) still hold this view. Our teacher education programs are filled with methods courses, and probably most of these are necessary. Yet at the same time, I think it's important to recognize that teaching is so much more than simply using appropriate methods; it's also about *relationship*. It's a process of interaction, of give and take, of connecting with our students. After all, we aren't machines! Unless we establish trusting and mutually respectful relationships in our classrooms, very little learning will occur. Yet so often, cultural misunderstandings can get in the way of the development of such relationships. A major part of our job as teachers is to find ways to be sensitive to these differences so that productive classroom relationships can be created.

During a recent visit to a fifth-grade classroom, an incident occurred that I still find troubling. The teacher (who was White) was verbally reprimanding one of his African American students for her slowness in coming to the table for small group instruction. The student's subsequent facial expression was perceived by her teacher as disrespectful, and so he continued to reprimand her, this time by giving her a punishment for her behavior. The student looked puzzled and asked, "but what did I do?" In fact, the student had to repeat this question several times, because to the teacher it was perfectly obvious what she had done. Finally he told her that he didn't appreciate her "bad attitude." The student still seemed confused, but the teacher was able to prevail (at least temporarily) through the sheer power of his position of authority.

This incident, to me, was a clear example of cultural misunderstanding. The student was responding in a way that was natural to her by looking away, rather than making direct eye contact with the teacher. Such nonverbal behaviors are reinforced among some cultural groups. For instance, some students have been socialized to look down when they are being reprimanded because it is viewed as a sign of disrespect to look someone in the eye. (Indeed, as one of my African American friends pointed out as she read this manuscript, Blacks have historically been punished for looking directly at Whites.) For this Anglo teacher, however, the student's failure to make eye contact was considered disrespectful, so he disciplined her. The result of such incidents, particularly if they occur regularly, is that the student-teacher relationship suffers. In fact, students and teachers often develop an adversarial relationship, to the point that everyone is miserable and very little learning occurs.

I have just finished reading Cynthia Ballenger's book, *Teaching Other People's Children*, about her experiences as a White preschool teacher working with Haitian children.[1] One of the most interesting episodes in this book is her description of how she finally learned how to manage the children in her classroom by watching the Haitian teachers and parents. By writing down exactly what the Haitian adults said to the children, particularly when they were dealing with the children's misbehavior, Ballenger learned how to change her style of interaction so that she was able to achieve the desired response. Significantly, she found that, consistent with their cultural values, Haitians tend to emphasize the community rather than individual values and behaviors in their reprimands. For instance, they might say something like "You need to respect adults—even people you see on the streets. You are taking good ways you learn at home and not bringing them to school. You're taking the bad things you learn at school and taking them home."[2] In other words, the "control talk" that was found to be effective with these children stressed the values and responsibilities of group membership. According to Ballenger, in using these kinds of reprimands, the adults assume that the children already share the adults' understanding of appropriate conduct; that there is a sense of shared knowledge about what constitutes good and bad behavior.

In contrast, Ballenger discovered, she had been using control talk that emphasized individualism, for example, referring to individual emotions ("You must be angry") or emphasizing individual consequences for a particular behavior ("If you don't listen then you won't know what to do"). Ballenger reports that once she learned and started using the Haitian style of reprimand, her children's behavior improved. In fact, she became more connected to her students when she was able to use the style of control to which they were accustomed. She reports that "there is intimacy in this kind of talk....I feel especially connected to the children in these instances in which I seem to have gotten it right."[3] She continues throughout the book to provide other examples of cultural differences and explains how she learned to appreciate and to adapt to her students' ways of "being in the world" through a careful examination and analysis of their responses.

The multicultural education literature is filled with admonitions to care for our students. In fact, study after study has shown that when students feel cared for by their teachers, they tend to work harder. Thus, caring for students is a critical component in effective teaching. Yet, as I was reading Ballenger's words, the thought occurred to me that as teachers, we may sincerely believe we are showing students that we care about them through our actions and behaviors, but our students may interpret our actions entirely differently. That is, it's not enough to care; we must also learn culturally appropriate ways for demonstrating that care. For me, what makes Ballenger's story so powerful is her willingness to observe and learn from the community that she serves. We don't have to go into our classrooms having all the answers, *but we must be willing to learn*.

To illustrate this, let's go back to the incident in the fifth-grade classroom I talked about earlier. Rather than just ignoring the situation and feeling that he was "in the right," the teacher might have had a conversation with his student after class to find out why she responded as she did. In fact, they could have had a very productive discussion about cultural expectations relating to eye contact. The teacher would have been making a conscious effort to learn from the student, and she would perhaps have learned more about dominant expectations for nonverbal behavior. At least, by taking steps to learn about the student's interpretation of the incident, the teacher would have been making an effort to mend the relationship. At the same time, this teacher might have engaged in a bit of research by looking closely at his interactions with the students of color in his classroom.

In *Subtractive Schooling*, Angela Valenzuela underscores the impor-
tance of caring relationships in schools and the need for teachers to learn how to care for their students.[4] Through interviews and observations in an urban high school, Valenzuela looked at the reasons why Latino/a youth tend to become disenchanted with school. One of the primary themes that emerged was that of caring; teachers felt that students just didn't care about school, and students felt that teachers didn't care about them. In effect, you might say there was a "Great Divide" in this school between teachers and students. Teachers expected their Latino/a youth to show that they cared about school by embracing the ideology of achievement and traditional school practices. Students, on the other hand, expected their teachers to care about them as individuals—to take a personal interest in them, to make the effort to learn why they respond as they do, to value their history and culture.

What tended to happen, according to Valenzuela, is that teachers put up boundaries between the public life of the school and the private life outside of school. Very few teachers in her study lived or participated in the students' predominantly Mexican community. Instead, they tended to have a paternalistic attitude toward the students they taught—a sense that their students (and, by association, their students' families and communities) were somehow "deficient" and that this deficiency led to their educational underachievement. The students, on the other hand, viewed their teachers as distant and uncaring, and felt alienated and even offended by the primarily Anglo curriculum which tended to denigrate their language and culture.

Because of this Great Divide, students and their teachers were unable to establish the reciprocal, trusting relationships that are necessary for learning, and very little learning occurred.

Unfortunately, school structures often impede opportunities for teachers to interact with students and families on a more personal level. Particularly in secondary schools, class sizes are often large, and teachers are expected to impart a certain amount of information in an efficient manner. In other words, the dominant model of education—one that sees teaching as transmitting information rather than entering into relationships—militates against the development of communities of care that would help to prevent failure among many of our youth. Is it any wonder that the student in my multicultural class was concerned about methods?

Yet it's important to recognize that if the teachers in Valenzuela's study had made the effort to get to know their students in a more personal way (and if school structures had supported it), they might have been surprised at what they discovered. For instance, as I discussed in my last letter, Valenzuela found that some students protected themselves from the pain of failure by *choosing* to do poorly. Think about this for a moment. Isn't it less threatening to our ego not even to try, rather than to try and then fail? I wonder how many of our students actually fall into this category? (And if we don't take the time to get to know our students, how can we know?) Many students in Valenzuela's study also struggled with conflicting identities, trying to "fit" into their own community and culture through dress and behavior which their teachers interpreted as being "anti-school." Take Carla, for example, who had a close relationship with her track coaches and was also enrolled in honors classes. When Carla changed her dress and her choice of friends, her coaches began to question her motives. Yet in her interviews, Valenzuela discovered that Carla was merely spending more time with people she had known all of her life, and that she was trying hard not to stand out in her neighborhood. Valenzuela points out:

> If the adults at school view her as separating herself from the academic identity they would prefer that she sustain, Carla may not get the guidance she needs at the point she most needs it. A breakdown in the process of authentic caring could

have extremely damaging effects. Carla's coaches care enough about her to notice apparent changes in her clothes and friends, but they fail to go beyond superficial assessments.... They view her as oppositional, when in fact, she continues to care deeply about her future in the very terms they value.[5]

What tends to occur when teachers become judgmental, Valenzuela suggests, is that students become defensive. Again, the trusting relationships that are so necessary for learning are sacrificed. Oftentimes age and cultural differences between students and teachers can lead to misunderstanding and misinterpretation. What stories like Carla's teach us is that instead of making judgments based upon only partial and superficial information, we need to listen to our students and learn from them.

When we don't make the effort to learn from our students and their communities, cultural incompatibility will result. I think this incompatibility takes a number of different forms. First, there can be differences between the values that are being taught in the home community and those being reinforced in the school. Clashes in values can sometimes be quite obvious, as when particular religious ideas differ from school norms; at other times, however, they can be more subtle. Second, there can be incompatibility in patterns of interaction, as Ballenger found in her work with Haitian preschool children. Not only can the students' preferred styles of interaction be misinterpreted by teachers, but learning can be hindered when the communicative style used in the classroom is different from that of the home. Third, as I've mentioned in previous letters, there is cultural incompatibility between what is taught as "official knowledge," and students' own language, histories, and literary traditions. Finally, there can be incompatibility between teaching methods and students' preferred learning styles. While individual research studies have tended to focus on single aspects of cultural incompatibility (students' learning styles, for example), I think all of them taken together contribute to the "subtractive schooling" that Valenzuela discusses.

Recently I have read several studies relating to the educational experiences of American Indian students. Although the issues relating to the education of Native youth are less prominent in my state of Kentucky than those relating to African American and Mexican American youth, nevertheless, I have learned a great deal from reading this research. Historically, the education of American Indian youth has been overtly assimilationist.[6] As I mentioned in my letter on racism, in the late 1800s and early 1900s, Native children were forced to attend boarding schools which were designed to strip them of their language and culture and teach them Anglo ways. In fact, in many cases students weren't even permitted to return to the reservation during the summer, but were sent to live with Anglo families. Of course, it's no secret that a consistent aim of schooling has been to "Americanize" immigrant children, Appalachian children, children of color, and any group that seemed to fall outside of the American mainstream. In the case of Native youth, however, this assimilationist objective was particularly aggressively pursued. Deirdre Almeida writes that "It was not unusual for Native children to be sent away to boarding school at the age of six or seven, and not to see their homes and families again until the age of seventeen or eighteen."[7]

While American Indian youth are no longer forced to attend boarding schools, the assimilationist legacy nevertheless continues in that students are expected to adopt Anglo beliefs and values. In her 10-year study of a Navajo high school, Donna Deyhle found that there was a significant conflict between the White ideology of the teachers and the ideology of the Navajo population.[8] Like the teachers in Valenzuela's study, the teachers in this particular high school (most of whom were Anglo) viewed their students' culture through a deficit lens, and believed that their role was to change their students so that they might embrace an Anglo value system. They saw their students as lacking in motivation to change their life circumstances, and believed that the answer for them was simply to work harder in school, get a college degree, and leave the reservation. This individualistic value system clashed with the value system of the students' Navajo community, "where individual jobs and educational success are used to enhance the family and the community and aggressive individualism is suppressed for the cooperation of the group."[9] This community-based value system is embedded in the reality of Navajos' lives, for they must depend upon the support of the extended family for their very survival. Further, Navajos have learned that moving to the city makes one dependent upon outside resources such as water and electricity, and therefore one's standard of living does not necessarily improve.

What is so revealing in this study are the overt and subtle forms of racism that existed both inside and outside of the school. Students were very aware of this racism and it informed their relationship with the educational institution on a daily basis, yet faculty and administrators remained oblivious to it. Navajo students knew that a glass ceiling existed for them; it was evident both through the tracking system of the school—which tended to sort Navajo students into vocational versus academic tracks—and through the lack of occupational opportunities available to them in the local community.[10] School personnel merely assumed that Navajo students would enter vocational fields, so they placed them in nonacademic tracks, which effectively limited their future options. Also, Deyhle found that most of the upper-level jobs in the local community were reserved for Anglos. Given all of this, most Navajo students chose to maintain their identities as Navajos—with the support system of family and community that was vital to their economic and psychological survival—rather than risk everything for the slight chance of individual upward mobility.

Given the reality of institutional racism, the students' choices made sense. Of course, the beliefs of populations that differ from our own can often appear irrational unless we take the time to understand them. Thus, the Anglo teachers viewed the students' culture as a barrier to be overcome. They believed that the students' families did not teach "school appropriate values," and saw those students who chose to remain on the reservation as failures. Yet Deyhle points out that education is highly regarded in the Navajo community and students are encouraged to finish school and even pursue undergraduate and graduate studies. What Anglo teachers often fail to acknowledge is the psychological cost to Native youth of attempting to live in two very different worlds.[11] Deyhle writes that "Navajos are not trying to 'get away' from Anglo culture, just from assimilation. Thus, they do want certain material goods and school success, but not at the expense of their cultural identity."[12]

Because the teachers in the high school Deyhle studied didn't value the Navajo culture, they didn't see any reason to learn from their students;

therefore, they were never able to see the educational institution from the perspective of the community that they were supposedly commissioned to serve. Indeed, if they had been willing to explore the Navajo perspective, they might have been surprised to learn that *the students who were the most successful in school were those who had a strong sense of their own cultural identity and were firmly rooted in the Navajo community.* Thus, the assimilationist policies of the school—which encouraged Native youth to embrace Anglo values and norms and to leave the reservation—were actually counterproductive to the very outcomes the teachers sought to realize.[13] This is a critical point, and I encourage you to take a moment to think about it. Do schools help students develop positive racial and ethnic identities, or do we encourage students to deny their identities and act White?[14]

"Acting White" not only involves embracing the ideology of White America, but it also involves adopting certain language and interactional styles. Consider, for example, the communication patterns of students of Asian descent. In reporting her work with Asian Pacific American (APA) students, Valerie Ooka Pang notes that these children tend to be less verbally aggressive than other students in the classroom. Thus, teachers are inclined to give them less attention than the more verbal students; the teachers may also erroneously assume that APA students are able to learn on their own and do not require teacher assistance. Here's how Pang describes this cultural misunderstanding:

> APA children can be seen in classrooms raising their hands for help, but not verbally calling out at the same time....After a few minutes, when APA students see their teachers are dealing with other young people and they do not get their attention, they lower their arms and stop waving. Students then turn to their peers who are sitting close by for help. Some teachers then assume that the APA students who stopped raising their hands, do not need tutoring and so begin to believe that these students are able to answer their own questions. Unfortunately, APA students may be disappointed that the teachers did not spend more time with them.[15]

Further, Pang writes that because of culturally learned patterns of communication, APA students may have difficulty participating in discussions and debates. That is, they may have been taught that it is disrespectful to question the teacher or to make their views known. Pang therefore suggests that teachers may need to encourage these students to share their thoughts and provide them with opportunities to interact in small groups prior to engaging in large group discussions. Pang also notes that Asian Pacific American students must continually deal with the "model minority myth," which brands them as being "nerds"or "eggheads" instead of "basketball stars" or "homecoming royalty." This sends the message that they will never be able to fully assimilate into the White institution because they are "different" (yet another instance of marginalization) .

A seminal study in differences in language use is Shirley Brice Heath's *Ways with Words*.[16] In this book, Heath carefully documents how individuals learn and use language in two communities in the Piedmont (the region east of the southern Appalachian mountains): Roadville, a White, working-class community; and Trackton, an all-Black, working-class neighborhood. Most relevant to the current topic of cultural incompatibility is Heath's finding that schools tend to have very specific, narrow ideas on what constitutes "literate" behaviors, and these behaviors are not those that come naturally to many of our children. In Trackton, for instance, Heath found that reading is almost always a shared and negotiated activity. For example, several folks might sit on the front porch together and read the evening newspaper, sharing personal stories and jokes and bringing their own interpretations to the text. Reading materials in Trackton are usually read and then discarded; Heath found that children in Trackton typically do not have books. In Trackton churches, there are formulaic ways of using both oral and written language whereby a phrase will be introduced in either oral or written form (e.g., a prayer or hymn), and the congregation will modify and build on this phrase. Words on a page are not "fixed," but rather are there to be used creatively; as Heath puts it, "each interaction between leader and congregation is unique."[17] This form of discourse is familiar to children in Trackton, who often use it in jump-rope songs, hand claps, and so forth; yet it is typically absent from most classrooms.

In Roadville, parents read bedtime stories and Sunday school materials to their preschoolers, and they generally ask questions as they read. What is instructive is the type of questions that they ask. For parents in Roadville, the text is absolute; there is no room for variation in interpretation. Children are encouraged to listen passively and to provide exact responses to questions; that is, they must give the "right" answer. Heath writes that "For Roadville, the written word limits alternatives of expression; in Trackton, it opens alternatives. Neither community's ways with the written word prepares it for the school's ways."[18] For instance, Heath suggests that in reading a book about fantasy characters such as Curious George, a mischievous talking monkey, children may react to it differently than we might expect:

> Roadville children have had little experience with such wild fantasy stories, and Trackton children have not heard stories about such animals read to them from books. Neither group of children has had the experience of helping negotiate with an adult the meaning of the story: "Isn't he crazy"?" "Do you think they'll catch him?" "What would have happened if… ?"[19]

I have often heard educators blame parents for early reading failure by stating that "the parents just don't read to their kids." Heath's research shows that the problem may not be a lack of reading in the home; *the parents may simply read to their children in a very different way*. Heath contrasts these story-reading behaviors with those of the middle-class residents of the town, who ask questions such as "What do you think will happen next?" and who use the children's knowledge to help interpret the text. Because these children's early interactions with written texts are consistent with those of the school, the book-reading behaviors of the school come naturally to them. So, of course, these children will undoubtedly appear "smarter" than those from Roadville or Trackton. Could it be that many of our children end up in special education and lower academic tracks not because of an inherent lack of ability, but because their early language and literacy experiences are simply *different* from those of the school?

It's also important to note that storybook reading—in contrast to discussing the newspaper on the front porch, for example—is generally a solitary activity. Thus, in cultures that value community over individualism, activities that encourage children to interact with others are often preferred to reading books. Further, consider that in contrast to the spoken word, the written word is "decontextualized"; that is, it is removed from its social context. Because of this, some cultural groups may simply prefer oral communication over written communication because talk is more "social" and tends to foster connection and interpersonal relationships. Therefore, while we may consider storybook reading to be "natural" for children, the reality is that for many of our students it is not.[20] Or, they may respond to books in ways that we don't expect.

In her work with Haitian preschool children, for example, Cynthia Ballenger was frustrated by the exuberance demonstrated by her children during storybook reading.[21] While she expected them to make comments that directly related to the text, her children seemed to be taking over the story line and largely ignoring the book. In addition, they interpreted the text in ways that fit their own view of the world—a world that was considerably different from Ballenger's. Yet after she thought about how adults talk about books in their informal conversations and studied typical Haitian storytelling forms, the ways that her children interacted with books began to make sense, and she was subsequently able to build on their prior experiences.

Another interesting example of cultural language variation in classrooms is the use of directives. White, middle-class teachers are likely to give behavioral instructions to children through the use of questions, such as "What are you supposed to be doing right now?" or "Where is that folder supposed to go?" In contrast, Black teachers will issue specific directives in the form of commands: "Jerome, take your seat." "Put the folder in the crate." In writing about this phenomenon, Lisa Delpit says that working-class mothers tend to use the more direct form of speech style with their children, whereas middle-class mothers tend to couch their directives in the form of questions ("Isn't it time for your bath?").[22] So, when they get to school, Delpit suggests that some children may misinterpret a teacher's indirect commands. Similarly, teachers who use this discourse style may be seen by Black students as lacking in authority. Delpit writes that "black people often view issues of power and authority differently than people from mainstream middle-class backgrounds. Many people of color expect authority to be earned by personal efforts and exhibited by personal characteristics."[23] Thus, in the eyes of many students of color, teachers do not automatically have authority because they are teachers; they must earn that authority through their behavior. So, while White teachers may try to reduce the power differential between themselves and their students through an affable and unassuming attitude, this is precisely the kind of behavior that loses points with Black students, many of whom will perceive this kind of teacher as weak and ineffectual.

Could this be why so many of our students of color end up being labeled as behavior problems? It seems that rather than always placing the blame for misbehavior and/or educational underachievement on our students, we ought to be looking at ourselves as teachers in order to determine what we might be doing (or not doing) that's contributing to the problem. Heath found that teachers of Roadville and Trackton children were often puzzled by their students' behavior and uses of language. Yet she also writes about teachers who were able to overcome their limited knowledge of their students' culture and adjust their instructional practices to make them more culturally compatible. Space does not permit an in-depth discussion of all of her findings, but suffice it to say that teachers in her graduate classes—through a careful analysis of classroom data—were able to discover many patterns of mainstream behaving and valuing that were in contrast to the patterns of the children they taught. What is important in this discussion, I think, is that these teachers were willing to learn from their students and that they then modified their instruction to meet their students' needs. This is very different from an assimilationist model that expects all students to adjust to the teacher's discourse style and to adopt the traditional ways of the school.

One more fairly large body of research that addresses cultural incompatibility in schools relates to students' learning styles. Some research has shown that African Americans, American Indians, Hispanics, and women are "field dependent" learners; that is, they tend to prefer to work with others instead of individually and tend to conform to the prevailing social context. "Field independent" learners, on the other hand, tend to be goal oriented, autonomous, and detached from others.[24] According to Theresa McCormick, "One way that oppression is maintained relates to the learning style that predominates in classrooms, that is, the field-independent mode that primarily favors white males."[25] While I think there's legitimacy to this position, I think we must also be careful not to apply data from this research too generally. Students are not only members of a particular group, but also individuals, and to assume that all students who are members of a certain population learn in a particular way would be erroneous and stereotypical. Further, as we have seen in this and other letters, there are many other factors that affect students' learning.

Certainly, as we have seen, it's important to try to adapt our instruction to our students' preferred ways of responding and interacting. It can make a difference. And sometimes, those ways of responding and interacting are culturally based. But research also teaches us that we cannot assume that certain things will work with certain groups of students. For instance, several researchers who worked with Hawaiian students found that making changes in instructional practice and classroom organization made a big difference in students' achievement.[26] In what was called the Kamehameha Elementary Education Program (KEEP), students worked in small, heterogenous groups rather than independently at their seats, and reading instruction became meaning-centered rather than "skill and drill." By allowing the children to engage in interactive talk as they jointly comprehended and reconstructed their reading texts, and by permitting them to help one another in small groups, the teachers were making their instruction more culturally compatible. In addition, the teachers adjusted their use of praise by praising group versus individual effort. When they tried the same techniques with Navajo students, however, the techniques didn't work. In fact, initially the results were almost disastrous. The investigators found that they first had to learn about their students, and then they were able to use what they had learned to adapt their instruction to make it more congruous with the students' culture.[27]

It's obvious that a lot of research has been done that links cultural incompatibility with educational failure. What is so disheartening is that despite all of the data, it seems that very few educators consider their students' cultural backgrounds in their teaching. Why is it so difficult for us as educators to make our teaching culturally appropriate? I think there are a lot of reasons. Certainly, we are constrained by curriculum guides, by the expectations of the institution, and by tradition. ("We've always done things this way.") It's hard to change, and often when we do try to change things we are ostracized by other teachers and administrators. Also, there may be several different racial and ethnic populations represented in a single classroom, so it's tempting just to teach the White canon rather than risk excluding a particular group. (Consider, though, that when we celebrate differences in our classrooms, we are actually validating *all* differences.)

But I think the fundamental reason why our schools remain culturally incompatible with many of our students is the pervasiveness of cultural racism. Schools support the basic belief that "White ways" are superior to the ways of others. Think about this for a moment. There is a fundamental belief that Standard English is superior to other languages and dialects; that the Anglo value system of individuality and upward mobility is superior to one that espouses a sacrificial commitment to extended family and community; that the interactional styles, dress, and mannerisms of White, upper/middle-class Americans are preferable to those of other groups. Because of cultural racism and classism, many educators don't feel that they need to learn about the populations they serve. If we are honest, don't we expect *them* to become like *us*? So what would be the point of learning about their worlds? Of course, when students resist our attempts at cultural assimilation, we become confused and perhaps even a little hurt. We only want what is best for them, we reason. And surely we know what is best, because, after all, we've "made it," and they haven't.

I'm ashamed to admit that, for years, I accepted these culturally racist assumptions. Because I came from a White, upper-middle-class home, I thought I had all the answers. My goal was to help poor people overcome their impoverished condition so that they might become more like me. Now I recognize that this is a very paternalistic stance that comes not from a position of equality, but from a position of perceived superiority. And while I was often distressed by the lives of some of the poorer children with whom I worked, it never occurred to me that there would be any value in learning about their culture so that my teaching might become more culturally compatible. I focused instead on learning about their individual struggles, which served as a useful excuse for their educational underachievement and helped to reinforce my own sense of cultural superiority. ("Well, no wonder he's such a poor reader. Just look at his home life.")

I truly believe that most teachers are compassionate and caring individuals who have only the best intentions for their students. But as I discussed in my third and fourth letters, most of us (particularly if we are Anglo) have been socialized to accept White, upper-class values and norms. Of course, the process of schooling, for the most part, merely reinforces these culturally racist assumptions. We have not had the opportunity to learn about other ways of seeing the world; it's as if our schooling experiences have given us tunnel vision. So, as teachers, it's vital that we make up for these years of miseducation by opening up our hearts and our minds and learning from our students and their families. We must literally grow as multicultural educators by recognizing that teaching is a reciprocal relationship; we teach our students, but they also teach us.

I want to conclude this letter to you with one final thought. Gloria Ladson-Billings, a well-known African American educator, points out that culturally relevant teaching (or, to use the terminology I have used through-out this letter, "culturally compatible" teaching), is fundamentally just good teaching.[28] That is, it's doing what we know in our hearts we ought to be doing. For instance, culturally relevant teaching means using our students' worlds as vehicles for learning. If they listen to rap music, then we incorporate it into our lessons. If they're concerned about violence, then we use it as a springboard for reading, writing, and discussing texts. If their primary language is Spanish, then we use it as a bridge to learning English. Good teachers have a competence versus a deficit model of learning; that is, like Cynthia Ballenger, they see their students as competent individuals regardless of their home backgrounds, and they value their students' language and cultural knowledge rather than view them as hindrances to learning. Because such teachers operate from a competence model, they insist upon academic excellence for all of their students. Finally, culturally relevant teaching means acknowledging that racism, classism, sexism, and other oppressive forces exist in our society, and preparing our students to fight against those forces. That is, it means helping students to develop "a broader sociopolitical consciousness that allows them to critique the cultural norms, values, mores, and institutions that produce and maintain social inequities."[29]

I think Ladson-Billings is making a critical point here. Ultimately, if our instructional practices are to be culturally compatible, they must be "consciously political." I'll be talking more about this concept in a future letter, but for now it's important that you understand that this does not mean talking about politics; it means bringing controversial topics, such as those that relate to the inequities in our society, into our classrooms. As I discussed in previous letters to you, we often think that what we teach is "objective," when the reality is that it always endorses a particular point of view—a particular perspective of what is considered "essential knowledge." Thus, our teaching can never be neutral. What is important to our students, however, is that our instruction become *intentionally* non-neutral through our discussion of how power works in our society and our encouragement of critical thinking and productive responses. We tend to want to avoid controversy, but remember, controversy does not have to be negative and unproductive! In fact, I question whether there can ever be any lasting, substantive change without it. (As I frequently remind my husband as he struggles through his midlife crisis, change can be good!)

Until next time,
Becky

Notes

1. Cynthia Ballenger, *Teaching Other People's Children: Literacy and Learning in a Bilingual Classroom* (New York: Teachers College Press, 1999).

2. Ibid., pp. 33–34.

3. Ibid., p. 38.

4. Angela Valenzuela, *Subtractive Schooling: U.S.-Mexican Youth and the Politics of Caring* (Albany: State University of New York Press, 1999).

5. Ibid., p. 83.

6. See, for example, Deirdre A. Almeida, "The Hidden Half: A History of Native American Women's Education," *Harvard Educational Review*, vol. 67, no. 4, Winter 1997, pp. 757–771; and Daniel McLaughlin, "Personal Narratives for School Change in Navajo Settings," in Daniel McLaughlin and William G. Tierney, eds., *Naming Silenced Lives: Personal Narratives and the Process of Educational Change* (New York: Routledge, 1993), pp. 95–117.

7. Almeida, "Hidden Half," p. 764.

8. Donna Deyhle, "Navajo Youth and Anglo Racism: Cultural Integrity and Resistance," *Harvard Educational Review*, vol. 65, no. 3, Fall 1995, pp. 403–444.

9. Ibid., p. 408.

10. Amazingly, Deyhle found that even though Navajo sixth graders from a local elementary school scored above the national norm in mathematics on the Stanford Achievement Test, all were placed in the lowest-level mathematics class when they entered secondary school because the administration felt that Navajo students would do better in these classes. The test scores were never used in making this decision. See Deyhle, "Navajo Youth," p. 415.

11. For an important discussion of the difficulties faced by American Indian youth in establishing a dual-world orientation, see Alan Peshkin, *Places of Memory: Whiteman's Schools and Native American Communities* (Mahwah, NJ: Lawrence Erlbaum, 1997).

12. Deyhle, "Navajo Youth," pp. 423–424.

13. For other ways in which Anglo educational institutions conflict with American Indian beliefs, see Carol Locust, "Wounding the Spirit: Discrimination and Traditional American Indian Belief Systems," *Harvard Educational Review*, vol. 58, no. 3, August 1988, pp. 315–333; and Lisa Delpit, "'Hello, Grandfather': Lessons From Alaska," in her book *Other People's Children: Cultural Conflict in the Classroom* (New York: The New Press, 1995), pp. 91–104.

14. See Signithia Fordham, "Racelessness as a Factor in Black Students' School Success: Pragmatic Strategy or Pyrrhic Victory?" in Tamara Beauboeuf-Lafontant and D. Smith Augustine, eds., *Facing Racism in Education*, 2nd ed.(Cambridge, MA: Harvard Educational Review, 1996), pp. 209–243. In this interesting study of high-achieving students of color, Fordham documents the cost of academic success for African

American students, who must give up aspects of their Black identity in order to achieve success as defined by the dominant culture.

15. Valerie Ooka Pang, "Educating the Whole Child: Implications for Teachers," in Valerie Ooka Pang and Li-Rong Lilly Cheng, eds., *Struggling to Be Heard: The Unmet Needs of Asian Pacific American Children* (Albany: State University of New York Press, 1998), pp. 265–304.

16. Shirley Brice Heath, *Ways With Words: Language, Life, and Work in Communities and Classrooms* (Cambridge: Cambridge University Press, 1983).

17. Ibid., p. 205.

18. Ibid., p. 235.

19. Ibid., p. 294.

20. See, for example, Delpit, "'Hello, Grandfather': Lessons from Alaska." Delpit documents the importance of social context in Alaskan students' interactions, and shows how cultural conflict can result when a teacher's words do not match her actions.

21. Ballenger, *Teaching Other People's Children*.

22. Delpit, "The Silenced Dialogue: Power and Pedagogy in Educating Other People's Children," in *Other People's Children: Cultural Conflict in the Classroom* (New York: The New Press, 1995), pp. 21–47.

23. Ibid., p. 35. For an alternate perspective, see Mary Phillips Manke, *Classroom Power Relations: Understanding Student-Teacher Interaction* (Mahwah, NJ: Lawrence Erlbaum, 1997).

24. For a summary of the research on cultural learning styles, see Jacqueline Jordan Irvine and Darlene Eleanor York, "Learning Styles and Culturally Diverse Students: A Literature Review," in James A. Banks and Cherry A. McGee Banks, eds., *Handbook of Research on Multicultural Education* (New York: Macmillan Publishing, 1995), pp. 484–497.

25. Theresa Mickey McCormick, *Creating the Nonsexist Classroom: A Multicultural Approach* (New York: Teachers College Press, 1994), p. 63.

26. Lynn A. Vogt, Cathie Jordan, and Roland G. Tharp, "Explaining School Failure,

Producing School Success: Two Cases," in Evelyn Jacob and Cathie Jordan, eds., *Explaining the School Performance of Minority Students*, theme issue of *Anthropology and Education Quarterly*, vol. 18, no. 4, December 1987, pp. 276–286. Also see Kathryn H. Au, *Literacy Instruction in Multicultural Settings* (Fort Worth, TX: Harcourt Brace Jovanovich, 1993); and Geneva Gay, *Culturally Responsive Teaching* (New York: Teachers College Press, 2000).

27. Vogt, Jordan, and Tharp, "Explaining School Failure," pp. 282–283.

28. Gloria Ladson-Billings, "But That's Just Good Teaching!" in Jana Noel, ed., *Sources: Notable Selections in Multicultural Education* (Guilford, CT: Dushkin/McGraw-Hill, 2000), pp. 206–216. Also see Patricia Cahape and Craig B. Howley, eds., *Indian Nations At Risk: Listening to the People* (Charleston, WV: ERIC Clearinghouse on Rural Education and Small Schools, 1992); and Eugene E. Garcia, "Chicanos/as in the United States: Language, Bilingual Education, and Achievement," in José F. Moreno, ed., *The Elusive Quest for Equality: 150 Years of Chicano/Chicana Education* (Cambridge, MA: Harvard Educational Review, 1999), pp. 141–168.

29. Ladson-Billings, "But That's Just Good Teaching!" p. 211.

Part Four

Straight Talk about Equitable
Schools and Classrooms

Letter Eleven

Multicultural Education as Democratic Education

Dear Readers,

In my own state of Kentucky, the term "equity" is used a lot. I'm on a committee called the Kentucky Education Equity Task Force, our state department has recently created a new Division of Equity, and schools are required to include an "equity component" in their long-term plans. I wonder, though, if people really understand what equity is all about. A few years ago I was at a meeting of higher educators and we spent at least an hour talking about the meaning of "equity." Even among my colleagues, many of whom teach courses in multicultural education, there was a lot of variation in our understanding of this term.

For me, to understand the notion of "equity," you have to have an understanding of democracy. We are supposedly a "democratic" nation, but do we really know what this means? After all, there are different forms of democracy. There's a representative form of democracy, where citizens participate largely through casting their ballots. Benjamin Barber calls this a "thin" or "protectionist" form of democracy.[1] In thin democracies, citizens aren't really an integral part of the governing process because the decisions are made primarily by their elected representatives. The idea behind a protectionist democracy is that those who are most fit to rule (an "aristocracy") will rise to the top. Thin democracy can be contrasted with a strong form of democracy, where citizens are actively involved in the act of governance. Perhaps the best example of a strong, participatory democracy was Athens, where citizens were chosen by lot to serve periodically as representatives.[2] (Probably the closest we come to this form of direct governance in our own country is our system of jury duty.)

Obviously, strong democracy becomes problematic for large states and nations. But in smaller institutions and communities, such as schools, direct citizen governance is possible. Even with a representative form of governing, it is possible to have active citizen participation. Of course, such participation is not without its problems. For instance, we have town meetings where we are able to talk about important issues and raise our concerns prior to a vote by the city council; the council, however, is not bound to follow our recommendations. In Kentucky we have a Site-Based Decision Making (SBDM) Council in nearly every school, made up of representatives from both the school and the community. Teachers who have served on SBDM councils have told me that they sometimes become frustrated when a particular individual (oftentimes the principal) dominates the decisions that are made. Another difficulty is that the parent representatives who are nominated and subsequently elected to serve on school councils are generally White and middle/upper-class. So, while I think these are all commendable attempts at promoting democracy, they nevertheless amount only to a representative form of democracy, and many groups still do not have a voice. To put it another way, with a protectionist form of governance, not everyone's interests are protected.

For me, equity is all about power. In fact, I define equity as the equal distribution of power. Democracy is an attempt to equalize power—to spread it out among those being governed. In a strong democracy, people have more decision-making power, and hence, there is more equity. In a thin democracy, our power is limited to voting for those individuals who, we think, will best represent our interests. And, as the examples above reveal, some are going to have more power than others simply because of their position within the institution or within society.

I think it's important to point out that our Founding Fathers never intended every individual to have decision-making power. Rather, societal inequities were accepted as natural, and power was limited to White males who owned land. So, while we live in a "democracy," from its inception our nation was not particularly "democratic"—at least, not as democratic as we might like to believe. Further, the history of democracy has been one of distrust of the masses. Even Plato felt that most people were not fit to govern. (With a few notable exceptions, so did our Founding Fathers.)[3] As

I discussed in my letter on marginalization, I think that John Wills and Hugh Mehan make a good point when they suggest that a study of U.S. history ought to center around the continuous struggle for civil rights.[4] We never really achieve democracy; it's always in process.

In an institution that is equitable, everyone has a voice in the decisions that are made. There is a concerted effort to make sure that all the populations that are being served have the opportunity to be heard, and their views are taken seriously. As Benjamin Barber puts it, there is an "aristocracy of everyone."[5] In schools that were serious about equity, for example, the teaching force and governing bodies would be representative of the community being served in terms of race, ethnicity, religion, and gender. Parents would become an integral part of the educational process, and structures would be developed to assure active parental participation. Small dialogue groups might be formed where parents would feel free to express their views about issues that affected their children. There would be genuine partnerships between parents and teachers, where teachers would learn how best to meet the needs of the children in their classrooms through continuous communication with the home. Think about this for a moment. Isn't this model quite different from the way that we are accustomed to operating in schools? This is a strong democratic model, where parents—*all* parents—have a voice in the education of their child.

Even with all of the rhetoric about "parent involvement," I still think that educational institutions typically tend to operate according to a protectionist model of governance. Deep down, don't we believe that we know what is best for the children we teach? After all, aren't we the experts? We encourage parental involvement, but not *too* much involvement; and, if we're really honest, we would prefer that some parents not be involved at all. So, what tends to happen is that communication breaks down. Equity is simply not possible in environments where some individuals want to hold most of the power. (The same holds true in classrooms where teachers are unwilling to relinquish any of their authority to students. I'll have more to say about this in another letter.)

Many of you are probably thinking that giving parents this strong a voice in schools is a naive idea. After all, parents can't possibly know about everything that goes on in classrooms, and as educators we are responsible for the learning and safety of all of our students. You might also argue that most parents won't get involved anyway. I can certainly relate to these arguments. What I primarily object to is the paternalism that seems pervasive in our educational institutions—a paternalism that is grounded in a White, upper/middle-class ideology, that sends the message to many of the families we serve that their cultural knowledge is inadequate and that we have nothing to learn from them. Rather, *we* have all of the answers for *their* child. Is it any wonder that parents don't get involved? How often do we invite them to become true partners in the educational process?

There's no doubt about it—democracy is hard. We have to learn to listen to one another, to understand the other person's position, and to compromise. When I urge teachers to involve parents more in their classrooms, they invariably bring up conflicts in cultural norms between the home and the school. One of the most typical conflicts involves different notions about the legitimacy of fighting in school. Two students will get into a fight and the parents may endorse it because they have taught their children that they should stand up for their rights. From the teachers' perspective, this is a terrible behavior to teach a child; however, from the perspective of the parents, many of whom live in rough neighborhoods where learning to fight is necessary for survival, this behavior makes perfect sense. This is a typical example of a breakdown in communication that is due to a paternalistic attitude on the part of educators who have made assumptions concerning the "rightness" of a particular action based upon their upper/middle-class experiences. Of course, for the safety of all of our students, we can't allow fighting in school. But rather than dismiss the parents' perspective, I think it's important that we try to see things from their point of view and acknowledge the legitimacy of their position. Then we can begin to communicate with them and explain the need to maintain order in school for the safety of all the students. I maintain that we can't have equity unless we learn to talk to one another on an "equal plane."

Often, however, I think we tend to confuse equity with equal opportunity. The two are not the same. For me, equal opportunity is consistent with a thin, protectionist form of democracy. We don't have to give everyone a voice; all we have to do is to make sure that everyone has an opportunity to obtain a position of power—to become a part of the ruling aristocracy. Equal opportunity leaves a lot of people behind, for there will always be those who just "don't make it." Equal opportunity is based upon a notion of *sameness*. That is, if we provide the same educational opportunities for everyone, then everyone will have an equal chance to succeed.

Consider that most of our educational policies are based upon the notion of equal opportunity, not equity. In Kentucky, for example, we have equalized funding across districts and have provided rural regions with advanced courses in science and mathematics through distance technology. Certainly, these are important reforms that have gone a long way to improve the educational opportunities for students in our state, and we need to celebrate these achievements. I would argue, however, that equal opportunity policies fail to consider the fact that many of our students need *more*, not the same. That is, we need to make an extra effort to give a voice to those parents and students who have traditionally been marginalized in our educational institutions. Thus, equal opportunity is a necessary, but not a sufficient, response to inequity in our society.

Consider, too, that equal opportunity promotes individual advancement over the needs of the group. For instance, if providing equal opportunities allows some to escape poverty, then we feel that we have succeeded. Equal opportunity policies can actually intensify competition, as the "space at the top" is still limited. Equity, on the other hand, involves community and emphasizes the needs of the whole group. Because an individualistic ideology is so pervasive in our society, I think it's difficult for us to think in terms of community.[6] Yet a strong democratic system is essentially one that promotes a shared vision and shared goals, rather than individual visions and goals. With equity, everyone is given power; we don't have to compete for it.

This past week I received a call from a student at a local college who was writing a paper on the question, "Is multiculturalism divisive?" Talk about a loaded question! He asked me to share my thoughts on this issue (in 10 minutes or less!). The issue of divisiveness is probably at the heart of the multicultural debate. We fear conflict and division; we really just want everyone to get along. The issue of divisiveness is very complex, and I'm sure I didn't answer his question adequately. But, it seems to me that whether "multiculturalism" is divisive or not depends upon how one views it. If "equity education" is seen just as providing equal opportunities for underrepresented populations, then I believe it may be potentially divisive. In fact, this is the approach that has been taken in the past. Consider that equality of opportunity does not require us to change the White canon; it does not require us to eliminate cultural racism; it does not require us to consider the perspectives of those from lower socioeconomic classes and other historically marginalized groups. It's not that I'm opposed to equal opportunity policies; I'm not. But I also believe that while such policies are necessary for addressing gross inequalities, they simply do not go far enough, in that they do little to address the classist and racist ideology in our schools and in society. Such an ideology endorses a competitive system that allows some individuals to advance, while those who are left behind generally have a sense of powerlessness, hopelessness, despair—and anger.

A multicultural education that is grounded in equity, however, can be potentially transformative. By giving legitimacy to the cultural knowledge and experiences of all of the populations we serve, common goals depending upon the cooperative effort of all involved can be realized. For instance, an equitable education in a rural area would give legitimacy to the expertise of local farmers, who would share their knowledge in countless ways with students. In their English and mathematics classes, students might study issues related to agriculture; they might write to their local legislators about various issues that affect agricultural production in their area; in their science courses, they might examine the effects of chemical crop applications. In urban areas, students might read literature addressing issues that directly impact their lives, and explore those issues through writing and drama. With the guidance of educators and community leaders, they might become involved in community projects directed at enhancing their neighborhoods. Parents would be invited to be true partners with educators and all would work collectively toward common goals. For instance, one teacher writes about the relationships she developed with her students' families when she planted a community garden in their urban neighborhood.[7] This is strong, participatory democracy in action.

Would such an education lead to divisiveness? Perhaps. Students would be involved in solving real problems in the real world, and decisionmaking often involves conflict. But I would argue that divisiveness comes not from collaborative inquiry and action, but rather from a focus on individual goals and desires. Our society is already severely divided, and we had better be willing to listen to one another and to work together to solve the problems that affect us all, or we will all go down together. I think the resistance to multiculturalism comes more from White, middle/upper-class parents who feel that they have something to lose by working toward common aims. Let's face it; it's easy to forget about our urban and rural poor and work toward our own individual goals. After all, we're not really affected personally until the violence starts to move into our neighborhoods or starts hitting our pocketbooks. What we fail to acknowledge, however, is that we are not just a bunch of individuals; we are a society. And what affects others in society ultimately affects everyone.[8]

The concept of strong democracy supports a way of life where there is interaction between diverse groups for the mutual benefit of all. For instance, John Dewey, the famous twentieth-century educational philosopher, viewed democracy as a process—as a way of living in community. Nel Noddings points out that

> Dewey did not look at democracy merely as a system of government in which everyone votes and the majority prevails. For Dewey, democracy was a mode of associated living, and decisions were to be made by a shared process of inquiry.[9]

Dewey believed that democracy can be characterized by two criteria: the sharing of interests and the communication of these interests among diverse groups. It is this second criterion that is particularly relevant for our discussion of multiculturalism. Dewey believed that democracy will break down when groups isolate themselves. The important question to ask, states Noddings, is whether there is interaction between various populations:

> Do people communicate freely across the lines of class, religion, race, and region? Whenever groups withdraw from connection, isolate themselves, and become

exclusive, democracy is endangered.... Dewey was not so concerned with the number of subgroups [in society] as with the quality of their association.[10]

The notion of equity as I have conceptualized it is consistent with Dewey's ideas of democratic life. Equity is a process of shared decision-making, where all persons participate. Thus, equity necessitates the association and interaction of various subgroups. Rather than being divisive, an education that is multicultural and equitable can actually bring individuals together in a process of mutual inquiry and collaboration.

Because democracy involves "associated living," Dewey opposed schooling practices and structures that promote competition. For instance, sorting students into separate academic tracks can actually hinder democracy, because it is counterproductive to the development of community. Tracking is consistent with an individualistic, equal opportunity ideology that reinforces individual advancement rather than the benefit of the group. Further, the practice of sorting students according to ability can lead to divisions within the student body, as students in the upper tracks come to define themselves along lines of intelligence, class, race, and/or ethnicity. Typically, we tend to judge the benefits of tracking solely on the basis of individual achievement. Yet perhaps we ought to be asking different questions. Joseph Kahne makes a critical point: "Policy analysts do not ask whether tracking promotes or inhibits students' ability to pursue goals collectively or how it shapes their commitment to and understanding of democratic communities."[11] Consider again Dewey's warning that "whenever groups withdraw from connection, isolate themselves, and become exclusive, democracy is endangered." Are we teaching students how to live democratically in our schools, or are we merely teaching them how to compete?

All of this discussion might seem very foreign to most of you. After all, we're not accustomed to talking about education in terms of democracy and democratic living. Rather, education has come to be associated with work and job training. Some of my graduate students even teach in districts where a "seal of approval" is affixed to students' diplomas indicating to prospective employers that the graduates are ready to enter the workforce. I recall an education forum held a couple of years ago at my institution, where a local superintendent spoke on the goals of education. The aims and related curricular options that he suggested were all connected to preparing students for future employment. When an astute student asked what the role of education would be for those students who would never be able to achieve upward mobility, he simply didn't know how to respond.

It has not always been this way. Schools were once seen as the primary institution for preparing students for civic life. It was felt that if individuals were to participate in a democracy, then they needed certain knowledge, skills, and values which could be provided through appropriate schooling. Thus, while early schooling was intentionally moralistic, its role nevertheless was to prepare students for democratic citizenship. According to Edward Stevens and George Wood,

> Jefferson's educational system, proposed in "A Bill for the More General Diffusion of Knowledge" to the Virginia Legislature in 1779, separated religion and education. Yet the proposed system of schooling was firmly based on a moral concept of citizenship. Moreover, all levels of schooling included education in "democratic principles" so that citizens would fulfill their civic duties and obligations.[12]

It was felt that if citizens were to be involved in democratic decisionmaking, then it ought to be *informed* decisionmaking, based both upon a sense of what is morally "right" and upon the ability to read and to communicate. Indeed, in the early history of our nation, job preparation was never considered to be the function of public schools. With the emergence of industrialization, however, business leaders began to link education with economic development and productivity. It was felt that "public education would provide a work force prepared for labor in the industries and businesses that would be attracted to the town precisely because of this educational preparation."[13] Today, not only are educational institutions viewed as job training grounds, but a major role of schools is to sort students for their future positions in the workplace—a result of the "social efficiency model" that emerged during the era of industrialization.

It is my sense that a focus on job preparation rather than preparation for civic life has contributed to the educational failure of scores of students. For many of our students in poverty, for example, the promise of upward mobility rings hollow. Like the "Hallway Hangers" in Jay MacLeod's study of urban adolescents, students of color and those from lower socioeconomic classes sense intuitively that the "good life" will always be out of reach.[14] No matter how much "official knowledge" they obtain, they simply lack the cultural capital (e.g., appropriate speech, dress, and social connections) to succeed by society's standards. And, they know that the curriculum typically taught in schools—one that emphasizes facts and information over real-world, power-related skills and knowledge—generally fails to provide the necessary cultural capital. (How often, for instance, do we diverge from our grammar books and put students in real social situations where they can learn and practice the "language of power"?)[15] Consider, too, the values that we impart to students when we equate education with upward mobility. Do we teach students that *all* productive work is valuable? Or do we tell them that some jobs are more valuable than others, but obviously only a few can attain them?

Given all of this, I would argue that we need to recapture a democratic imperative for schools. Schooling ought to be less about job preparation (although, of course, this will always be one function of schools), and more about preparing future citizens to live and work together in such a way as to realize a strong democratic community. A focus on individual upward mobility tends to undermine such communities by fostering competition and divisiveness. In *Democracy*, Anthony Arblaster contends that "without the sense of a common interest, it is clear that democracy itself is at risk."[16]

This is a strong statement. We tend to take democracy for granted, and have convinced ourselves that threats to our democratic way of life are largely external rather than internal. Yet Arblaster argues that when so much power is held by institutions outside of government—such as large multinational corporations—it no longer makes sense to think that the requirements of democracy have been met through a system of elections. Traditionally, democracy has been understood to involve the "power of the people"; hence, "the concentration of so much power in non-accountable hands, outside the control of elected bodies, is incompatible with democracy."[17] As Carole Edelsky argues in *Making Justice Our Project*, in a genuine democracy "participation is a participation among equals, negotiation among equals, not participation in which a few are more equal than the rest."[18] A system that perpetuates class, race, and gender privilege is simply inconsistent with a strong democracy.

If we truly believed that our democratic way of life was being threatened, would we view education differently? I think we would. Arblaster suggests that several conditions must be in place for the realization of a strong, participatory democracy. First, there must be freedom. Individuals must feel free to express their views without fear of reprisal. In other words, democracy requires freedom of thought and diversity of opinion. Even in representative democracies such as ours, Arblaster suggests, choice requires debate, and debate requires a certain degree of freedom. However, it is not enough that we *feel* free to make independent choices, for we can feel free and still be manipulated. Thus, education is necessary so that citizens become aware of the persuasive powers in society that can influence their capacity to think freely. Note that Arblaster is not advocating an education that encourages conformity by teaching standardized facts and information; he is arguing for an education that promotes critical thought and diversity of ideas: "If people are exposed to the variety of opinions that normally exist in relation to any major issue, the likelihood of their being easily manipulated by unscrupulous opinion-makers is greatly reduced."[19]

In contrast to the ideas of Dewey and Arblaster, popular opinion holds that to achieve unity as a nation and to preserve democracy, we all must share the same values, beliefs, and knowledge. This "conformity leads to unity" ideology underlies the popular "cultural literacy" perspective of theorists such as E. D. Hirsch, who argue that the role of schools is to provide everyone with identical knowledge so that all might have an equal opportunity to succeed.[20] Dewey would argue that conformity is an artificial substitute for real community. Reflecting Dewey's ideas, Kahne writes that conformity holds us together "in the absence of dialogues that recognize differences in individual and group interests but which seek to accommodate them through shared decision-making."[21] It is not conformity of ideas, but the interaction and mutual decisionmaking that occurs in strong democratic communities that creates unity.

Consider, too, that conformity often results from the misuse of power; those who are dominant—whether it be in a small group like a school SBDM council or in the larger society—are those who have the power to set the standards. Arblaster makes a critical point when he states that "Closed societies, marked by a high degree of coherence in belief and custom, can be found throughout history. They are often, and perhaps even typically, characterized by authoritarian rather than democratic forms of government."[22] Indeed, it has been the authoritative power of dominant groups, who have generally set the standards for conformity, that has led to resistance and educational failure in our schools.

I would add that schools have always operated on the principles of cultural literacy, and it simply hasn't worked. Because textbooks often define what is taught in our educational institutions, the information that students learn is very similar in every school, regardless of the racial or ethnic composition of the student body and regardless of whether one is looking at a school in eastern Kentucky or Los Angeles.[23] As I have argued throughout this book, this "official knowledge" has resulted in the marginalization and alienation of many of our students, who view it as "White" and see it as essentially irrelevant to their lives. Indeed, schools have always assumed the role of "Americanizing" those groups that fell outside the mainstream—immigrants, American Indians, Appalachian mountaineers—so that they might learn to conform to the dominant standards. Yet, despite these attempts at forced conformity, it's apparent that we still remain seriously divided as a nation. The movement toward a standardized national curriculum, however, illustrates just how strongly we still believe that conformity—rather than "associated living"—will result in a unified society.[24]

How does all of this relate to multicultural education? For me, multicultural education *is* democratic education. As James Banks, a prominent multicultural scholar, argues, "Students must develop multicultural literacy and cross-cultural competency if they are to become knowledgeable, reflective, and caring citizens in the twenty-first century."[25] He suggests that multicultural education ought to be conceived as "equity pedagogy," as an education that gives all students "the knowledge, skills, and attitudes needed to function effectively within and to help create and perpetuate a just, humane, and democratic society."[26] I agree. The knowledge, skills, and attitudes that are necessary for democratic participation can only be nurtured within an equitable learning environment, where diverse ideas are sought and validated. Both teachers and students must learn that theirs is not the only opinion that counts—that there are other legitimate perspectives that can contribute to our collective understanding. For me, this is what "liberal education" is all about. It's opening our minds to alternative ideas, so that we might develop the capacity to think more critically and thoughtfully—in essence, so that we might not only become knowledgeable, but also become wise.

It's also important to recognize that true community emerges not from conformity, but from struggle. It's a process of give-and-take, of compromise, of deliberation, of considering opinions that differ significantly from one's own. Developing a genuine community isn't easy. But rather than being divisive, such a community can ultimately result in shared agendas and common aims. As I have suggested throughout this letter, it is this kind of community that is required for a strong, participatory democracy. And I would argue that it can only be realized through an education that is both multicultural and equitable.

Imani,
Becky

Notes

1. Benjamin R. Barber, *Strong Democracy: Participatory Politics for a New Age* (Berkeley: University of California Press, 1984). Barber also examines several subgroups within these two basic categories. David Sehr conceptualizes these two basic forms of democracy as "privatized" and "public." See David T. Sehr, *Education for Public Democracy* (Albany: State University of New York Press, 1997).

2. Anthony Arblaster, *Democracy* (Minneapolis: University of Minnesota Press, 1987), p. 19. Arblaster points out that women, foreigners, and slaves were excluded from participation.

3. Arblaster, *Democracy*. Also see Joel Spring, *Wheels in the Head: Educational Philosophies of Authority, Freedom, and Culture from Socrates to Paulo Freire* (New York: McGraw-Hill, 1994).

4. John Wills and Hugh Mehan, "Recognizing Diversity Within a Common Historical Narrative: The Challenge to Teaching History and Social Studies," *Multicultural Education*, Fall 1996, pp. 4–11.

5. Benjamin R. Barber, *An Aristocracy of Everyone: The Politics of Education and the Future of America* (New York: Ballantine Books, 1992).

6. Robert N. Bellah, Richard Madsen, William M. Sullivan, Ann Swidler, and Steven M. Tipton, *Habits of the Heart: Individualism and Commitment in American Life* (New York: Harper and Row, 1985). For an interesting discussion on how classical liberal theory, modern liberalism, and postmodernism have influenced educational theories and practices, see Landon E. Beyer and Daniel P. Liston, *Curriculum in Conflict: Social Visions, Educational Agendas, and Progressive School Reform* (New York: Teachers College Press, 1996).

7. Joan Tibbetts, Case 13, Commentary #1, in Judith H. Shulman and Amalia Mesa-Bains, eds., *Diversity in the Classroom: A Casebook for Teachers and Teacher Educators* (Hillsdale, NJ: Lawrence Erlbaum, 1993).

8. I am indebted to Cornel West and his insights into the nihilistic threat faced by African Americans, and the effects of this nihilistic threat on society. See *Race Matters* (Boston: Beacon Press, 1993).

9. Nel Noddings, *Philosophy of Education* (Boulder, CO: Westview Press, 1995), p. 35. Similarly, Henry Giroux declares that "Put simply, democracy is both a discourse and a practice that produces particular narratives and identities in-the-making informed by the principles of freedom, equality, and social justice. It is expressed not as moral platitudes but in concrete struggles and practices that find expression in classroom social relations, everyday life, and memories of resistance and struggle. When wedded to its most emancipatory possibilities, democracy encourages all citizens to actively construct and share power over those institutions that govern their lives." Henry A. Giroux, *Living Dangerously: Multiculturalism and the Politics of Difference* (New York: Peter Lang, 1993), p. 13.

10. Noddings, *Philosophy of Education*, p. 35.

11. Joseph Kahne, *Reframing Educational Policy: Democracy, Community, and the Individual* (New York: Teachers College Press, 1996).

12. Edward Stevens, Jr., and George H. Wood, *Justice, Ideology, and Education: An Introduction to the Social Foundations of Education*, 2nd ed. (New York: McGraw-Hill, 1992), p. 113. Also see Thomas S. Popkewitz, *A Political Sociology of Educational Reform: Power/Knowledge in Teaching, Teacher Education, and Research* (New York: Teachers College Press, 1991).

13. Howard Besser, "Education as Marketplace," in Robert Muffoletto and Nancy Nelson Knupfer, eds., *Computers in Education: Social, Political and Historical Perspectives* (Cresskill, NJ: Hampton Press, 1993), p. 43.

14. Jay MacLeod, *Ain't No Makin' It: Aspirations and Attainment in a Low-Income Neighborhood* (Boulder, CO: Westview Press, 1995).

15. I examine these ideas in depth in my book, *Literacy as a Moral Imperative: Facing the Challenges of a Pluralistic Society* (Lanham, MD: Rowman and Littlefield, 1999). Also see Lisa Delpit, *Other People's Children: Cultural Conflict in the Classroom* (New York: The New Press, 1995); and James Paul Gee, *Social Linguistics and Literacies: Ideology in Discourses* (New York: The Falmer Press, 1990).

16. Arblaster, *Democracy*, p. 78.

17. Ibid., p. 64. Also see Giroux, *Living Dangerously*.

18. Carole Edelsky, ed., *Making Justice Our Project: Teachers Working Toward Critical Whole Language Practice* (Urbana, IL: National Council of Teachers of English, 1999), p. 10.

19. Arblaster, *Democracy*, p. 96.

20. E. D. Hirsch, Jr., *Cultural Literacy: What Every American Needs to Know* (Boston: Houghton Mifflin, 1987).

21. Kahne, *Reframing Educational Policy*, p. 35.

22. Arblaster, *Democracy*, p. 19.

23. In their five-year study of American high schools, Theodore Sizer and his colleagues found that high schools were remarkably similar. Sizer writes: "In most schools, I visited biology and social studies classes, and I could soon predict the particular topics under study during a given month in Bio I or U. S. History, whatever the school." Theodore R. Sizer, *Horace's Compromise: The Dilemma of the American High School* (Boston: Houghton Mifflin, 1984), p. 6.

24. For an interesting discussion of the English/Welsh National Curriculum and the aims of education, see John White, *Education and the Good Life: Autonomy, Altruism, and the National Curriculum* (New York: Teachers College Press, 1991).

25. James A. Banks, *Educating Citizens in a Multicultural Society* (New York: Teachers College Press, 1997), p. 13.

26. Banks, *Educating Citizens*, pp. 78–79. Also see Theresa Perry and James W. Fraser, "Reconstructing Schools as Multiracial/Multicultural Democracies," in Theresa Perry and James W. Fraser, eds., *Freedom's Plow: Teaching in the Multicultural Classroom* (New York: Routledge, 1993), pp. 3–24; David Sehr, *Education for Public Democracy*; and George H. Wood, "Democracy and the Curriculum," in Landon E. Beyer and Michael W. Apple, eds., *The Curriculum: Problems, Politics, and Possibilities* (Albany: State University of New York Press, 1988), pp. 166–187. Sehr and Wood both list several values, attributes, and capacities for democratic citizenship that they argue schools ought to be developing and nurturing in students.

Letter Twelve

Assessment Issues

Dear Readers,

I just returned from a visit to a primary classroom, where the children were doing practice exercises in preparation for a national achievement test that is required in my state. With the teacher's guidance, they were filling in "bubbles" on worksheets and then checking their answers together. The teacher told me that they do this for at least an hour every week.

We might be tempted to criticize this activity as a waste of valuable instructional time. But the reality is that schools have been "under the gun" to produce higher and higher academic gains. Thus, teachers are under tremendous pressure to teach to the test. This comes during a period in our history where our schools are becoming increasingly diverse. It's assumed that the test scores are relatively accurate—at least accurate enough to make decisions on students' abilities and the quality of instruction that they are receiving. It's also assumed, I think, that the tests are unbiased and that they test every child fairly.

In order to understand how standardized tests gained such prominence in this country, I think it's important to put the testing movement in historical context. Earlier in this century, there was an effort to mold educational institutions around an industrial model so that the process of schooling could become more efficient. In an earlier letter, I talked about how this "social efficiency" model led to sorting and grouping students into separate academic tracks. Intelligence tests provided an important measurement tool in determining who would end up in the various tracks. It was felt that intelligence was fixed and based upon one's heredity; therefore, a child's environment had little to do with his or her intellectual abilities, which were innate. It was reasoned that if intelligence was solely based upon nature, not nurture, then it would be a simple matter to determine one's intelligence; culture simply didn't count.

The population used in the standardization of IQ tests was typically White and middle-class. Lewis Terman of Stanford University, the designer of the Stanford-Binet Intelligence Test, intentionally sought a standardization group that was White, middle-class and English-speaking in establishing the norms for the test. Interestingly, when girls outperformed boys on the original 1916 version, Terman revised it, replacing verbal items with nonverbal ones in order to raise boys' scores. While there were also differences in scores between rural and urban children, children from various socioeconomic classes, and children from various racial and ethnic groups, these differences were viewed as normal and so Terman saw no need to revise the test to accommodate them. The development in 1920 of the National Intelligence Test (NIT), which was a group-administered IQ test, similarly omitted students of color from the norming population. Richard Valencia, who has studied testing issues associated with Mexican American youth, notes that

> With respect to norming, the NIT was just as exclusive as the Stanford-Binet: no Mexican American, African American, or American Indian children were part of the standardization sample.[1]

Such exclusive norming practices contributed to the perception that students of color were genetically inferior in intelligence—a legacy that continues to this day with the publication of books such as *The Bell Curve*.[2]

Today, IQ tests are used less frequently than before, but standardized achievement tests are common, and are used for everything from sorting students to achieving school and district accountability. Achievement tests and instruments such as the Scholastic Aptitude Test (SAT), which are designed to be predictive measures, have also been found to be culturally biased. An item on a test is considered to be biased when it is determined to be more difficult for one group to answer than another group, given that the groups are of equal ability levels. Terry Meier sites the following example from the Scholastic Aptitude Test:[3]

RUNNER : MARATHON
(A) envoy : embassy
(B) martyr : massacre
(C) oarsman : regatta
(D) horse: stable

The correct answer, (C), requires that students have knowledge of marathons and regattas. Citing a study by John Weiss, Meier writes that questions appearing on various forms of the SAT require students to be familiar with such things as polo, minuets, pirouettes, property taxes, melodeons, and golf.[4] Hence, standardized tests often become tests of experience, not ability. Unfortunately, test scores can then confirm teachers' limited expectations of certain students, contributing to a self-fulfilling prophecy.[5]

At this point, you may be thinking "but surely it's possible to create a test that would eliminate cultural bias." In response to this suggestion, Meier points out that

> Those who argue that it is possible to make standardized tests less discriminatory by removing their cultural bias seriously underestimate the enormity of their task. What is a "culture-fair" test in a multicultural society? And who could design such a test?[6]

I think it's important to probe this idea a bit further. For starters, content validity—or the appropriateness of the items included on a test—is only one concern among many.

When you consider, for instance, that every test is administered within a social context that involves relationships of power and potential intimidation, then test results become questionable. I think some of the most interesting work that has been done on the effects of social context on test results is that of sociolinguist William Labov, who demonstrated that children of color are not verbally deprived, as had been previously thought. It seems that when Black children were faced with an investigator (typically White) in a testing situation, they were basically nonverbal. Unwilling to accept these results, Labov documented the children's linguistic behavior in their natural surroundings—on city streets, while communicating with their peers—and an entirely different picture emerged. Like most of us, these children were intimidated by a situation in which they felt uncomfortable, and it affected their linguistic performance. Labov concluded that

> the social situation is the most powerful determinant of verbal behavior....an adult must enter into the right social relation with a child if he wants to find out what a child can do; this is just what many teachers cannot do.[7]

In previous letters, I've emphasized the need for teachers to learn from the children they teach so that they might develop trusting and productive relationships. Through such relationships, we can begin to see students' competence. Given the social constraints of any testing situation, it seems evident that the "right social situation" for determining a child's competence simply does not exist. Yet we make decisions every day based upon test data, and sometimes these decisions profoundly affect the future life chances of a child.

Intimidation can even be as subtle as being required to mark one's race or ethnicity on the evaluation instrument. Claude Steele and his colleagues at Stanford have done some interesting research on what they have termed "stereotype threat," the fear that failure will reinforce a negative stereotype about one's group. The researchers have shown through experimentation that stereotype threat can lead to underachievement on tests by students of color, even among those who identify strongly with school. Steele hypothesizes that students of color feel the burden of overcoming the negative stereotypes associated with their race, and this pressure and anxiety causes them to underachieve.[8] When stereotype threat is eliminated, for example, by telling students that the purpose of the test is to examine how certain problems are solved and not to measure ability, then Black students' performance matches that of their White peers. Steele suggests that it is stereotype threat—and not a lack of self-confidence—that is at the heart of Black students' academic problems. When under pressure, they often try *too* hard in an effort to avoid mistakes and therefore to disprove a negative stereotype. Researchers have determined that stereotype threat can also be a factor in the underperformance of women on tests of mathematical ability.[9]

An added problem in placing so much emphasis on test scores is the language barrier. Increasingly, English is not the primary language of many of our students. Data from the U.S. Department of Education indicate that since 1984, there has been a 70 percent increase in the number of limited English proficient (LEP) students in our public schools.[10] These students typically come from homes and communities where a language other than English is spoken; hence, they often do poorly on verbal, English-language tests. In examining this problem, Richard Figueroa and Eugene Garcia find that the most popular solution is either to have a bilingual adult translate the test for the child, or to produce a comparable version of the test in another language. They suggest that both solutions are inadequate because bilingual learners are not like monolingual learners. The constant interaction of two languages results in a unique and complex linguistic profile. According to Figueroa and Garcia,

> Extensive research from both Europe and the U.S. also points to the disadvantage that bilingual learners face when asked to perform encoding tasks in the weaker language. Not only is the process potentially slower, it is also more amenable to blockage due to stress, task complexity or noise. For tasks such as reading, where naming speed is critical for comprehension, the bilingual learner can be put at a considerable disadvantage when artificially induced speed or timed tasks (such as in tests) are required.[11]

The authors also cite data on the limited capacity of standardized measures to predict the achievement of limited English proficient students. Interestingly, research shows that even with well-known and respected instruments, the greater the use of a language other than English in the home, the lower the predictive validity of the tests. Given all of the problems associated with testing LEP students, Figueroa and Garcia recommend that all norm-based assessments and high-stakes testing of diverse learners be abandoned.

Language barriers may be even more subtle, however. For example, some children come to school with more experience answering "test-type questions" than other children. Recall my discussion in Letter Ten on the research conducted by Shirley Brice Heath, who found that White, middle/upper-class children were accustomed to responding to test-like questions during storybook reading. In contrast, Heath found that children in the working-class Black community of Trackton were seldom asked such questions. These children tended to be asked genuine questions—those to which the adult did not have a prefabricated "correct" answer.[12]

Even though there is currently a general acknowledgment that standardized tests are not without bias, we often act as if they are. (Consider, for example, the incredible popularity of *The Bell Curve*, which uses test data to argue for the superior intelligence of upper/middle-class Whites.) Because tests are regarded as "scientific," we frequently make decisions based upon the assumption that the results of tests are reliable and accurate. I recall several years ago in Appalachia working with a first-grade teacher who sincerely believed that all of her children were capable and intelligent, and who worked hard to ensure their success. Yet even she was duped by standardized tests in language development that supposedly "proved" that Appalachian children are linguistically deprived. Tests carry with them a weight of scientific authority that often overrides our own intuitions about children.

Consider, too, the fact that different cultural groups respond to test items in culturally specific ways. Even major national organizations involved with testing acknowledge the complexity of the problem in testing diverse populations. Figueroa and Garcia cite a chapter entitled "Testing Linguistic Minorities" in the *Standards for Educational and Psychological Testing* manual, which, among other concerns, discusses the fact that the linguistic genre typically used in testing—which elicits short versus elaborate responses—may invoke culturally appropriate ways of responding rather than test-appropriate ways.[13] "The issues raised in the chapter on 'Testing Linguistic Minorities' in the *Standards* virtually preclude the use of psychometric and normative tests with linguistically and culturally diverse individuals in the U.S."[14]

Perhaps the greatest indictment of standardized tests, however, is that they tend to measure lower-level skills as opposed to the creative and critical thinking (e.g., problem solving, decision making, etc.) that is essential for participating in a democratic society. For instance, items on reading tests given to young children often test the ability to decode versus the ability to read and understand connected text; even the accompanying "comprehension questions" are based upon short, contrived passages and are therefore generally trivial and meaningless. In mathematics, correct responses are encouraged over divergent thinking that might tap alternative ways of arriving at a solution. Indeed, skills that we should be encouraging, such as bilingualism and creative thinking, can actually become handicaps on standardized tests. Research suggests that when tests have been instituted for purposes of accountability, the use of teaching methods that would lead to higher-order thinking (e.g., research projects, discussions, essay writing, laboratory work, etc.) has actually declined.[15]

To illustrate, allow me to share a personal story. My stepson, Michael, is extremely bright, and has always received straight As in his academic subjects. Until this past year, he devoured literature. In fact, when he was in the fourth grade, he was already reading Stephen King novels. During his freshman year in high school, however, his English teacher placed a great deal of weight on the multiple choice tests which accompanied a popular program that is supposedly designed to motivate students to read. In this particular program, points are awarded when a certain mastery level is attained. Because Michael was accustomed to reading literature for its aesthetic value rather than to recall bits and pieces of relatively trivial information, he had a great deal of difficulty passing these tests. This subsequently affected his grade in English, and he ended up hating reading.

Whether intentionally or not, standardized tests have generally been used to sort students. Because students come to school with differing backgrounds and abilities, it is inevitable that some will do well, and others will do poorly. The reality is that standardized testing reinforces institutional racism and classism (and sometimes even sexism) because students are labeled and tracked according to their performance on measures that can never be completely free of cultural bias. The result is that students who need the very best our schools have to offer end up receiving an even greater dose of "skill and drill" in their curriculum. Linda Darling-Hammond writes that

test-based decisionmaking has driven instruction toward lower order cognitive skills. This shift has created incentives for pushing low scorers into special education, consigning them to educationally unproductive remedial classes, holding them back in the grades, and encouraging them to drop out.[16]

Schools and the testing industry have established practices that virtually assure the success of some students and the failure of others, and these institutional racist practices continue and are legitimized because they are seen as providing "scientific evidence" of ability and worth—evidence that justifies and perpetuates economic and social class divisions in the larger society.

It is estimated that 100 million standardized tests are given to 40 million students in our schools each year. (I don't know about you, but I find these figures almost incomprehensible.) The costs of administering and scoring these tests are also mind boggling; it is estimated that between 70 and 107 million dollars are spent annually on testing programs.[17] Testing is big business. Because most of the tests that are administered are designed to measure overall achievement rather than specific skill development, they provide little information that will aid teachers in improving instruction. Further, research suggests that testing often limits teachers' motivation and creativity as they are forced to adopt a prescribed and narrowly conceptualized curriculum in order to prepare students for the tests. In this way, mandated testing programs contribute to the "deskilling" of teachers, as they become mere workers (as opposed to professionals and autonomous decision makers) whose job is to "teach to the test."[18]

I would argue that we need to be asking some serious questions about educational testing. For instance, is it really worth all of the money that is being invested? Is it worth the instructional time that is being spent on teaching and practicing lower-level skills? In what ways are our testing programs and policies affecting the curriculum and the ability of teachers to make professional decisions based upon the needs of their students? And through our obsession with testing, how many highly capable, insightful, creative individuals are being left behind? Given the fact that within a very few years our schools will primarily consist of students of color, and that these students have always fared poorly on standardized tests, I think it's time we faced the limitations of testing. Surely, our multicultural, democratic society demands more of its citizens than the ability to answer multiple choice questions. It demands that we should be able to communicate with others in a variety of social and cultural contexts, that we should be able to get along with one another in our shrinking global society, and that we should be sensitive to the perspectives of those who differ from ourselves. It also requires the capacity to analyze, to think critically, to lead, to embrace moral values. Perhaps the most vital question we ought to be asking is this: As a society, can we really afford to continue to plan our curriculum around a narrow set of skills and information simply because these can be easily measured?

By now, many of you may be protesting that some form of assessment and accountability is necessary for evaluating students' progress. I agree. After all, in order to ensure that all students are receiving a quality education, we need to have ways to determine their progress. When test scores are disaggregated by race, gender, ethnicity, and socioeconomic status and are used to hold school districts accountable for maintaining high standards for *all* students, then perhaps a limited use of such evaluation measures is justified.[19] Whether standardized test scores have been used to improve the quality of instruction for students of color, however, is debatable; often the blame for underachievement is placed on the students' homes and communities rather than on the schools themselves (the "victim blaming" syndrome that I talked about in an earlier letter). Hence, it's often felt that instructional intervention would be fruitless. Further, as I mentioned previously, standardized measures generally don't easily translate into recommendations for improving instruction. So what, if any, are the alternatives?

One alternative is to use authentic assessments that are conducted as students are actually engaged in the completion of a particular task or that evaluate actual student products. Such assessments include portfolios, student self-assessments, checklists, rubrics, teacher observations, inventories, debates, exhibits, oral presentations, constructions, videotapes, collections of students' written work, and so forth. Authentic assessments are more consistent with instruction, and therefore can lead to improved pedagogy when they are used to inform practice. Also, authentic assessments tap students' competence as the students are involved in legitimate and meaningful learning experiences. Such performance-based assessments can be used for the purposes of school or district accountability by establishing local norms and then evaluating student progress over time.

Simply changing the methods of assessment, however, is not enough. Linda Darling-Hammond makes the critical point that "changes in the forms of assessment are unlikely to enhance equity unless we change the ways in which assessments are used as well."[20] Like standardized tests, assessments based upon actual student performance can be misused and can perpetuate class and race divisions. For instance, if they are used to sort students into various tracks, then the negative outcomes for traditionally underserved populations will continue. Further, if the assessments are unrelated to actual student learning, then they will have little value for improving instruction. For example, when the Kentucky Education Reform Act (KERA) was first initiated, outside examiners were hired to test performance while students were engaged in various tasks. The examiners gave a specific assignment to a group of students (constructing an electric circuit, for example), and analyzed their performance as they completed the task. These types of tests were abandoned in Kentucky when their reliability was questioned. When performance tests are conducted and scored externally—outside of the classroom setting by individuals other than the classroom teacher—teachers are left with only a superficial understanding of what the assessments are designed to measure and how instruction might be improved by using test outcomes.

If evaluation measures are to be used to inform instruction rather than to sort students for the purposes of social efficiency, then we will need to change how we view these measures. This is no easy task; the scientific authority of tests and the entire testing enterprise are firmly entrenched in the culture of the school (as well as in many legislative chambers and board-rooms). Yet a countermovement is emerging even within the testing industry itself, as the efficacy and ethics of using standardized multiple choice tests to evaluate a diverse student population have come under increasing scrutiny.

An assessment program that is truly equitable, however, involves more than just using authentic assessments; it also involves the use of a variety of measures in tapping students' competence. In consistency with Howard Gardner's theory of multiple intelligences, students enter our classrooms with different ways of knowing and with preferred ways of demonstrating competence.[21] Because students have different strengths and learn in different ways, it's important that a variety of assessments be used in evaluating their performance. For instance, in Michael's case, the teacher might have permitted him to write personal responses to the books he read rather than insisting that he take multiple choice tests. Other students in his class might have preferred to create dramatic interpretations or to give oral reports. By giving students a choice in how they might demonstrate learning, we help to assure their success.

It's also advantageous to seek student input as to the criteria that will be used in evaluating their work. I recall a middle-school teacher (I observed him as part of my dissertation study) who believed in the democratic process and had involved his students the entire year in curriculum decisions. The students became so empowered that one day they told him to take a seat—*they* were going to set the standards for evaluating their projects! He sat at one of the student's desks and watched in amazement as they proceeded to outline a point system on the board. Teachers who use such democratic practices in assessment often tell me that students set higher standards for themselves than the teachers would have set for them. At the same time, the students feel that they are an integral part of the assessment process and have a clearer sense of how they will be evaluated. Establishing specific criteria and guidelines ahead of time is a much more fair and equitable way of determining student progress than keeping students "in the dark."

Let's look at a couple of examples to see how these principles might work in the classroom. In evaluating a piece of student writing, for instance, you might write down the expectations, with student input, and then allow students to correct their work prior to receiving a grade. In *A Fresh Look At Writing*, Donald Graves suggests that if we are working on particular writing skills—for example, capitalization and punctuation—students should be asked to choose a piece of their writing to submit for a grade specifically on the proper uses of capitalization and punctuation.[22] Students are told that this is what will be graded, and their pieces are evaluated only on these skills. If you are evaluating social studies projects, then you might develop assessment standards in cooperation with your students and write them on a chart so that the students can refer to them as they complete their projects. Over time, what tends to occur is that students begin to internalize the standards for quality work.[23]

One caveat is in order, however. It's important to keep in mind that the criteria that you develop for assessment must relate directly to the learning objectives you have established, and they must also reflect the fact that high standards are expected of *all* students. I've seen many committed teachers who have allowed for student choice in completing a project, yet the final product shows little evidence of learning. For example, if you are completing a unit of study on the environment and students choose to design posters for the school, the posters should reveal an understanding of the concepts that were addressed throughout the study; they shouldn't merely read "Don't pollute!" When we allow students to get by with demonstrating very little knowledge, then we convey to them that we really don't *expect* them to learn. I'm reminded of an instance reported by Kati Haycock of the Education Trust, in which high-school students were asked to color posters in response to literature they had read. When the teacher was asked about this assignment, she said that her students simply were not capable of writing a coherent written response.[24] *When we settle for mediocre performance, then we abdicate our responsibility to our students to teach them to the very best of our ability.* As I have suggested throughout my letters, it's critical that we maintain high expectations for *all* students, and these expectations need to be reflected in our assessment practices.

These are sound evaluation procedures for all students. They become particularly important, however, in classrooms where there is a great deal of student diversity. Some educators would argue that we need to modify the standards for some students to accommodate language and cultural differences. For instance, they would suggest that students' essays and portfolios not be graded on standard English usage. I strongly disagree with this position. In fact, I think we do students a great disservice when we don't hold them accountable for reaching certain standards. Requiring less of some students merely assures that they will remain relatively powerless in our society; we need equity *and* excellence. At the same time, however, it's critical that students understand *why* they are learning dominant knowledge and discourses. Much as we would like to believe otherwise, our society is not equal, and learning the standard form of language and other canonical information is required if our students are to attain status in our society.

Holding all students to high standards also places certain responsibilities on us as teachers. Mainly, we need to make sure that we are actually teaching what students need to know, and this will require effort and creativity. For instance, we need to make sure that we place students in situations where they must actually *use* and *practice* the standard discourse; doing grammar exercises in a textbook is simply ineffective.[25] Non-canonical knowledge needs to be integrated and infused with traditional knowledge so that what we teach is relevant and meaningful to our students. (I'll have more to say about this in my next letter to you.) And of course we need to have structures in place that will provide assistance when students need it. Essentially, I'm making two points here: first, we need to have high standards for *all* students; and second, we need to make sure students are actually learning what we intend to assess. Holding students accountable for meeting high standards without providing the support necessary for them to achieve those standards is not only unprofessional, it's also unethical. I hope you agree.

Until next time,
Becky

Notes

1. Richard R. Valencia, "Educational Testing and Mexican American Students: Problems and Prospects," in José F. Moreno, ed., *The Elusive Quest for Equality: 150 Years of Chicano/Chicana Education* (Cambridge, MA: Harvard Educational Review, 1999), p. 124. Terman wrote of students of color: "Their dullness seems to be racial, or at least in the family stocks from which they come." Cited in Jeannie Oakes, *Keeping Track:*

How Schools Structure Inequality (New Haven, CT: Yale University Press, 1985), p. 36. Also see Jane R. Mercer, "Alternative Paradigms for Assessment in a Pluralistic Society," in James A. Banks and Cherry McGee Banks, eds., *Multicultural Education: Issues and Perspectives* (Boston: Allyn and Bacon, 1989), pp. 289–304.

2. In *The Bell Curve: Intelligence and Class Structure in American Life* (New York: The Free Press, 1994), Richard Herrnstein and Charles Murray suggest that genetics accounts for 60 percent of an individual's intelligence.

3. Terry Meier, "Why Standardized Tests Are Bad," in Bill Bigelow, Linda Christensen, Stan Karp, Barbara Miner, and Bob Peterson, eds., *Rethinking Our Classrooms: Teaching for Equity and Justice* (Milwaukee: Rethinking Schools, 1994), p. 174.

4. John G. Weiss, "It's Time to Examine the Examiners," *The Negro Educational Review*, vol. 38, nos. 2–3. Cited in Meier, "Why Standardized Tests Are Bad," p. 174.

5. See, for instance, Donna Y. Ford and J. John Harris, III, *Multicultural Gifted Education* (New York: Teachers College Press, 1999).

6. Meier, "Why Standardized Tests Are Bad," p. 175.

7. William Labov, "The Logic of Nonstandard English," in Pier Paolo Giglioli, ed., *Language and Social Context* (New York: Viking Penguin, 1985), p. 191.

8. Claude M. Steele, "Thin Ice," *Atlantic Monthly*, vol. 284, no. 2, August 1999, p. 44. Also see Claude M. Steele and Joshua Aronson, "Stereotype Threat and the Test Performance of Academically Successful African Americans," in Christopher Jencks and Meredith Phillips, *The Black-White Test Score Gap* (Washington, DC: Brookings Institution, 1998), pp. 401–427. The researchers have found that all groups are affected by stereotype threat. For instance, when a group of White males were told prior to taking a test that Asians generally perform better than Whites, they did less well than White males who did not receive this information.

9. Steven J. Spencer, Claude M. Steele, and Diane M. Quinn, "Stereotype Threat and Women's Math Performance," *Journal of Experimental Social Psychology*, vol. 35, no. 1, 1999, pp. 4–28.

10. Richard A. Figueroa and Eugene Garcia, "Issues in Testing Students From Culturally and Linguistically Diverse Backgrounds," *Multicultural Education*, vol. 2, no. 1, Fall 1994, pp. 10–19.

11. Ibid., p. 17.

12. Shirley Brice Heath, *Ways With Words: Language, Life, and Work in Communities and Classrooms* (Cambridge: Cambridge University Press, 1983).

13. American Educational Research Association, American Psychological Association, and National Council on Measurement, *Standards for Educational and Psychological Testing* (Washington, DC: American Psychological Association, 1985). Cited in Figueroa and Garcia, "Issues," p. 16.

14. Figueroa and Garcia, "Issues," p. 16.

15. Linda Darling-Hammond, "Performance-Based Assessment and Educational Equity," *Harvard Educational Review*, vol. 64, no. 1, Spring 1994, pp. 5–30.

16. Ibid., p. 8.

17. Reported in Sonia Nieto, *Affirming Diversity: The Sociopolitical Context of Multicultural Education*, 3rd ed. (New York: Longman, 2000).

18. Sonia Nieto, *Affirming Diversity*. For interesting discussions on the deskilling of teachers, see Michael W. Apple, *Teachers and Texts: A Political Economy of Class and Gender Relations in Education* (New York: Routledge and Kegan Paul, 1988); Joe L. Kincheloe, *Teachers as Researchers: Qualitative Inquiry as a Path to Empowerment* (New York: Falmer Press, 1991); and Rebecca Powell, *Literacy as a Moral Imperative: Facing the Challenges of a Pluralistic Society* (Lanham, MD: Rowman and Littlefield, 1999).

19. For instance, the State of North Carolina has recently implemented an accountability system that requires all students to meet statewide standards for promotion. When individual students' scores fall below the established level, various interventions are provided, such as smaller classes, special tutoring, summer school courses, and personalized educational plans. See *Questions and Answers About Student Accountability Standards* (Raleigh: Public Schools of North Carolina, State Department of Public Instruction, July 1999). At the same time, such accountability systems can lead to high levels of stress among students. See Wendy Cole, "Feeling Crushed By Tests at Age 11," *Time*, May 7, 2001, p. 61.

20. Darling-Hammond, "Performance-Based Assessment," p. 7.

21. Howard Gardner, *Frames of Mind* (New York: Basic Books, 1983).

22. Donald H. Graves, *A Fresh Look at Writing* (Portsmouth, NH: Heinemann, 1994).

23. For additional alternative assessment ideas, see Bill Bigelow, "Getting off the Track: Stories From an Untracked Classroom," in Bill Bigelow, Linda Christensen, Stan Karp, Barbara Miner, and Bob Peterson, eds., *Rethinking Our Classrooms: Teaching for Equity and Justice* (Milwaukee: Rethinking Schools, 1994), pp. 58–65; and Kenneth Cushner, Averil McClelland, and Philip Safford, *Human Diversity in Education: An Integrative Approach*, 3rd ed. (Boston: McGraw Hill, 2000).

24. Kati Haycock, "Distinguished Speaker: Kati Haycock," video produced and aired by KET, The Kentucky Network (November 15, 1999), 600 Cooper Drive, Lexington, KY, 40502-2296.

25. I examine this issue in greater depth in my book, *Literacy As a Moral Imperative*. Also see James Paul Gee, *Social Linguistics and Literacies: Ideology in Discourses* (New York: The Falmer Press, 1990); and Theresa Perry and Lisa Delpit, eds., *The Real Ebonics Debate* (Boston: Beacon Press, 1998).

Letter Thirteen

Curriculum

Dear Readers,

Today I was talking with a veteran teacher (who is White), and our conversation drifted toward multicultural education. She said she thought the problem associated with diversity in our schools was that so many persons of color tend to live in the past. She said, "We have African American history month. We read multicultural books. I think we're moving in the right direction. What else do they want?" I think this teacher is expressing the sentiments of a lot of White teachers. This comment also shows how we still tend to see our society in terms of "us" and "them"— White, Western culture versus "the Other"—rather than acknowledging our collective identity as a diverse nation.

I have intentionally put this chapter on curriculum near the end of the book, because I wanted you to get a broader concept of multicultural education before we talked about curricular issues. Too often I think we reduce multicultural education to the curriculum. As the teacher said to me today, we think that if we occasionally include multicultural perspectives in the curriculum, then equity is being adequately addressed and we are "multicultural educators."

Of course, including multicultural perspectives is important, but I would argue that multicultural education is so much more than celebrating African American History Month or Women's History Month, or using multicultural literature. The reality is that in most schools, these are easy things to do. They are relatively nonconfrontational, probably because they do little to challenge the status quo. Please don't misunderstand me. I'm not criticizing these activities; certainly they are important and valuable. But multicultural education is not just about changing the curriculum to make it more culturally inclusive; it's also about equity. And equity is all about shared power, about ownership, about justice—that is, about who has power in our society, and who doesn't. At its very core, multicultural education is anti-racist, anti-classist, anti-sexist education. At least for me, that's what it's all about.

The problem with focusing *only* on a multicultural curriculum is that it allows us to ignore issues of power. To put it another way, we can read and talk about the historical contributions and experiences of diverse populations and yet never have to confront the reality of White privilege, and the ways that privilege gets reinforced on a daily basis through culturally racist and classist practices. Part of being privileged is that we never really have to *see* our privilege. And then we wonder why persons of color can't seem to "forget about the past." In my own experiences, many teachers teach multiculturally, yet in many ways they end up trivializing multicultural education by ignoring the reality of inequities both in schools and in society—inequities that are perpetuated by cultural racism and based upon a system of White privilege. Thus, we never have to change our tracking and grouping practices, our assessment practices, or our expectations of the students we teach. After all, our students read multicultural literature, so aren't we "multicultural educators"?

The problem, it seems, isn't that we conceptualize multicultural education merely as making modifications in the curriculum; rather, it's that we tend to stop there. That is, we tinker with change by adding information on various populations without seriously challenging mainstream White knowledge. For instance, often the books that we choose are "safe," that is, unlikely to generate controversy. Other books may potentially lead to conflict, but we intentionally (or perhaps even unintentionally) direct students' reading of these texts so that an examination of racism, classism, and sexism is avoided. For example, it would certainly be valuable to have our high-school students read Elie Wiesel's *Night* as a tragic story about the holocaust and to discuss the profound human suffering of millions of Jews under the Nazi regime.[1] Indeed, in my opinion, every teacher and student ought to have the experience of reading this powerful book. Yet as multicultural educators, it would also be important to have our students read other literature that examines the experience of human bondage and to study the forces that perpetuate such abuses of power. How does oppression affect the oppressed? How does it affect the oppressor? Students might also read about current instances of inhumanity, both in their own communities and around the globe. In this way, they not only develop empathy for the victims of oppression, but they also understand what drives individuals to persecute others. They might then begin to realize how we all have the potential to become both oppressors and the oppressed.

Most of the multicultural curricular changes that I have seen in schools are of the safe, "let's all just get along and celebrate our differences" variety. This type of curriculum is grounded in what has been called the human relations approach to multicultural education, where the goal is to teach tolerance and respect for those who differ from ourselves.[2] Of course, there's nothing wrong with this approach; it's just that it doesn't go far enough. When you think about it, tolerance is a very low-level response to human difference. When you tolerate people, you don't really have to listen to them or to learn from them, nor do you have to challenge your prejudicial image of them; you merely have to try to get along with them. (I might tolerate my son's messy room, but that doesn't solve the conflict we have over it!)

The other problem with the human relations approach is that it does nothing to challenge the status quo. It's based upon a melting pot ideology that would like us all to "melt" into a single culture, which generally means the culture of those who have the power to define it. This is the assimilationist perspective that I have talked about throughout this book. Consider that when things melt, they no longer maintain any defining characteristics. To take the metaphor a step further, the chef who is in charge of the final product also determines the ingredients that will be added to the pot, and how that product will ultimately turn out. So, the distinct identities of Appalachians, Jews, American Indians, and others are sacrificed in order to ensure conformity to a single standard of being "American." Their unique historical and cultural identities are denied them in the effort to shape a singular American identity.

It's commendable that we add a few "ingredients" to the pot along the way, through occasionally learning about the experiences of diverse populations. During African American History Month, we teach about the contributions of famous Black leaders such as Howard Thurman, Martin Luther King, Jr., and W.E.B. Du Bois. Posters of scientific pioneers such as George Washington Carver, Lewis Latimer, and Elijah McCoy adorn our walls. We might even read works written by famous Black authors such as Ralph Ellison, Toni Morrison, and James Baldwin. During Women's History Month, we similarly extol the contributions of famous women throughout our history. Yet our students still sense that the truly important knowledge—the information that they must know in order to pass the tests and to get into the prestigious universities—is that of Whites (and predominantly males). Although the recipe is changed a bit, the basic pot is still the same.

Multicultural educators who are committed to social justice view the curriculum as an opportunity for struggle and conflict, that is, as a means for addressing problems in society. Ira Shor refers to this type of curriculum as "problem posing pedagogy," whereby a basic problem is established and students then explore the many facets of the problem through reading, writing, and discussion.[3] For instance, in a high-school English classroom, students might choose to examine the problem of violence in their school or community. To try to better understand the problem and its potential solutions, they would read and discuss various texts that related to the topic of violence (poems, novels, newspaper articles, etc.) and would also explore their ideas through writing and/or drama. The ultimate aim would be to come up with some recommendations for reducing violence and to present their ideas to the public.

In Kentucky, the elimination of tobacco subsidies is a big issue since tobacco is a major source of income for many farmers. Using a problem posing curriculum, students might investigate the history and economic impact of tobacco in the state and explore the viability of alternative crops. I can envision numerous activities that might be necessary to this study: interviewing farmers, writing articles, calculating the past and future economic impact of tobacco, researching environmental conditions for various crops, studying the health hazards of smoking, examining the effects of smoking on the poor, participating in debates, and so on. You might protest that this doesn't sound very "multicultural." I disagree. Tobacco has had a tremendous impact on the life and culture of rural communities not only in Kentucky but elsewhere, and too often I think policymakers from urban environments do not fully understand the problems of families living in rural areas. Our students need to be able to talk about these problems critically and intelligently and see all the sides of an issue. This is real-world learning that will help students to live and work in a democracy, not just acquire information so that they can pass a test.

During the past couple of months I have been interviewing fifth-grade students from central Kentucky and their teachers on a project that they did last year called "Saving Black Mountain." The children selected this project from among several options because they were interested in learning more about strip mining on the highest peak in Kentucky. The children decided that in order to learn more about the problem, they would need to visit the mountain. So, the teachers arranged for a field trip to eastern Kentucky so that the children might see firsthand the destruction that was occurring there and its impact on the environment. While they were there, the children examined water samples from wells and streams and took pictures of the scarred mountainside. They also interviewed students whose parents depended upon coal mining for their livelihoods. In the process, they not only learned about the negative effects of strip mining, but also about eastern Kentucky and its inhabitants' dependence on the coal industry. The children subsequently came up with several recommendations that showed a sensitivity to both perspectives; for instance, they suggested that the coal company be permitted to continue mining at the bottom of the mountain and that the land at the top be purchased for a wildlife preserve. They wrote letters to newspapers, legislators, and potential funding sources; they wrote songs, reports, and articles; they made telephone calls and interviewed people who lived in the region; they spoke before a legislative committee and presented their findings to coal industry representatives.[4] They also made a second visit to eastern Kentucky and worked with students, teachers, and environmental activists there in an effort to save the mountain. The students' efforts finally paid off when the Kentucky General Assembly voted to buy part of Black Mountain from the coal company so that the state's highest peak could be preserved for future generations. This is an example of strong, participatory democracy in action.[5]

When I interviewed these students a year after the completion of the project, they were still filled with excitement. It wasn't merely the fact that they had "won"; in fact, a debate is currently going on in the General Assembly as to whether the project will still be funded. Rather, their excitement emerged from the fact that they realized that their learning really mattered—that they were a part of something important and their lives and their literacy made a difference. The teachers told me that the students who really benefited were those who were designated as students with "special needs." Through the Black Mountain project, they came to feel that they were an integral part of the community and their contributions were valued. In one of the group interviews that I conducted, several of the students boasted about one of the boys in the group who had written a letter to a professor at a local university and the fact that, as a result of that letter, they had received a sizeable contribution. Another boy told me that prior to the project he really hated to read and write (he even went to "special reading" classes), but now, if his teacher asked him to choose between playing outside or writing for the project, he said, "I'd probably write."

As I said earlier in this letter, I think it's important to think of multicultural education more broadly than just including information on the history and experiences of diverse populations. In fact, James Banks calls this the "additive approach" to multicultural education.[6] Textbooks use an additive approach when they include information on various subordinated populations in "special sections" of the text, such as those infamous "Let's Think About" boxes. Teachers use an additive approach when they create units of study on special topics, such as "A Study of Native Americans" before Thanksgiving. Schools use an additive approach when they plan special activities and events for African American History Month. The overall result of the additive approach is that students and teachers continue to view the information presented as nonessential knowledge. In other words, it still is seen as the knowledge and experiences of "the Other," not of *us*. Thus, while introducing students to information about non-White and non-Western cultures certainly has some value, it does relatively little to advance our understanding of the social, political, and economic issues associated with human diversity or to challenge the "official knowledge" of the school.[7] Perhaps even more critically, it does little to unify us as a society—to help us to see the histories, experiences, and problems of "the Other" as *our* history, *our* experiences, *our* problems.

Projects such as Saving Black Mountain, however, move beyond the additive approach toward what James Banks refers to as the "transformation approach."[8] In the transformation approach, understanding the histories and experiences of various populations becomes vital to understanding the history and experiences of this nation. For instance, in order to appreciate the problem posed by strip mining the mountain, students had to learn from the people who lived in the Appalachian region. Through interviews and discussions, they came to appreciate the aesthetic value of Black Mountain to the people who lived there; at the same time, however, they also began to understand the impact that the coal industry has had in eastern Kentucky. They learned that "coal is king" there, and that many of the communities were originally established by mine operators who had such power that they paid miners with company scrip that could only be cashed in at the company store. They also learned how corporate power continues to work in eastern Kentucky as they listened to local residents complain about mountain streams and well water that have been contaminated by strip mining while mine officials turn deaf ears. Finally, they learned how the legislative process works in a democracy, and how they might use this process to effect change. Perhaps most importantly, they learned about the power of literacy—*their* literacy—for transformation.

When the curriculum goes beyond preparing students for a test and addresses real-world problems, then we no longer have to bribe students to learn, through stickers or grades. Students are internally rewarded, and learning about the experiences of those who differ from themselves becomes a natural and integral part of the discovery process. Students learn about historical conflicts and struggles because a knowledge of history is vital to understanding present-day issues. Yet to be useful, the study of history must include a study of the conflicts that emerged as diverse populations struggled for power, sovereignty, and human rights. As I suggested in an earlier letter, our entire history as a nation can be conceptualized as a continuous fight for civil rights.[9] How did various groups interact during different events in our history? How do past cultural conflicts relate to those we are experiencing today? For instance, how do the institution of slavery, the subjugation of Native peoples, the conquering of the west, and the capitalistic exploitation of Appalachia relate to current social and economic problems? Many of the issues we face as a society and as a nation have roots in the economic exploitation of large segments of our population and the denial of freedom and democratic rights to them. Thus, while I think it's important that we celebrate the fact that America has been the land of opportunity for many, it seems that avoiding a study of the negative aspects of our history in order to maintain a safe, "let's just all get along" curriculum will result in a real danger of repeating the mistakes of the past.[10] In this age of local and global violence, can we really afford to do that?

When we talk about curriculum issues, it's important to keep in mind that the curriculum is never neutral. That is, we make choices about what to teach and how to teach it, and these choices are always the result of what someone has deemed important to know. Michael Apple argues that controversies about the curriculum "involve profoundly different definitions of the common good, about our society and where it should be heading, about cultural visions, and about our children's future."[11] Given the vast amount of knowledge in the world, who decides what gets taught in our schools? When I ask my graduate students this question, they usually reply "the state department of education." Of course, departments of education often have a substantial influence over curricular decisions; but at the same time, they merely endorse what society has determined to be essential knowledge. This is where power and privilege enter into the equation: Who has the power to decide? I encourage you to think about this question carefully. Do low-income parents have much power over the curriculum? Do Native American parents? How about corporate executives, or the Religious Right?

In an earlier letter, I dealt with the question of the feared divisiveness of multicultural education. I would argue that the traditional canon—one that endorses a singular, monocultural perspective—is actually much more divisive than one that is multicultural. The traditional canon is exclusive; it divides us into "winners" and "losers," "insiders" and "outsiders." A multicultural curriculum, in contrast, is based upon equity or shared power. With a multicultural perspective, no voices are marginalized or devalued; rather, every student is validated through what is being taught. Such a curriculum is consistent with a multicultural democracy that espouses freedom and equality for all. In the words of Linda Spears-Bunton,

> A multicultural perspective labels no part of humanity as trivial; it unsilences humanity's voices, and it seeks and welcomes opportunities to include and honor diverse cultural ways of creating knowledge and metaphorical ways of understanding.[12]

A multicultural curriculum affirms and validates. It also invites us to struggle with the controversies that inevitably arise through our human differences, and to create community out of conflict. Perhaps the reason why some view multicultural education as divisive is that a curriculum that is truly multicultural is not a "safe" curriculum; rather, it is one that presents multiple perspectives in the search for truth. Dialogue becomes central as both teachers and students are encouraged to consider views that differ from their own and to reconsider their own taken-for-granted assumptions about the world. As I mentioned in one of my earlier letters, we are all limited by our experiences, and hence we all have biases. A curriculum that is genuinely transformative challenges us to confront these biases and to work for a more equitable and just society and world.

In this way, a curriculum that is multicultural can potentially unite; for unity comes from acknowledging our common humanity, our common destiny, our common purpose. As in the example of the children of central and eastern Kentucky who joined together to save a mountain, it also comes from establishing common goals and working toward the common good. At the same time, a transformative curriculum will undoubtedly be resisted by those who have a vested interest in maintaining the status quo—that is, by those who benefit the most from the current system of privilege. A multicultural curriculum that is grounded in equity is not for the fainthearted.

Nevertheless, I am blessed to know many fine teachers who believe in their power to transform society, and who are willing to take risks to make a difference. I encourage you to be that kind of teacher.

Courage,
Becky

Notes

1. Elie Wiesel, *Night* (New York: Bantam Books, 1960). For an interesting discussion on how children's literature can be used to examine various social issues (e.g., sexism, classism, racism), see Herbert Kohl, *Should We Burn Babar? Essays on Children's Literature and the Power of Stories* (New York: The Free Press, 1995).

2. For a comprehensive discussion of the human relations approach, see Christine E. Sleeter and Carl A. Grant, *Making Choices for Multicultural Education: Five Approaches to Race, Class, and Gender*, 2nd ed. (New York: Macmillan, 1994).

3. Ira Shor, *Empowering Education: Critical Teaching for Social Change* (Chicago: University of Chicago Press, 1992).

4. For an informative look at how the arts can be used in schools to combat racism, see Karen B. McLean Donaldson, *Through Students' Eyes: Combating Racism in United States Schools* (Westport, CT: Praeger, 1996).

5. For a more detailed description of this project, see Rebecca Powell, Susan Chambers Cantrell, and Sandra Adams, "Saving Black Mountain: The Promise of Critical Literacy in a Multicultural Democracy," *The Reading Teacher*, vol. 54, May 2001, pp. 772–781.

6. James A. Banks, *An Introduction to Multicultural Education*, 2nd ed. (Boston: Allyn and Bacon, 1999).

7. Michael W. Apple, *Official Knowledge: Democratic Education in a Conservative Age* (New York: Routledge, 1993).

8. James A. Banks, "Multicultural Education and Curriculum Transformation," *Journal of Negro Education*, vol. 64, no. 4, Fall 1995, pp. 390–400. For additional information

on developing a multicultural curriculum, see Leonard Davidman and Patricia T. Davidman, *Teaching with a Multicultural Curriculum: A Practical Guide* (New York: Longman, 1997); and Carl A. Grant and Christine E. Sleeter, *Turning On Learning: Five Approaches for Multicultural Teaching Plans for Race, Class, Gender and Disability* (New York: Merrill, 1989).

9. John Wills and Hugh Mehan, "Recognizing Diversity Within a Common Historical Narrative: The Challenge to Teaching History and Social Studies," *Multicultural Education*, Fall 1996, pp. 4–11.

10. For instance, consider the economic exploitation of recent immigrant populations. See Karen J. Hossfeld, "Hiring Immigrant Women: Silicon Valley's 'Simple Formula,'" in Fred L. Pincus and Howard J. Ehrlich, eds., *Race and Ethnic Conflict: Contending Views on Prejudice, Discrimination, and Ethnoviolence*, 2nd ed. (Boulder, CO: Westview, 1999), pp. 162–179; and Joan Moore and Raquel Pinderhughes, "Latinos and Discrimination," in the same volume, pp. 180–194. Moore and Pinderhughes write of Latino neighborhoods in U.S. cities: "These neighborhoods are likely to remain as pockets of unrelieved poverty for many generations to come" (p. 188).

11. Apple, *Official Knowledge*, p. 52.

12. Linda Spears-Bunton, "All the Colors of the Land: A Literacy Montage," in Arlette Ingram Willis, ed., *Teaching Multicultural Literature in Grades 9–12: Moving Beyond the Canon* (Norwood, MA: Christopher Gordon, 1998), p. 21.

Letter Fourteen

Classroom Environment

Dear Readers,

When you think of a typical classroom, what comes to mind? Desks in straight rows? The teacher expounding on some topic in the front of the room? Boring lectures as the students take notes? Until recently, you could walk into any classroom in nearly every school in the United States and observe this scenario. Schools have been designed for efficiency, and a "factory model" of education has been the norm.

Consider the social dynamics that exist in such classrooms. The teacher is obviously dominant, and this dominance is displayed in several ways. First, she's providing information as the students take notes, and therefore she is the only really active participant in the learning process; the students are relatively passive. The teacher controls and directs the learning, both in terms of what counts as important knowledge, and in terms of how that knowledge is to be learned. Further, she controls the rewards that students receive in the form of grades or praise. She controls the amount of work that students are required to do, and the form of that work. She also controls the elements of classroom communication, that is, who is permitted to speak, and when. In many cases, she even controls the discourse, because many of the questions that we ask students have only one correct answer.[1] Given this dynamic, our students often feel relatively powerless in our classrooms.

Indeed, most teachers want it this way. After all, teachers are charged with maintaining order, and students won't learn in an environment where there is chaos. Yet research shows that often teachers control students not solely by using behavior management techniques, but by controlling the information that students receive and the ways the information is presented. In her ethnographic study of social studies classes in four different high schools, Linda McNeil found that teachers engage in what she calls "defensive teaching," using teaching methods and evaluation procedures that will help make completion of their task more efficient and will lead to the least amount of student resistance. For instance, she found that teachers tended to reduce complex topics to a series of disjointed facts that were to be memorized for a test, and generally failed to explain their interconnectedness. Such fragmentation of knowledge was often accompanied by what McNeil refers to as "mystification," the tendency to silence discussion of important or complex topics in an effort to hide the teacher's lack of knowledge or to enhance trust in America's institutions. A third strategy that teachers used to control students was that of omission. That is, teachers simply refused to discuss certain topics, particularly those that might lead to controversy. Finally, they engaged in what McNeil calls "defensive simplification," winning students' commitment and compliance by telling them that the study wouldn't demand much effort or time on their part. In writing about the teachers in her study, McNeil states that "*Their patterns of knowledge control were, according to their own statements in taped interviews, rooted in their desire for classroom control*" (emphasis in original).[2]

The discouraging thing to me about this research is that McNeil found that even teachers who believed in transformative teaching used these control strategies. That is, while some teachers gave their students more freedom, they generally expected little from them in terms of academic effort and became apologetic when topics became challenging. According to McNeil,

> The philosophical values the individual brings to the classroom are not in all cases the same. Yet the strategies for instruction are quite similar: *control students by making school work easy*. The result is content that neither the teachers nor the students take very seriously.[3] (emphasis in original)

After experiencing years of such pedagogy, students developed what McNeil refers to as a "client mentality." They became passive receivers of information and learned not for the joy of knowing, but rather so that they might acquire future payoffs (grades, a diploma). That is, students were externally versus internally motivated. In this sense, they became consumers of information, taking just what they needed to get by while never actually becoming actively engaged in any real learning. Similarly, teachers tended to lower their expectations of students and rarely expected them to *want* to learn.

It has been my experience that many teachers are reluctant to grapple with difficult issues and to make their instruction truly relevant to their students' lives because they fear chaos. It's easier to maintain control by presenting information in fragmented bits and by not delving into topics too intensely. In other words, we can control students' behavior by providing lower-level knowledge and by keeping them relatively passive. Presenting challenging topics like the continuous struggle for civil rights (in our social studies classes), the increasing income gap (in our mathematics classes), and the oppressive forces of racism and classism (in our literature classes)—and actually *engaging students in dialogue* about these topics—is taking a risk that many teachers are not willing to take. So, we often settle for teaching students fragmented, low-level knowledge so that they might pass a standardized multiple choice test, rather than grappling with issues that would help prepare them to live and work in a democracy.

Recently I was fortunate enough to hear a presentation by Kati Haycock, president of the Education Trust, an organization that examines the achievement gap between White students and students of color. In her presentation, she shared the story of a girl named Tamika who had suffered sexual abuse and had lived in several foster homes. When teachers were asked "What does Tamika need?" they generally gave answers like "counseling," "a stable home life," and so on. Yet when Tamika was asked this same question, she responded, "Teach me!"[4] Consistent with other research findings, Haycock made the point that students in our society receive substantially different instruction based upon their income and race/ethnicity.[5] She also stated that *the most important factor in student achievement is the quality of teaching.* Haycock cited a Dallas study that showed the impact of effective teaching on student achievement: students who had the most effective teachers for three years in a row scored in the

76th percentile on standardized tests, whereas those who had the least effective teachers for three years in a row scored in the 27th percentile. When we lower our standards and "water down" the curriculum in an effort to maintain control and/or placate students, then their achievement suffers and we ultimately do them a tremendous disservice. And we tend to do this most with students who need us the most—those in the lower academic tracks.

What does all this have to do with the classroom environment? The main point I am trying to make is that when we control student behavior by controlling knowledge, then we ultimately undermine the life chances of our students—especially those students like Tamika who depend on us to give them the knowledge they need to create new options for their lives. Yet this is precisely what happens in classrooms all around the country. Students who are in the lower academic tracks (as well as those from disadvantaged communities where fear of anarchy is the highest) must endure more teacher control, not just in the form of behavior management, but in the form of control of knowledge.[6] As I mentioned in my letter on curriculum differentiation, research shows that the curriculum is often less rigorous for these students because it is felt that they just cannot engage in higher-level thinking or that they need more "structure."

I also suggest that when control of behavior is manifested through control of knowledge and students are treated as mere "clients," then the relationships between teachers and students suffer. Students don't trust that teachers will give them what they really need to know, and teachers don't trust that students might actually *want* to learn (or that they are even capable of learning). Students are viewed as "vessels to be filled" or as objects on the educational assembly line, rather than as thoughtful, reflective, and passionate human beings. (Consider how often we hear students referred to as "products"!) The famous Brazilian educator Paulo Freire aptly refers to this kind of teaching as "banking education": the teacher makes deposits in the minds of students, which they later withdraw for a grade.[7] As in the case of the college student I mentioned in a former letter, whose professor did not even know her name, banking education leads to disengagement and depersonalization; teachers never really get to know their students on a more personal level and never develop the caring, mentoring relationships that are so essential for learning to occur. Throughout this book, I have suggested that we must be advocates for our students, particularly for those who have very few supportive networks and whose cultural capital puts them at a disadvantage. Yet *how can we become advocates for students when we don't even know them?*

I would argue that if we are truly to prepare students for living and working in a democracy, then our classrooms need to be places where democracy is practiced. As I discussed earlier, a strong democracy is a participatory democracy—one where all share in the decision-making process and all are given a voice. Of course, the teacher must be the primary authority in the classroom, and we must be able to maintain a structured environment that is conducive to learning. But I maintain that a classroom where the teacher's voice is the only one that is heard is simply inconsistent with a democratic state. Further, such classrooms fail to teach equity, because they reinforce inequitable relationships of power.

As a teacher educator, I must admit that I have rarely witnessed classrooms that were genuinely democratic. Nevertheless, those that I have seen are truly exciting places. In these classrooms, the teachers are willing to turn over some of their power and authority to their students. Students participate in everything from designing the room and planning the bulletin boards, to determining criteria for evaluation, to choosing the topics and accompanying activities for study. For instance, I recall a middle-school teacher who allowed his students to design and paint their lockers every year. He also gave them choices as to how they would meet his learning objectives. Another middle-school teacher simply asked his students what they wanted to study that year in social studies. Because they lived in eastern Kentucky, they decided they wanted to study what happened to coal when it left their community. This topic led to a year-long study of the environmental impact of coal emissions and other related issues. The students worked collaboratively and developed surveys, wrote rap songs, and made presentations throughout the state on their findings. To meet state mandates, their teacher occasionally used the required social studies text, but the students were generally able to engage in activities of their choice to learn the material.[8]

For teachers, turning over some of their authority to their students can be highly liberating. Teachers who practice a democratic pedagogy claim that they could never go back to the traditional way of teaching. The learning environment is transformed from one that is grounded in competition to one that is centered around equity. As a result, teachers report that status problems among students virtually disappear; that is, students begin to value the expertise of their peers and the classroom becomes a genuine community, not a group of individuals competing for a grade. Not only do teachers get to know their students on a more intimate level, but stereotypes break down as students get to know one another in ways that are not based upon race or socioeconomic class. Trusting relationships form, and their classrooms become "safe spaces" in which students can take risks in their learning without fear of failure.

There is another important reason for creating a noncompetitive, democratic classroom environment, however, and this has to do with the isolation that students of color often experience in the high academic tracks. As I mentioned in previous letters, students will often choose to under-achieve rather than risk alienating their peer group by appearing to "act White." In her research with high-achieving Black high-school students, Signithia Fordham hypothesized that the students' identity as African Americans—or what she describes as their sense of "peoplehood"—causes them to establish boundaries between themselves and their White peers. The students' loyalty to this "fictive kinship system" causes tremendous conflict as they attempt to operate within an institution that tends to marginalize and devalue their cultural and ethnic identity. In essence, they are torn between pursuing academic achievement in a competitive, culturally racist environment and thereby separating themselves from their peers, or maintaining a sense of solidarity with their group. Fordham puts it this way:

> The mere act of separating Black adolescents from those who are racially similar suggests to them that they are, in some important intellectual and nonintellectual ways, different from other Black people and...clones of their White peers. Separating Black adolescents and other non-dominant-group children—both spatially and psychologically—from their peers and other adult members of their

communities, regardless of its benign intentions, appears to exacerbate the conflict such students experience around academic achievement and school success.[9]

These conflicts for students of color do not have to persist, however. Fordham goes on to suggest that in addition to implementing a multicultural curriculum that values and affirms students' identities, teachers can create classroom communities where the achievement of the group takes precedence over individual accomplishments. She cites several studies where students of color made incredible gains when teachers began to implement a group-centered approach to learning. For instance, a teacher in a junior high school in New York City implemented a system whereby students were rewarded according to the performance of their class or team rather than their individual achievement. When the students entered his classroom, they ranked near the bottom in reading skills; by the end of eighth grade, they were reading above grade level. Fordham concludes that when a multicultural curriculum is combined with working toward team goals and individual competition is minimized, the students perceive that schooling is compatible with their cultural identity, which tends to favor service to the group versus individual accomplishment. In other words, structuring learning in this way is consistent with students' "fictive kinship system" and therefore supports and promotes a positive racial identity.

Compounding the conflicts experienced by students of color is the fact that they tend to work in isolation rather than to seek the help of their peers. Fordham found that the high-achieving Black students in her study tended to have a distorted sense of self-reliance and therefore were reluctant to collaborate with fellow students. This finding is supported by research conducted by Philip Uri Treisman, who examined the differences between the study patterns of African American and Chinese university students.[10] Treisman was concerned that large numbers of Black and Hispanic students were failing the introductory mathematics course, despite remedial efforts and interventions designed to assure their success. At the same time, Chinese students did well in these courses. He decided to find out what factors made the difference, by comparing the study habits of African American and high-achieving Chinese students. Treisman discovered that the Chinese students studied together and had developed a highly effective academic support network, whereas the African American students tended to study in isolation. In reporting on Treisman's work, Mano Singham writes,

> They [the Chinese students] had an enormously efficient information network for sharing what worked and what didn't. If someone made a mistake, others quickly learned of it and did not repeat it. In contrast, the black students partied together, just like the Chinese, but then went their separate ways for studying....This tendency resulted in a much slower pace of learning, as well as the suffering that comes with having to learn from mistakes.[11]

In response to this discovery, Treisman restructured his math classes by forming heterogenous study groups. Students were required to work in these groups and to share information and solve problems together. In a sense, he required his students to assume a teaching role and to develop problem-solving strategies together. Through this learning structure, students came to discover the value of group effort. Treisman also gave his students challenging math problems so that there was no embarrassment when they were unable to solve them. At the same time, because the students knew that the problems were difficult, they experienced a high sense of accomplishment when they were successful. Treisman found that African American and Hispanic students were able to achieve at higher levels in a learning environment that promoted group collaboration versus individual advancement. As I noted in Letter Eleven, such environments are consistent with Dewey's idea of democracy as "associated living," that is, a system that values collaborative inquiry and the equitable distribution of power.

Creating a democratic classroom community, however, is not easy. A few weeks ago I had the pleasure of reading *Round Peg, Square Hole: A Teacher Lives and Learns in Watts*, by John Gust.[12] In this book, Gust shares his experiences as both an elementary teacher and a resident in this low-income community in Los Angeles. He was committed to erasing the barriers between himself and his students and to promoting more productive, equitable relationships in his classroom. He was also committed to becoming a member of the community that he served. He subsequently acted on this commitment, moved into his students' neighborhood, and began the process of turning over more responsibility to his students. At first there was chaos, and Gust questioned whether he had made the right decision. Even the students began to question the soundness of this newly formed classroom environment. Yet rather than giving up, Gust decided to bring the problem to the class. Through discussion, they talked about their goals for their classroom. Here's how Gust describes the process:

> So I explained about the three different ways that we could organize our pure, rather than representative, democracy. In language that they could understand, I explained participatory input, majority rule, and consensus building. After I was finished, they all just sat there looking at me, until Angela asked, "Can we use all three?"
>
> Somewhat confused, I asked, "What do you mean?"
>
> "Well," she continued, "sometimes you could get ideas from us and decide for the class. Other times, we could have a vote. And other times, we could talk things out until we all agree." What an intelligent kid Angela was! Why didn't I think of that? I guess, sometimes it takes a kid to figure things out. [13]

The students in his class subsequently envisioned what they wanted their classroom to be like—respectful, helpful, loving, clean, friendly—and they established several ground rules for participation that would help them to achieve their goals. As a result of the classroom climate that Gust was able to establish, his students became so empowered that they successfully procured money for and built a new playground in their community. State-mandated objectives in basic reading, language, and mathematics were learned through the process of completing this real-world project.

As I mentioned in a previous letter, I have recently had the good fortune of interviewing fifth-grade students in central Kentucky who were part of such a classroom last year. They chose to study the problems of strip mining on Black Mountain, and subsequently they were able to influence state legislators to buy a portion of the mountain so that it might be saved from further destruction. One of their teachers, Mrs. Adams, told me that the students had total ownership of this project. They planned field trips, wrote to legislators, conducted research, developed presentations, created songs, planned events, wrote reports, and so on, all in an effort to "save the mountain." These children subsequently received several national and state awards for their efforts. What impressed me so much about this project, however, was not what they were able to accomplish, but the commitment that these children had to learning. All of their reading and writing was for a purpose, and even a year later their motivation has still not diminished. Something else that impressed me in the interviews was the high regard that these students had developed for one another's abilities and achievements. It was not unusual for them to talk about a letter or report that a peer had written, or to speak with pride about a classmate's accomplishments. Finally, the students talked about relationships that developed as a result of the project. They talked about the love they felt for their teacher, Mrs. Adams, even though she made them work hard and insisted on high standards. Several students also talked about their class as being like a family. From the many hours they spent together outside the classroom and their commitment to a common goal, they grew from a classroom of individuals to a genuine caring community. For me, this is what equity is all about.

When we structure our classrooms around the principle of equity, then our relationships with our students change. We are no longer the "all knowing expert," but we become partners with our students in the exciting adventure of learning. Our students teach us as much as (if not more than) we teach them. We open up our classrooms to genuine dialogue, where students feel free to exchange ideas and provide new insights. Knowledge acquisition is no longer controlled, but teachers and students co-construct the curriculum. In such classrooms, teachers send the message to their students that they are significant and that their lives can make a difference. They communicate their belief not only that each and every student can learn, but also that they are capable of teaching others. A democratic classroom is empowering for both teachers and learners.

Thus, multicultural education isn't just about *what* we teach; it's also about *how* we teach. If we teach about equity yet fail to practice it, what message are we sending to our students? If we believe in the need to end racism, classism, sexism, homophobia, and other oppressive forces in our society, yet reduce complex social issues to a series of facts, what message are we sending to our students? If we believe in democracy yet practice aristocracy in our classrooms, what message are we sending to our students? If we believe that our job is to promote student achievement, yet fail to uphold high standards and expectations for all students, then what message are we sending them? Finally, if we believe that our role as teachers is to develop citizens who will work for a better society, yet fail to affirm and empower our students, what message are we sending them?

Teaching is all about *relationship*. As I said in an earlier letter, students aren't machines. The environments that we establish in our classrooms must be such that they enable us to develop positive, trusting, caring relationships with our students. The heart of multicultural education is equity, and therefore equity ought to guide all of our teaching practices.

Keep the faith,
Becky

Notes

1. Several educational researchers have examined the discourse patterns that are prevalent in American classrooms. For example, David Bloome talks about "text reproduction," whereby the aim is to reconstruct (rather than to challenge) the information found in a text. Roland Tharp and Ronald Gallimore discuss the use of recitation through the use of "scripts," which promote rote learning and student passivity. See David Bloome, "Reading as a Social Process in a Middle School Classroom," in David Bloome, ed., *Literacy and Schooling* (Norwood, NJ: Ablex, 1987), pp. 123–149; and Roland G. Tharp and Ronald Gallimore, *The Instructional Conversation: Teaching and Learning in Social Activity,* Research Report 2 (Santa Cruz: University of California, National Center for Research on Cultural Diversity and Second Language Learning, 1991).

2. Linda M. McNeil, *Contradictions of Control: School Structure and School Knowledge* (New York: Routledge, 1988), p. 159. A similar pattern has been found in elementary classrooms. In describing her observations in a fifth-grade classroom, for example, Mary Phillips Manke notes that the teacher "had succeeded in using activities that called for strictly limited student responses to promote her agenda of student control and (she believed) enhanced learning." Mary Phillips Manke, *Classroom Power Relations: Understanding Student-Teacher Interaction* (Mahwah, NJ: Lawrence

Erlbaum, 1997), p. 70.

3. McNeil, *Contradictions*, p. 184.

4. Kati Haycock, "Status of the Nation." Presentation to the Minority Student Achievement Task Force: Critical Barriers to Equitable Student Achievement, Lexington, KY, May 17, 2000.

5. For instance, in what is now a classic study, Jean Anyon found very different pedagogical practices in schools of low-income and working-class students when compared to schools of high-income students from professional homes. See Jean Anyon, "Social Class and the Hidden Curriculum of Work," reprinted in Etta R. Hollins, *Transforming Curriculum for a Culturally Diverse Society* (Mahwah, NJ: Lawrence Erlbaum, 1996), pp. 179–203.

6. Jeannie Oakes, *Keeping Track: How Schools Structure Inequality* (New Haven, CT: Yale University Press, 1985).

7. Paulo Freire, *Pedagogy of the Oppressed* (New York: Continuum, 1970/1993).

8. These teachers' classrooms are described in greater detail in Rebecca G. Eller, "Teacher Resistance and Educational Change: Toward a Critical Theory of Literacy In Appalachia," unpublished doctoral dissertation, University of Kentucky, 1989.

9. Signithia Fordham, "Peer-Proofing Academic Competition Among Black Adolescents: 'Acting White' Black American Style," in Christine E. Sleeter, ed., *Empowerment through Multicultural Education* (Albany: State University of New York Press, 1991), pp. 76–77.

10. See Philip Uri Treisman, "Studying Students Studying Calculus: A Look at the Lives of Minority Mathematics Students in College," *College Mathematics Journal*, vol. 23, no. 5, November 1992, pp. 362–372.

11. Mano Singham, "The Canary in the Mine: The Achievement Gap Between Black and White Students," *Phi Delta Kappan*, vol. 80, no. 1, September 1998, p. 13.

12. John Gust, *Round Peg, Square Hole: A Teacher Lives and Learns in Watts* (Portsmouth, NH: Heinemann, 1999).

13. Ibid., p. 36.

Letter Fifteen

Evaluating Your Classroom

Dear Readers,

   If you're like me, you value the information you get from reading about research and instruction, but at some point you need something concrete. The purpose of this letter is to summarize the ideas presented in this book in the form of a checklist that you can use to evaluate your classroom. All of the guidelines that follow are based upon the notion of equity and how it can be achieved through our instructional practices. In consistency with previous letters, the criteria are categorized under the headings of curriculum, assessment, and classroom environment. I have also developed another category, "Other," to include important criteria that did not fit neatly into any of the other categories. I hope that you will find this checklist to be helpful as you work toward developing an equitable, inclusive, and democratic classroom.

Best wishes,
Becky

Curriculum

_____   The curriculum is relevant to students' lives and addresses contemporary problems and social issues.

_____   Multicultural themes and resources are an integral part of the curriculum. Learning about diverse perspectives is not seen as an "add on" (learning about "the Other"), but rather as essential knowledge (learning about "us").

_____ I give students choices and allow them to contribute to the development of the curriculum (e.g., by posing questions, by providing
suggestions for topics of study, etc.).

_____ I involve students actively in the learning process.

_____ I value the cultural knowledge of my students and frequently
integrate it into the curriculum.

_____ Many of the materials that I use and the learning experiences in
which my students are engaged are designed to raise their social
consciousness.

_____ I implement a curriculum that is anti-racist, anti-classist, anti-sexist,
and anti-homophobic by addressing issues that require students to
examine their cultural assumptions and confront their own biases.

_____ I use activities and materials that challenge students to confront the
forces of privilege and oppression in our society.

_____ I use activities and materials that support various learning styles and
cultural ways of knowing.

_____ I consistently provide students with learning experiences that
empower them to become change agents in order to promote a more
equitable, just, and compassionate society and world.

Assessment

_____ I allow students to have a voice in how they are assessed and the
criteria that will be used in evaluating their performance.

_____ I try to minimize the problems with formal assessments by making
frequent use of authentic, performance-based assessments which

allow students to demonstrate competence in a variety of ways.

_____ The assessments that I use encourage critical, higher-order thinking.

_____ I use assessment data from a variety of sources in evaluating students.

_____ I use assessment data primarily to determine student needs and to further student learning, rather than to assign grades.

_____ The assessments that I use are always linked directly to the goals and objectives that I have established for a particular unit of study, and reflect high standards and expectations for all students.

_____ I continuously monitor my cultural assumptions and perceptions of students so that I might be fair in assessing them.

_____ I examine tests for cultural bias and I value student input on their perceptions of bias in particular tests.

Classroom Environment

_____ I make sure that my classroom reflects our human diversity (in terms of books, displays, posters, etc.).

_____ I strive to make my classroom a noncompetitive, collaborative community where group effort is encouraged.

_____ I model respectful, caring relationships so that every student will feel valued and affirmed, and I expect the same from students.

_____ I try hard to get to know each of my students on a personal basis and to let them know that I care.

_____ Through my seating arrangements and my interactions with students, I try hard to make each individual feel that she or he is an important and integral part of the classroom.

_____ All of my rules and policies encourage the realization of a democratic community in my classroom. That is, students are expected to have decision-making power in all aspects of classroom life.

_____ I maintain rigorous academic standards for every student, and I expect that every student will be able to meet those standards.

_____ I try to convey to all students, through both words and actions, that I expect them to meet the established standards.

_____ I continuously monitor my interactions with students to make sure that I use effective interaction patterns with both high and low achievers (in terms of praise, wait time, rephrasing of questions, use of their ideas, etc.).

_____ I avoid ability grouping of students.

_____ I promote networks such as peer study groups to enhance the academic achievement of all students.

_____ I am continuously seeking culturally appropriate, culturally compatible ways for teaching and responding to the students that I teach.

_____ I try to convey to all students that I value them as individuals and that I believe in their ability to succeed, and I try to help them to believe in themselves and to empower them to effect change.

_____ I try hard to establish trusting relationships with my students and to make my classroom a place where students are comfortable and feel safe enough to take risks.

_____ I promote dialogue and encourage the free exchange of ideas.

_____ I welcome diverse opinions and perspectives, even when I do not agree with them.

_____ I recognize that I am a learner as well as a teacher and I am always learning from my students and their families.

Other

_____ I view my students' parents as true partners in the education of their children, and I try hard to develop positive working relationships with them and to involve them in making educational decisions.

_____ I work hard to learn about my students' home community and to be viewed as a part of that community.

_____ I value the strengths of my students' families and believe that most parents are vitally concerned about their children's education.

_____ I am an advocate for my students, especially for those who seem to have few advocates.

_____ I continuously reflect on how my own identity (in terms of my race, ethnicity, gender, socioeconomic class, sexual orientation, etc.) impacts my teaching and my relationships with students.

Letter Sixteen

Multicultural Education as Humanizing Education

Dear Readers,

In my second letter, I asked you to think about how you perceive multicultural education. Now, at the close of this book, I invite you to revisit those initial ideas. Have your perceptions changed in any way? For me, being an effective multicultural teacher means continually questioning and reflecting upon what we teach and how we teach it, and interrogating our role as educators in a diverse society. I find that my ideas about multicultural education are constantly expanding as the result of new understandings, insights, and experiences, and I continue to grow as a multicultural educator and scholar. Hopefully, you will, too. You will undoubtedly come away with different opinions and ideas as a result of reading this and other works. My hope, however, is that the one essential point that you will have gained from reading this book is that multicultural education is vital in a pluralistic democracy.

In my own state of Kentucky, there are many school districts with very few students of color. It's not unusual for educators in these districts to believe that multicultural education simply isn't necessary in their schools. "After all," they claim, "we really don't have any diversity here. So why do we need multicultural education?" Of course, such a perspective ignores the fact that our job as educators is to prepare students to live and work in a society that is yet to be—a society that will require an increasing level of understanding of persons whose cultural assumptions and perspectives differ from our own.

But beyond this, as I have suggested through my various letters to you, multicultural education is much more than studying the perspectives and contributions of diverse populations. It involves the ways in which we conceptualize education in general and the role of schooling in our society. For me, and for many other multicultural scholars, the essence of an education that is multicultural ought to be the promotion of social justice by challenging classism, racism, sexism, and other inequities.[1] That is, we believe that as educators, we're not just preparing students to live and work in a diverse society; we're also preparing them to *change* that society so that freedom and justice for all might become a reality. This reality includes the civil rights of women, persons of color, gays and lesbians, the poor, and any other group that historically has been disenfranchised and oppressed.

Several years ago I presented a paper at the annual conference of the National Association for Multicultural Education on the topic of "White hegemony," that is, the dominance of the White race which is sustained through the perpetuation of a White cultural ideology (essentially what I have referred to in this book as "cultural racism"). In this paper, I stated that

> to suggest that one is "not prejudiced" (as many Euro-Americans often do) is simply erroneous. In effect, we are inevitably biased, and hence it becomes crucial that we identify and interrogate our cultural assumptions so that we might examine how they affect our relationships with others and our expectations of the children we teach.... it is precisely because our whiteness is generally regarded as unproblematic, precisely because Anglo, middle-class society is seen as normative, that we as European American educators must examine critically our own conceptions of diversity.[2]

Following my presentation, a teacher approached me and asked if he could have a copy of the paper to use with his students. He told me that he taught at an elite preparatory school in the Washington D.C. area, and that he felt that his students particularly needed to hear the message of the paper. I agree with him. I argue that multicultural education is especially needed for those who have known privilege, for it is those students who are the most oblivious to that privilege. An education that is multicultural enables us to confront our own cultural assumptions and to see the world from different perspectives. In this sense, multicultural education is consistent with liberal education in that it helps to "open the minds" of both teachers and students.

Further, I suggest that those of us who are privileged have the greatest power to transform society, and thus it is our responsibility to educate ourselves and to work side-by-side with marginalized populations to fight for their basic rights as citizens and as human beings. The students in that preparatory school are being groomed to be our future political leaders, yet their daily school environment is all-male, essentially all-White, and upper-class—even less diverse than a typical high school. Should we say therefore that these future leaders don't "need" multicultural education because they live and work in a community where diversity is limited? I think most would agree that it is essential for these particular students to be taught to consider various viewpoints and to examine social issues relating to race, class, gender, and other human differences, because they have the appropriate cultural capital to acquire positions where they will have decision-making power (the right language, the right connections, etc.). In fact, I argue that these students ought to be required to confront their privilege in all of its forms and to be provided with experiences that will help them to understand the struggles that many individuals must face on a daily basis just to survive. (I also argue that this same process ought to be required of educators.)

In my philosophy of education class, I continually ask my students to return to the question "What is an educated person?" At some point in the semester, I generally read excerpts from a chapter written by David W. Orr, who writes about Hitler's minister of armaments, Albert Speer.[3] Speer was condemned by the Nuremburg Tribunal to serve 20 years at Spandau Prison for his contributions to Hitler's regime. In his memoirs, Speer writes that he learned to become oblivious to human suffering:

> I saw a large pool of dried blood on the floor. There on June 30 Herbert Von Bose, one of Papen's assistants, had been shot. I looked away and from then on avoided the room. But the incident did not affect me more deeply than that.[4]

In these same memoirs, he writes:

> the tears I shed are for myself as well as for my victims, for the man I could have been but was not, for a conscience I so easily destroyed.[5]

Speer was a highly educated man; he attended a distinguished private school and various institutes of technology in Karlsruhe, Munich, and Berlin. Yet rather than use his knowledge to create a better society, Speer chose to use it for destruction. He admits in his memoirs that his education was essentially apolitical: "It never occurred to us to doubt the order of things."[6]

Similarly, in *Education and the Good Life*, John White compares Great Britain's 1987 National Curriculum proposals with the curriculum of Stalin's Soviet state, and finds very few differences. He writes that "[Stalin's] list is almost identical to Mr Baker's ten foundation subjects,"[7] despite the fact that Stalin's curriculum was designed to prepare students to live in an autocracy, while Baker's was to prepare students for a democracy. White goes on to argue that

> The only defensible form of national curriculum is one that is genuinely committed to democratic principles, not least equality of political power. A minimum test of its commitment is whether it includes among its goals preparing all young people to become equal citizens of a democracy.[8]

What comes to mind when you think of an "educated person"? An individual who has a great deal of "book knowledge"? Someone who has achieved mastery in mathematics or science? Someone who has published extensively? Or is an educated person someone who can see a problem from various perspectives and will subsequently act with both insight and compassion?

At the risk of sounding trite, I think it's important to recognize that knowledge can be used either for good or for evil. That is, knowledge alone isn't enough; students need to be encouraged to use that knowledge for the betterment of society rather than for economic gain or personal power. It's interesting that we rarely think about education in this way. All too often, we talk about education solely in terms of individual advancement: You need to go to school so that you can get a good job. The problem with this approach isn't just that the promise of future rewards rings hollow for so many of our students; it's also that we trivialize education when we speak of it only in terms of personal economic gain. Of course, preparing students for employment is one function of education. Yet is this the only reason we educate? Isn't our role as teachers to prepare our students for the future? What kind of future do we want? I encourage you to take a moment to think about these questions carefully.

It seems that everywhere we look, persons are being "dehumanized"—that is, they are being treated more as objects or images on a screen rather than as genuine human beings. Turn on any news broadcast or open any newspaper and you can see this process at work. We see tremendous human suffering and yet we are reluctant to take a stand or to get involved. For instance, a couple of years ago I tried to mobilize students to participate in the boycott of a large company that exploits women in developing countries. Investigations found that the conditions these women worked under were inhumane, and their wages were so low that they didn't even make enough money to feed their families. When it was felt that they weren't being productive, they were denied bathroom breaks or forced to stand for hours in the hot sun as punishment. Despite the obvious atrocities of this major U.S. manufacturer, not one student responded to the boycott. Typically we can always come up with excuses for not getting involved—excuses that tend to justify our privilege and wealth while ignoring others' humanity. ("Well, at least they have a job," was one I heard frequently.) How easily we become oblivious to human misery, even when that suffering is caused by our own economic greed.

Even many of our own children and youth must personally endure an environment that devalues human life on a daily basis. In this age of technology, it is all too easy to become numb to the pain and suffering of those around us and to accept inequity as "the order of things." As I have argued throughout this book, schools have contributed to this process of dehumanization by conceiving of students as "products," by viewing the curriculum as if it were "neutral," by devaluing students' cultural knowledge, by treating students as if they were invisible. In fact, like those who were forced to study biology in the boiler room, some students are even dismissed as being unworthy of our efforts. Such an education is simply inconsistent with a democratic state that professes to provide equality of opportunity for all.

A humanizing education is one that helps students to empathize, to act with compassion, and to recognize injustice in all of its forms. It is one that helps them to "read the world" at the same time that they "read the word"—to understand how power works in society both to privilege and to oppress.[9] That is, a humanizing education is an education that is driven by a desire for equity, both in schools and in society. It is not apolitical (as was Speer's), but rather "consciously political" in that both what students learn and how they learn it are intentionally designed to promote democratic aims.

Perhaps the greatest humanizing educator was Paulo Freire, who believed that the primary purpose of education is to end oppression and who worked toward that aim in his literacy work with peasants in Brazil. Freire was subsequently exiled from his homeland for his liberatory efforts. The goal of education, according to Freire, is the empowerment of those who are oppressed, and the role of the oppressor is to achieve solidarity with the oppressed and fight side-by-side with them to end injustice. For Freire, education is potentially transforming. Yet transformation can never occur when we fail to see others as fully human, when we perceive someone who differs from ourselves as "the Other." Freire argues that true liberation is a process of humanization, and that a desire to work toward liberation emerges from understanding our common humanity:

> The oppressor is solidary with the oppressed only when he stops regarding the oppressed as an abstract category and sees them as persons who have been unjustly dealt with, deprived of their voice, cheated in the sale of their labor—when he stops making pious, sentimental, and individualistic gestures and risks an act of love.[10]

How often do we see others—even the students we teach—as "abstract categories"? Freire goes on to state that "*to affirm that men and women are persons and as persons should be free, and yet to do nothing tangible to make this affirmation a reality, is a farce*" (emphasis mine).[11]

I believe that education is a continuous journey. And I believe that this journey should be one that promotes goodness, compassion, and care, rather than one, like Albert Speer's, that never causes students to "doubt the order of things." In other words, education ought to be a process of humanization, where students are valued and affirmed for just who they are, and where they are taught to value and affirm others. The process of humanization is also a process of empowerment, where students—*all* students—come to recognize their capacity for transformation. For me, multicultural education is an ideology—a set of beliefs—about the role of education and our responsibility as educators in a democracy. Anything less trivializes our calling and reduces education to superficiality.

As we come to the close of this book, I encourage you to be the kind of educator who will refuse to accept "the order of things." In his letters to teachers, Paulo Freire writes that "It is impossible to teach without the courage to love, without the courage to try a thousand times before giving up."[12] For me, multicultural education is a humanizing education that can only be realized through love—love for humankind, love for our profession, love for our society and world, and most of all, love for the students that we teach. Will you have the dedication, the determination, and the fortitude that it takes to be the kind of teacher who can make a difference?

Faith and Courage,
Becky

otes

1. See, for instance, Rudolfo Chávez Chávez and James O'Donnell, *Speaking the Unpleasant: The Politics of (non) Engagement in the Multicultural Education Terrain* (Albany: State University of New York Press, 1998); bell hooks, *Teaching to Transgress: Education as the Practice of Freedom* (New York: Routledge, 1994); Sonia Nieto, *Affirming Diversity: The Sociopolitical Context of Multicultural Education* (New York: Addison Wesley Longman, 2000); and Christine E. Sleeter, *Multicultural Education as Social Activism* (Albany: State University of New York Press, 1996).

2. This paper was subsequently published. See Rebecca Powell, "Confronting White Hegemony: Implications for Multicultural Education," *Multicultural Education*, Winter 1996, pp. 12–15. Reprinted in Fred Schultz, ed., *Annual Editions: Multicultural Education 98/99* (Guilford, CT: Dushkin/McGraw-Hill, 1998).

3. David W. Orr, "The Dangers of Education," in Ron Miller, ed., *The Renewal of Meaning in Education: Responses to the Cultural and Ecological Crisis of Our Times* (Brandon, VT: Holistic Education Press, 1993), pp. 25–37.

4. Albert Speer, *Inside the Third Reich* (Boston: Houghton Mifflin, 1970). Cited in Orr, "Dangers of Education," p. 28.

5. Ibid., p. 29.

6. Ibid., p. 28.

7. John White, *Education and the Good Life: Autonomy, Altruism, and the National Curriculum* (New York: Teachers College Press, 1991), p. 14.

8. Ibid., p. 17.

9. Paulo Freire and Donaldo Macedo, *Literacy: Reading the Word and the World* (South Hadley, MA: Bergin and Garvey, 1987).

10. Paulo Freire, *Pedagogy of the Oppressed* (New York: Continuum, 1970/1993), pp. 31–32.

11. Ibid., p. 32.

12. Paulo Freire, *Teachers as Cultural Workers: Letters to Those Who Dare Teach* (Boulder, CO: Westview, 1998), p. 3.

Index

Studies in the Postmodern Theory of Education

General Editors
Joe L. Kincheloe & Shirley R. Steinberg

Counterpoints publishes the most compelling and imaginative books being written in education today. Grounded on the theoretical advances in criticalism, feminism, and postmodernism in the last two decades of the twentieth century, Counterpoints engages the meaning of these innovations in various forms of educational expression. Committed to the proposition that theoretical literature should be accessible to a variety of audiences, the series insists that its authors avoid esoteric and jargonistic languages that transform educational scholarship into an elite discourse for the initiated. Scholarly work matters only to the degree it affects consciousness and practice at multiple sites. Counterpoints' editorial policy is based on these principles and the ability of scholars to break new ground, to open new conversations, to go where educators have never gone before.

For additional information about this series or for the submission of manuscripts, please contact:
>Joe L. Kincheloe & Shirley R. Steinberg
>c/o Peter Lang Publishing, Inc.
>275 Seventh Avenue, 28th floor
>New York, New York 10001

To order other books in this series, please contact our Customer Service Department:
>(800) 770-LANG (within the U.S.)
>(212) 647-7706 (outside the U.S.)
>(212) 647-7707 FAX

Or browse online by series:
>www.peterlangusa.com